Volume 76   Number 3   September 2004

American Literature

Contents

Aesthetics and the End(s) of Cultural Studies

Book Reviews

Christopher
Castiglia
and
Russ
Castronovo

A "Hive of Subtlety": Aesthetics and the
End(s) of Cultural Studies

A talking head on the evening news in spring 2004, describing the Democratic primaries underway at the time, claimed that there was so little disagreement between candidates running for president that, at best, their differences were "aesthetic." What the commentator meant by *aesthetic* is unclear; probably, he simply meant superficial. In the current cultural moment in the United States, aesthetics have come to seem superficial and even suspect; even television, in its distaste for anything that smacks of the scripted (much less crafted), has taken to passing off the implausible and highly artificial as "reality" to avoid the taint of the aesthetic. And in the public and professional cultures of academia, this aversion to aesthetics has been claimed as particularly salutary, allowing criticism and interpretation to concentrate on the real political matters that demand our attention.

But let's assume that the commentator was going a little deeper. Could he have meant, literally, that difference per se is (related to the generation of the) aesthetic? Ian Hunter describes aesthetics as the dreamwork of a fractured subject, a sanctuary of illusion where coherence and symbolic unity can be imagined.[1] In an era in which subjects conceive of themselves increasingly as self-divided (between, just to take Jane Austen's list, sense and sensibility or pride and prejudice), when American citizens in particular are encouraged to fracture their self-conceptions on the hard edges of panic and plentitude, suspicion and sympathy, particularity and universalism (the novels Austen never wrote), the desire for integration, however contingent and fleeting, drives the subject into a space withdrawn from the unsatisfying and incomplete work of intimacy and democracy. There the citizen can

American Literature, Volume 76, Number 3, September 2004. Copyright © 2004 by Duke University Press.

construct, through aesthetic contemplation or activity, the psychic scrim onto which are projected fantasies of integrated and enriched personhood. Elsewhere Hunter suggests that literary hermeneutics represents a negative aesthetic activity that allows a different sort of dreamwork, namely, the spiritual exercise of self-examination, which takes the place of politics.[2] As Hunter cautions, "when it comes to their roles as citizens . . . it is important for literary theorists not to take their work home with them" lest they mistake the delicate operations of introspection, what Michel Foucault in a different context calls "an aesthetics of existence," for truer forms of civil engagement.[3] But in an American climate where political difference is reduced to spectacle, can aesthetics be uncoupled from the citizen's withdrawal into a space of contemplation masquerading as agency, a space not of debate but of deliberation? Might not interests in spectacle, fantasy, and form be the only things left in a house that has been repeatedly ransacked by rather strict notions of realpolitik?

The talking head probably didn't mean to invest aesthetics with such power. But if he knew the history of cultural studies and its treatment of aesthetics, he might have. It's become conventional to treat aesthetics as synonymous with formalism, with "high art," and with effete (read: academic) hair-splitting detached from the hair-raisings of the real world. But let's allow a moment of speculation here. Hunter suggests that aesthetics may occasion a "becoming" in which, contemplating the divided world, the subject reinvents the self in previously unconfigured ways. Such aesthetic becomings are often unexpectedly politicized, however. Cultural studies, with its attention to the social conditions and settings that make aesthetic contemplation a privilege available to relatively few, keeps us alert to the dangers of making aesthetics inherently progressive. In a corollary and countervailing gesture, however, cultural studies, with its attention to the unpredictable nature of these social conditions and settings, keeps us alert to the parallel fallacy of discarding aesthetic process as inherently conservative. The title of this special issue captures this schismatic sensibility: at one moment, aesthetics prove resistant to the sociological nature of becoming and thus figure as the transcendent end or limit to cultural contexts; at the next, aesthetics reactivate and defamiliarize the social forces and political possibilities that are ends or horizons of cultural analysis.

Take, for instance, Herman Melville's novella, *Benito Cereno*.

Readers easily recognize this narrative, with its emphasis on historical source material, slavery, and racial misrecognition, as a cultural
text. But *Benito Cereno* is also a tale of perspective, sensation, and projection, which combine either to confer or withhold subjectivity. It is,
in other words, a text that politicizes aesthetics. The blindness of the
American captain, Amasa Delano, who stumbles into a slave rebellion
aboard a Spanish trading ship, both precludes a social vision and is
itself a social vision whose effects can neither be controlled nor cal-
culated. Delano continually faces a world riven by conflict and contradiction, most obviously related to racial difference and the imperial
traffic in human bodies. Delano himself is perilously divided by the
contradictory demands of his New England liberalism, which requires
both a sympathetic heart and a head given over to order, particularly
the order of racial hierarchy. Delano energetically attempts to suture
the resulting rent in his consciousness but ultimately withdraws (the
majority of the story takes place as Delano's interior monologue) in
order to contemplate the self and to engage in an aestheticizing act of
synthesis that culminates in a moment of new becoming. Indeed, confronted with the racial, national, and class divisions that are continu-
ously at play on the Spanish ship, Delano repeatedly aestheticizes the
slave-revolt-in-progress into a drama that allows him to imagine himself as an increasingly patient, indulgent, and benevolent man. This
illusion is the cause of great satisfaction until, of course, the scales
fall from his eyes and the reality of the revolt, of a social and economic world so divided that violence and mutiny are the status quo,
is revealed. Delano's retreat into aesthetics is an effort to assert his
liberal freedom when faced with the violent systems of subjugation —
of unfreedom — that make liberalism possible in the first place. (After
all, forced labor purchases the liberal subject the time for aesthetic
contemplation.) Faced with the violent revolt that would make such
leisure impossible, Delano's aesthetic contemplation may be said to
be a freedom of last resort. The American captain, in short, engages in
aesthetic contemplation in order to end the cultural study of his own
liberal investments that the specter of blackness would force upon his
consciousness.

Aesthetics, however, need not be a turning away from differences.
As our fanciful rendering of the television talking head implies, aesthetics can be the point of incalculable rupture. So while Delano exemplifies the aesthetic contemplation of self that functions as a mode of

retreat, Babo, the leader of the slave revolt, commandeers aesthetic representation as a mode of confrontational engagement. In the violently erotic scene when Babo shaves his master, the American captain likens the slave's unctuousness to "a Nubian sculptor finishing off a white statue-head."[4] His worldview threatened once more by what he sees right in front of him, Delano sails off blithely toward the safe harbor of his own interior musings. But what he must contemplate even in this moment of inwardness and hermetic safety is the prospect of aesthetics as a tense, dialectical exchange. Babo lubricates, crafts, and ultimately manipulates the white head that he controls. In contrast to the idea that aesthetics comprise the compensatory dreamwork within our own heads, Babo forces us to grapple with another possibility: aesthetics can be the site at which we shape the heads—perspectives, ideologies, sympathies—of others. This is illusion with a vengeance. In *Revenge of the Aesthetic*, Michael Clark argues that far from being associated with a logic of domination—such, of course, is Delano's worldview, which is able to assimilate all observation within a presumably pleasurable schema of enlightened racialism—aesthetics provide a "source of autonomy and resistance to the status quo."[5] The slave revolt, too, requires the generation of difference between black disobedience and white command that takes on an aesthetic dimension. More than anything, then, Babo uses Delano's fantasies for the ends of revolution.

A significant part of Babo's revolutionary aesthetic is its challenge to ideas of individual autonomy. Aesthetic experience entails far more than the bounded dimensions of an American captain's consciousness. Melville's novella sketches aesthetics as an aleatory relation in which Babo acts on the Spaniard by treating him as an aesthetic object. That is, aesthetics are always transitive: they take an object, oftentimes, by force. For Hunter, aesthetic transformation is an individual phenomenon (the transformation of self) but Babo whets this ontology, giving it a much sharper edge by presenting aesthetics as an unsettling of self. Aesthetics, in this guise, are never (only) about self-transformation; rather, they invite the possibility of constituting and producing subjects at the site of dialogue and power. Whether it is the TV talking head or the white statue-head that is up on the block, aesthetics contain the possibility of articulating differences, not in a namby-pamby mode of liberal retreat but in a manner that radically reconfigures reconciliation so that it can no longer secure stability or an identity that rests on oneness. Where aesthetics produce difference, the materiality of the encounter is too bumpy and uneven to allow one to rest one's head on the pillow of an introspective dreamwork.

To say that reconciliation—in the form of the stability or fixity of oneness—is unsettled in the aesthetic moment is not to deny, however, the capacity for aesthetics to ground a post-identity collectivity. For all its antagonism, the primal scene of Babo shaving his master, in which one individual subject is confronted by another individual denied subjectivity, does not go far enough in suggesting the possibly collective nature of aesthetic transformation. Notions of performance, illusion, and beauty suggest much more than the domain of the singularized liberal subject, implying a fuller and richer field of community feeling and action. And yet aesthetics cannot shake off the criticism that the sociality it generates is only an empty reflection of true social content. Aesthetics fall prey to an inescapable formalism hostile to the gritty materiality, history, and contingencies of the real that jar and disrupt abstract criteria of judgment. Reflecting on "the current aesthetic revival," Fredric Jameson expresses this worry, suggesting that the collective nature of aesthetic transformation is only its false image. What looks like social engagement, he argues, is actually an "epistemological repression" that prevents sociality from coming into focus.[6] In place of some truer manifestation, an apparition of sociality takes the world-historical stage, passing off its shadowy outlines as the dimension of social content. Aesthetic form supposedly only counts as social content "when you are no longer able to acknowledge the content of social life itself."[7] Melville is not so sure. The slave revolt requires the generation of difference that takes on an aesthetic dimension. Babo stages a play for Delano's consumption in order to manipulate the aesthetic practices that he predicts, rightly, Delano will bring to the spectacle of racial suffering. By placing the tense difference *between* aesthetic practices at the heart of revolution, Melville's entire cast of willing, unwilling, and unaware actors shows that illusion, masquerade, deception, artifice, and any other terms that connote the ultimate ideological bankruptcy of aesthetic practice can, in fact, facilitate collective becoming, and, with it, collective social interests. In suggesting this reading of Melville's aesthetics, we not only want to hold open the possibility of collective transformation within the aesthetic moment but also the possibility that such transformations might become instances of what Lauren Berlant and Michael

Warner have called "world-making" or of imagining what Judith Butler has described as the not-yet-real.[8] What kind of politics could we have if politicians were better able to aestheticize: to see the unseen (civilly and socially dead citizens), to attempt new expressions (unarticulated social possibilities), to imagine social possibilities previously untried (or badly tried), to understand those constructions as negotiable and changeable over time, and to feel an emotional connection to very public possibilities of creating, of *becoming*? That, indeed, would be an aesthetic difference.

Cultural critics have, of course, been skeptical of the collectivizing potential of aesthetic experience, from Karl Marx's claims that performativity and poetics are counterrevolutionary through Roland Barthes's claim that "Revolution excludes myth" to Terry Eagleton's sustained analysis of how the major chords of aesthetic theory give voice to bourgeois ideology.[9] While Barthes brilliantly showed how critics could demystify the socioeconomic matrix and penetrate the deeply political character of seemingly innocent objects, such analysis was purchased at the cost of pleasure and fellowship, precisely because cultural analysis unveils the falseness of affect, image, illusion, beauty, and ugliness, rendering them powerless. While it is by no means a straight path from Barthes's study of culture to cultural studies, the abandonment of aesthetics remains nearly unmitigated. While frequently denying the collectivizing pleasures made possible by aesthetics, cultural studies, especially after its migration to U.S. institutional contexts, has debunked the essentialized identities and sanctioned intimacies at the base of most contemporary community formations, without supplying in their stead grounds for collective life that are affectively satisfying as well as theoretically plausible. It is this bind that arguably has revitalized the study of aesthetics, which traffics in affective sensations that promise—without necessarily providing—post-identity or non-normative forms of collectivism. The essays in this volume recommend aesthetics as a means for generating, through the sensations of the body and play of the imagination, broader collective—and collaborative—identifications, without necessarily tying them to hegemonic social formations. Taking up the challenge of post-identity interiority, the essays in this volume show two things that all critics working in the field of aesthetics should bear in mind. First, aesthetics may be most interesting as a site for locating and naming moments of affective fullness, which, especially as the traditional modes of interiority disintegrate, will make aesthetics, and its politics, increasingly important. The second, and related, point is that there is nothing fundamentally predictable about the interiorities or collectivities produced by aesthetics. Rather, aesthetics, like all affective formations, operate within institutional and disciplinary frameworks that seek to orient sense and sensation toward desired outcomes: those framings, the object of cultural studies, make aesthetics either conservative or progressive.

The essays in this volume grant aesthetics an agency far beyond what traditionally has been credited by cultural studies. For James Dawes, the power of aesthetic emotion lies in its capacity for disrupting the rational belief-systems that structure reality's common sense. Using both philosophy and cognitive science to address the question of why readers enjoy being scared by gothic fiction, Dawes argues for the pleasures of experiencing "emotions [that] sweep over us in sudden violation of all our most reasoned background assumptions (but safely, since we have willed the circumstances that predictably produce this violation)," thus allowing us to "experience the wondrous and absurd revelation that we are, in conscious thought, only dancing on the surface of what we truly are." This fissure in ontology characterizes Delano's experience in (and ours of reading) *Benito Cereno*. In the end, Delano is able to leap to safety, as we are able to close Melville's book. But in the process we have come to realize, if only affectively, the misconceived rationales of white social order.

Most of the essays in this volume are less interested in disrupting the subject than in formulating new—and usually collective—subjects. Paul Gilmore begins, like Dawes, with the assumption that aesthetic sensation has the power to surpass the limits of conventional cognition. Claiming that "aesthetic experience is the sensual and conscious experience of the suspension and ecstatic transcendence of the interested self," Gilmore doesn't leave us with the abstractly transcended or fragmented self. Like the American and British romantic writers he addresses, who believed that aesthetic experience supplied an electric charge not confined to the singularity of private consciousness, Gilmore asserts that "the aesthetic moment's potential political power derives from its ability to engender an imagined community that, unlike the one described by Benedict Anderson, transcends racial, social, and national boundaries." From Samuel Taylor Coleridge to Ralph Waldo Emerson and from Lord Byron to Walt Whitman, aesthetic sensation was electric, a material charge that could pass from body to body, becoming the basis for a collective experience that would transcend the limitations of identity. Gilmore's articulation of "a kind of egalitarianism" within aesthetics "that can be translated to the political sphere" suggests why the political projects of both Babo and Delano—both oriented toward nationalist understandings (both men want to return to a homeland they imagine as sites of freedom)— are forestalled by their dialectic aesthetics. Concluding that aesthetics need not signify a withdrawal from the world into consciousness and form "but a particular kind of engagement with the world," Gilmore helps us understand why Melville's drama of revolution takes place not within geographical boundaries but in the transnational space of the high seas.

Other critics, however, while conceding the collectivizing possibilities of aesthetics, are less sanguine about aesthetics' utopian outcomes. Tracing the rise of aesthetic theory in the aftermath of eighteenth-century revolution, Elizabeth Dillon argues that aesthetics ensured the continuation of liberal freedoms in a moment that called for law and social order. For Dillon, aesthetics opened up the individual capacity for evaluation and judgment central to juridical notions of consent, while simultaneously attaching those individual judgments to shared conventions of taste that allowed for collective order (or what Kant famously calls law without law). For Dillon, the liberal aesthete was not, finally, an individual subject but a member of a community of taste. In this regard, Dillon places sentimentalism—which constituted, first, liberal community generally and female community later—at the center of aesthetic production. At the same time, the attachment of aesthetic judgment to external "laws" rendered the liberal subject's freedom provisional at best, a point taken up powerfully by Wai Chee Dimock. Claiming Kant "as a patron saint of cultural studies," Dimock argues that the core of aesthetic experience is (the hope for) a species-wide awareness that could, potentially, become the basis of a "global civil society," allowing "for multilateral ties, more complex and far-flung than those dictated by territorial jurisdictions." The forces leveled against such a global collective are powerful, however, as Dimock demonstrates in her analysis of the fracas that followed the 1949 awarding of the Bollingen Prize to a poet who had been denounced as a national traitor—Ezra Pound. Close reading, which Dimock describes as a method of interpretation that privileges language over national taxonomy, removes critical judgment from the circumscribed horizon of Americanness. And in doing so, such aesthetic interpretation posits a community of taste that necessarily stands in oppositional excess of the nation, suggesting to Dimock a "not altogether unhopeful condition" of debate and divisiveness that, much like the gap-ridden deposition produced by the Spanish provincial authorities in Melville's novella, never congeals into a single univocal perspective that goes by the name of patriotism.

If aesthetics exist as nationalism's other, what value do notions of style, manner, and affect have in the globalism of what Christopher Nealon calls "late-late capitalism"? In the willfully obsolescent, often utopian, and always innovative work of post-Language poets, political possibilities become fluid and multiple when the critic cruises sites of damage, waste, and irrelevance—all effects of capitalism's unprecedented expansions—with the detachment and ironic sensibility of the flaneur. By charting the engagement of contemporary poets such as Kevin Davies, Rod Smith, and Lisa Robertson with the temporal unruliness of Frankfurt school meditations about where and when human history is headed, Nealon suggests that we can rethink our attachments to the materials of the future. The question is not what aesthetic objects signify now. Rather, as Nealon puts it, political significance is always "pending"; it is something we must wait for, resisting the critical temptation to finalize meaning. Theoretical power consists in "our being unable to pin down when the performance is finished." When will these poems stop meaning? The question is in many ways unanswerable because post-Language writing always awaits its objects, always refuses the possibility of a whole story, putting up "resistance to the idea" that there is "any one thing we know." In short, Nealon's essay echoes its own objects, featuring its own unfinished sentences, casual asides, and prophesies that extend interpretation. In place of aesthetic theory, then, Nealon gives us aesthetics *as* theory.

The sublime example of Martin Luther King Jr., as Thomas Kane illustrates, suggests aesthetics as practice. King's dreamwork has, after all, set the horizon for political action for the last half of the twentieth century. But King's dream was also deeply melancholic, tinged with the sadness of knowing that his utopian project would remain unfinished. The struggle for civil rights in this sense is an open-ended aesthetic project whose incompleteness stages a scene of witnessing: the audience watches and listens with a poignant sense of impending loss, yet simultaneously experiences loss as an opening of history, through which they may step—or march—as agents. With King's death, which he himself prophesized through an aesthetics Kane calls "automortography," this anxiety and promise become historically real. Now, four decades after King's assassination, the National Civil Rights Museum relies on an interactive aesthetic that continues the work of melancholy. Located in the motel where King was shot, the museum seeks to preserve the history of segregation and civil demand. If automortography depicts subjects becoming objects (in death), the engagement with melancholic objects in this museum allows spectators, through aesthetic contemplation, to remember in ways that bring political consciousness back to life. At the same time, the institutional logic of the museum, inviting "inward reflection and a detached rumination," may counter the collective action King sought to engender though his speeches, while the artificiality of museum display creates a misleading aura of immediacy and presence, shuttling visitors "between the plastic falsity of the objects on display and the temporal plasticity of our own fantasy." Showing how the National Civil Rights Museum, enshrining death, institutionalizes King's legacy as a matter of exhibits, facsimiles, reproductions, and representations, Kane's essay speaks provocatively to Nealon's: are the open futures recovered from the wreckage of capitalism threatened by the institutional aesthetics of supposedly historical consciousness?

Melville well understood both the danger and the potential of aesthetic encounters across histories, cultures, and institutions. It is not the American recapture of the *San Dominick* but the discursive postmortem of the mutiny that finally ends the rebellion. The American captain of Melville's novella, of course, employs aesthetics against expanded notions of historicity, exhorting his Spanish colleague, Benito Cereno, to forget the past and live in an eternal present, a natural-seeming stasis that is at once social and temporal, providing consolation in "yon bright sun . . . and the blue sea" (754). And Babo's manipulation of heads and minds, his subjective power in sculpting white interiority and psychology, is brutally punished when his own head, "that hive of subtlety," is "fixed on a pole," staring down the whites who would dare look at it (755). How thoroughly negated is the subjective power that Babo found in aesthetics as he himself becomes an object of the grotesque! Still we might also take this as a question: indeed, how thoroughly is Babo disempowered, as sculptor becomes sculpture? Not at all, is the answer that the final paragraph of *Benito Cereno* provides. Even though the spectacle of retribution replaces the fanciful Nubian objet d'art with a decapitated head, a defiant and scheming subjectivity nonetheless lingers in "the hive of subtlety." Babo continues to meet the "gaze of the whites," his head a *memento mori* to mutinous collective agency (755). Whiteness remains shot through with the image of blackness; rebellion persists within the scene of punishment; unpredictable meanings still circulate within the workings of an authority so severe and final that, at first glance, nothing would seem to be left to chance. But Babo's gaze demands a closer look at the spectacle, artifice, display, political staging, psychological attachments, liberal identifications, and insurgent possibilities that are all part of the aesthetic and its effects.

Taken together, the essays in this special issue suggest what the dialectical gazings of Babo and Delano also suggest: that aesthetics invite a process of (at least) second looks. If the first look sees aesthetics as a celebration of timeless transcendence, a second look shows us the historical development of theories, objects, sensations, and actions made possible through aesthetics; if a first look suggests that aesthetics provide a foundation for liberal subjectivity, a second look reveals that aesthetics disrupt the individual subject and provide the groundwork for an alternative, post-identity collectivism; if a first look discerns aesthetics' apolitical concern with ephemera, a second look reveals those objects as the historical manifestations of loss and possibility, of waste and wishfulness, as deeply political movements of sensation and sensibility; if a first look tells us that the overly formal subject of aesthetics does not merit close cultural investigation, a second look reveals the ways nationalism and globalism, consent and coercion, materiality and universalism, fear and pleasure, even life and death are mediated through aesthetics. Aesthetics require and enable not just first and second looks but also different tastes. Over the course of this special issue, our contributors shift back and forth, testing out cultural approaches to aesthetic objects (such as texts, poems, and speeches) and utilizing aesthetics as a methodology for discerning communities of taste, as in Dillon's sense. At times, such taste is distinctly pleasurable, allowing for the formation of sympathy, common sense, and other potentially reciprocal relations; at others, the hegemonic formation of taste under the sign of the nation and its sanitized history is so bitter that it burns. Faced with these multiple treatments and deployments of aesthetics, this special issue puts aesthetics on the pike of investigation and becomes the site of object lessons about representation and critique, community and citizenship, and prophesy and possibility. Always loaded, aesthetics are indeed a "hive of subtlety," one moment fixed in place, the next moment staring back at us, providing insight into the unpredictable and contingent cultural forces that create, identify, and unite subjects. The place of aesthetics in cultural studies is, for the moment at least, a problem, but a productive one, giving critics room to maneuver, to speculate, and, once again, in pursuing our ends, with eyes wide open, to attempt more promising beginnings.

Loyola University Chicago
University of Wisconsin, Madison

Notes

1 Ian Hunter, "Aesthetics and Cultural Studies," in *Cultural Studies*, ed. Lawrence Grossberg, Cary Nelson, and Paula Treichler (New York: Routledge, 1992), 347–72.

2 Ian Hunter, "Literary Theory in Civil Life," *South Atlantic Quarterly* 95 (fall 1996): 1059–1134.

3 Hunter, "Literary Theory in Civil Life," 1130; Michel Foucault, "On the Genealogy of Ethics: An Overview of Work in Progress," in *Ethics: Subjectivity and Truth*, ed. Paul Rabinow, trans. Robert Hurley and others, volume 1 of *The Essential Works of Michel Foucault, 1954–1984* (New York: New Press, 1997), 274.

4 Herman Melville, *Benito Cereno*, in *Herman Melville: Pierre or, The Ambiguities; Israel Potter: His Fifty Years of Exile; The Piazza Tales; The Confidence-Man: His Masquerade; Uncollected Prose; Billy Budd, Sailor* (New York: Library of America, 1984), 720. Further references are to this edition and will be cited parenthetically in the text.

5 Michael P. Clark, introduction to *Revenge of the Aesthetic: The Place of Literature in Theory Today* (Berkeley and Los Angeles: Univ. of California Press, 2000), 17.

6 Fredric Jameson, "Marx's Purloined Letter," in *Ghostly Demarcations: A Symposium on Jacques Derrida's "Specters of Marx,"* ed. Michael Sprinker (London: Verso, 1999), 52–53.

7 Ibid., 52.

8 See Lauren Berlant and Michael Warner, "Sex in Public," in *Intimacy*,

ed. Lauren Berlant (Chicago: Univ. of Chicago Press, 2000), 311–30; and Judith Butler, "The Force of Fantasy: Feminism, Mapplethorpe, and Discursive Excess," *differences: A Journal of Feminist Cultural Studies* 2 (summer 1990): 105–25.

9   See Karl Marx, *The Eighteenth Brumaire of Louis Bonaparte*, in *Marx's Eighteenth Brumaire: (Post)modern Interpretations*, ed. Mark Cowling and James Martin (London: Pluto Press, 2002); Roland Barthes, *Mythologies*, trans. Annette Lavers (New York: Hill and Wang, 1972), 146; and Terry Eagleton, *The Ideology of the Aesthetic* (Oxford, Eng.: Basil Blackwell, 1990).

James Dawes

Fictional Feeling: Philosophy, Cognitive Science, and the American Gothic

An interest in the deep structure of aesthetic pleasure and in the emotions that shake us when reading has in recent
years come increasingly to the fore in literary and cultural studies.[1]
This coalescing interest has gathered strength with the waning of
reader-response criticism in the nineties, which had long been criti-
cized for its tendency to privilege meaning over feeling and interpreting over imagining in its account of the reading experience,[2] and
with the concurrent and important rise of sensibility studies in Americanist research, which legitimized readerly emotion as a category of
analysis but tended to do so primarily insofar as it could illuminate
urgent political or cultural anxieties and needs.[3] In this essay I want
to contribute to the discipline's renewed interest in the feelings of
reading, its anticipated return to the "tears and prickles" of literature dismissed so long ago by Wimsatt and Beardsley.[4] I will do so by
using Charles Brockden Brown as a case study in the experience of
fright. Fear is an especially suitable emotion for study, as I will argue,
because of its illuminating extremity, and Brown is an especially suitable author. His works, as I hope to reveal, are among the most brilliant examinations available in the American literary tradition of what
happens when readers read.[5]

One of the most frightened (mis)readers in all of Brown's fiction is
Baxter in "The Man at Home." A character developed from Brown's
observations of the yellow fever epidemics in Philadelphia in 1793 and
1797, Baxter falls ill and dies because he believes, falsely, that he has
just witnessed the midnight burial of a fever-infected corpse and has
therefore been exposed to the disease. This death scene, which Brown

American Literature, Volume 76, Number 3, September 2004. Copyright © 2004 by
Duke University Press.

returned to and replayed more extensively in his novel *Ormond* (1799), offered a paradox so compelling to Brown that he could only resolve it through a new, more vigorous conception of "the force of imagination."[6] How could the observer of a danger *not real* nonetheless be physically stricken by it?

Brown's fictions are built upon this paradox and are, as I will argue, self-conscious about it. Like the later British sensation novels tracked by D. A. Miller, Brown's books function corporeally to touch the reader: they render our (real) bodies susceptible to the same physical symptoms of fear and anxiety that afflict the (unreal) characters we observe.[7] As a reviewer in 1819 declared of Brown's writing, "It produces throughout the liveliest sense of danger. . . . If we do not return to [his novels], it is to avoid suffering, and not that they want fascination, and a terrible one, if we are willing to encounter it more than once."[8] Another asserted that the author was unparalleled in his ability to keep the reader's "anxiety alive from first to last" and to excite "breathless apprehension."[9] Alone in our bedrooms, we read that Clara Wieland, orphaned by disease, is alone in hers. She is trying to sleep but is anxious and agitated. The toll of midnight triggers thoughts of her father's mysterious death—but thought ceases suddenly when she hears a whisper from lips close to her ear. Something is in the room with her. Our pupils dilate slightly, we feel a sudden chill as the down on our arms and legs bristles. Later in the novel, Clara will suspect that this intruder, a man plotting her murder, has returned and is hiding in her closet. She approaches the closet slowly, step by step. The small muscles of our fingers, forehead, jaw, and feet contract. She lays her hand on the lock, pauses, and prepares to open it. The increasingly agitated, fractional movements of our reading bodies are a myriad of aborted, preconscious gestures of physical rescue.[10] In *Arthur Mervyn* (1799), the protagonist enters a house heaped with bodies dead from the plague. Without warning, a contagious vapor assails him like a specter. This brutal surprise is reproduced later in the sudden appearance of a villain's face in a mirror, and still later in the ghoulish visitation of a disease-ravaged man apparently come back from the dead. And for each of these brief, terrible moments, we are Arthur, just as we are Clara when we pause before the closet. Our heart and breathing rhythms change slightly, the blood-flow to our extremities increases, and peptides are released into our bloodstream. We are in danger. Later, for just a moment, we may be Baxter: we will notice the cough, feel the bodies crowded around us in the city. We are in danger. "We are sometimes oppressed and sickened," one review concluded of Brown's plague depictions. "The reality seems too near" ("BLW," 70).

How can we be made to fear a fiction, to experience trepidation in the face of a danger not real, encountered and even courted precisely because it is not real, because it bears no consequences? How does the fictional spill over into the actual, the "near"? Questions of the ontology of fictional beings and environments are made urgent in the gothic because it is, when successful, so irreducibly physical, so inescapable. It is not only a question of how fiction makes us care, but how it makes us sick.

Brown's plague epic, *Arthur Mervyn*, presents us with three related paradoxes: Why do we seek stimuli that we avoid? How do fictional characters acquire existence in the real world? What are we feeling when we feel fear but are not afraid? I will provide answers to these questions by bringing together studies on cognition from multiple disciplines, including aesthetics, philosophy, neurology, and cognitive psychology.[11] In part 2, I will take up the first two (morally linked) paradoxes, developing what is at stake in each but not yet fully answering either question. In part 3, I will turn to the third question—what are we feeling when we feel fear but are not afraid?—to consider three replies from the philosophical tradition. Characterizing each reply as a faulty or incomplete conception of how readers respond, I will propose an alternative theory that is a hybrid of the three. In part 4, I will draw upon cognitive scientific approaches to emotion and belief in order to develop this hybrid conception of the "feeling of reading" as well as an account of our emotional lives more generally. This will allow me, in the conclusion, to return to the questions of part 2 (Why seek aversive stimuli? How can fictional characters be real?) so that I can, finally, reveal the answer that is most complexly embedded in Brown's gothic tales.

Following Brown, I will use contagious disease as a model for clarifying basic aspects of readerly experience. For Brown, disease was the most sensational of reading topics. "Of all dangers," he writes, "those allied to pestilence, by being mysterious and unseen, are the most formidable." We recoil from its final display, he continues, "with unconquerable loathing."[12] Infection is as frightening as a ghost or a predator, as Brown puts it in a letter to his brother James: "Plague operates by invisible agents, and we know not in what quarter it is about to attack us. . . . We fear it as we are terrified by dark."[13] For Brown, however, disease not only elicits strong feelings from readers but also models *how* they feel. Brown highlights the homology between the properties of disease and the transmission of emotion through art,[14] as does Leo Tolstoy in a document that repeatedly refers to the "infectiousness of art" and describes art's "power to infect people against their wills": "If a man is infected by the author's condition of soul, if he feels this emotion and this union with others, then the object which has effected this is art. . . . And not only is infection a sure sign of art, but the degree of infectiousness is also the sole measure of excellence in art."[15]

I will emphasize two key features of the experience of disease in modeling readerly emotion and cognition—features emphasized by Brown in his own plague accounts: namely, disease's blending of willed and unwilled experience, and its transformation of the body into a sign. First, disease breaks down the distinction between cognition (as a willed experience) and automatic bodily processes (as a coercive, unwilled experience). Disease is foremost an experience in irresistibility. It is the experience of being unable to decide to run or to walk, unable to decide to rise or to remain conscious, unable to choose not to have it. And yet as Baxter's hypochondria reveals, this bodily coercion can begin and sustain itself through the operations of choice and conscious, directed thought. Second, disease transforms the body into a series of cues for our feelings. Like Baxter, who vigilantly watches and, in his hyperreading, inevitably discovers in his body the signs of disease, we become readers of ourselves when ill, taking our lead from what our bodies show us. These points, which I will bracket for now, will become crucial at the completion of my argument in part 4.

■ ■ ■

Brown thematized the problems of the first paradox I mentioned— Why do we read horror?—from his earliest appearances in print. In "The Man at Home" he reflects upon our seemingly natural tendency to suffer when contemplating suffering:

I have heard of men who, though free themselves from any uncommon distress, were driven to suicide by reflecting on the misery of others. They employed their imagination in running over the catalogue of human woes, and were so affected by the spectacle, that they willingly resorted to death to shut it from their view. No doubt their minds were constituted after a singular manner. We are generally prone, when objects chance to present to us their gloomy side, to change their position, till we hit upon the brightest of its aspects.[16]

Why, then, in fiction especially but not exclusively, do so many of us derive pleasure from focusing intently upon the macabre? Continually throughout his stories, Brown gives us characters, from Baxter and Clara to Edgar Huntly and Arthur Mervyn, who cannot look away but are, like the readers he relies upon, irresistibly drawn and held by scenes or narratives of terror. The enigmatic pleasure of pain was taken up for serious consideration in the eighteenth century by philosophers including Edmund Burke and David Hume, whom Brown read. The issue had particularly strong moral implications in turn-of-the-century America, where religiocentric control of representations of heinous crime was being replaced by the rise of a sensationalist print culture and a native gothic fiction. Execution sermons that abstracted away from the particularity of crimes in favor of a view of man's common evil and the grace of God who redeems it gave way, according to Karen Halttunen, to a new cult of horror that luxuriated in the spectacular details of murder and the unapproachable monstrosity of the criminal. By 1830, the now familiar drama of the murder trial as entertainment was already a public fixture. In his prosecutorial closing speech at the trials of John Francis Knapp, Daniel Webster lamented the public's "morbid interest" in the actions of the accused. The "very horridness of the crime rendered it attractive. The monster presented to us, was rendered beautiful by its superlative ugliness." Human imagination was a shameful paradox: "So strangely was the mind of man constructed," Webster concluded, "that pleasure could be gathered from the elements of pain, and beauty seen in the Gorgon head of horror."[17]

Plague was especially popular. Mathew Carey's nonfictional account of the yellow fever outbreak later depicted in Brown's *Arthur Mervyn* was a wild success, quickly going through several editions. The pamphlet is, quite simply, a horror story: it opens with a vision of the ruined, anguished body (symptoms include "a vomiting of matter, resembling coffee grounds in colour and consistence, commonly called the black vomit, sometimes accompanied with, or succeeded by hæmorrhages from the nose, fauces, gums, and other parts of the body—a yellowish purple colour, and putrescent appearance of the whole body") and continues with scenes of the "universal terror" that struck even those who had "hundreds of times faced death without fear, in the field of battle" ("Who, without horror, can reflect on a husband, married perhaps for twenty years, deserting his wife in the last agony . . . parents forsaking their only children—children ungratefully flying from their parents . . . even on suspicion of the fever?").[18] Brown's Arthur Mervyn, self-described as a man with an imagination "delighting to be startled by the wonderful, or transported by sublimity" (*AM*, 350), makes himself into a symbol of Carey's eager readership when he reflects thus upon reports of the rise of the fever in his Philadelphia:

> A certain sublimity is connected with enormous dangers, that imparts to our consternation or our pity, a tincture of the pleasing. This, at least, may be experienced by those who are beyond the verge of peril. My own person was exposed to no hazard. I had leisure to conjure up terrific images, and to personate the witnesses and sufferers of this calamity. This employment was not enjoined upon me by necessity, but was ardently pursued, and must therefore have been recommended by some nameless charm. (*AM*, 347)

Why do we seem to enjoy the disgust and horror generated in us by the imagination of violence, disease, or injury visited upon other people? There are a variety of explanations available. In his *Poetics*, Aristotle notes that "we enjoy looking at accurate likenesses of things which are themselves painful to see" because learning provides enjoyment (iv, 3–10). David Hume argues that "sentiments of beauty" in art transform the passions of fear and pity into delightful movements of the soul.[19] In *Beyond the Pleasure Principle*, Freud explains the human impulse to return continually to moments of suffering with an account that delineates the ways we acquire control over traumatic events by repeating and replaying them in controlled frameworks. Literary critic Norman Holland uses psychoanalytic models of sexual desire, aggression, and fear to argue that readers derive through stories the gratification of managing repressed fantasies.[20] On the other hand, it could be argued that we like stories that provoke revulsion because it gives us pleasure to think of ourselves as the type of people who experience revulsion when witnessing violence.[21] Burke explains through analogy how "pain can be a cause of delight": just as regular physical excitation through labor is necessary for the pleasurably healthy functioning of our bodies, mental excitation through terror can be a mechanism for the healthy operation of our mental capacities.[22] Psychologist Marvin Zuckerman summarizes contemporary biosocial theories of sensation-seeking that claim pleasure is produced by an optimal level of cognitive stimulation, and that repressed behaviors or dangers encountered within protective frames are particularly stimulating as novelty;[23] others argue for the intrinsically positive valence of "arousal jag" (that is, negative stimulation followed by relief).[24] Evolutionary accounts of social behavior point to the survival advantages enjoyed by creatures drawn to "gratifying and thrilling literary entertainment": works that elicit strong emotion help "humans refine their skills for obtaining and disseminating information about emotions and thus become better adapted to the mind-reading, mind-revealing, and mind-concealing requirements of their lives."[25] A broadly developed romantic view, espoused in different ways by critics and philosophers ranging from Max Weber and Georges Bataille to Leslie Fiedler, asserts that in secularizing societies characterized by disenchantment—and in modernizing societies increasingly dominated by wage labor and, consequently, microregulation of body, behavior, and space—the encounter with evil and bodily violation substitutes for a lost spiritual transcendence, and the transgressions of crime and horror represent a form of liberation and an attractive Faustian heroism.[26] On the other hand, it could be argued that depictions of terror captivate precisely because they present an anxiety-inducing challenge to ethical and social order only to ritualistically and satisfyingly banish it. Consider John Mitchell Mason's post–yellow fever sermon, "Mercy Remembered in Wrath," which narrates the plague as a manifestation of God's control and the reliability of his mercy, earned through our "sorrowful review" of both our sins and their punishment.[27] Haltunnen answers this question of anomalous return and attraction by negating it. She argues that the invention of humanitarianism with the eighteenth-century cult of sensibility redefined the "distinctively modern" revulsion from pain as instinctive or natural.[28] Why *wouldn't* we enjoy representations of suffering? Humans have always, quite naturally, been fascinated by pain. Only in the modern world are we trained to believe we are not attracted to what attracts us.

Brown's first, most explicit, answer to this apparent paradox combines the cognitive with the romantic (his texts give a more deeply embedded answer, as I noted earlier, that I will reveal in the conclusion). Why are representations "of murders, ghosts, clanking chains, dead bodies, skeletons, old castles, and damp dungeons" the "most certain of being perused," Brown asked years after he abandoned the gothic in an essay on the popularity of romantic fiction. As an answer, he points to the "tameness and insipidity of common life and common events." Echoing an argument put forward by David Hume, Brown writes: "We awake in the morning, dress ourselves, go out shopping or visiting, and return in perfect safety to the same employments or amusements this day that we returned to yesterday, and which will probably engage our time to-morrow." But in the end it is only the dull who need the crude thrills of fear and wonder to divert themselves, Brown continues. Indeed, he suggests, there is something morally suspect in gothic amusement: the curiosity it generates is "very incompatible with tenderness of frame, or purity of mind."[29] Earlier, in a letter to his first love and superego, Henrietta G., he writes of the *Iliad*: "Who does not turn with anguish and aversion from the spectacle of slaughter and destruction which is continually presented to him? You could not possibly receive pleasure from [such] brutalities."[30]

Throughout all his novels, Brown figures curiosity as blameworthy. Baxter peeping from his neighbor's fence in *Ormond* is a pathetic spectacle. As *Arthur Mervyn* progresses, the novel trains us increasingly to suspect the integrity and honesty of its protagonist. Delighted at his capacity to peep anonymously and with impunity, like the reader, into "the most secret transaction" of private lives, Arthur spends much of his time poised quietly before keyholes or entering homes without permission; and as the range of scenes he witnesses expands, he is increasingly desensitized to individual value and human suffering. In *Edgar Huntly* (1799), the hunger of such "lawless curiosity" drives the protagonist to intervene wantonly in the lives of others.[31] The "pleasure" Edgar derives from bringing to light all the details of Clithero's jealously guarded story (reading private correspondence, breaking into locked chests) is narcissistic and finally murderous. By forcing Clithero to play the role of reader's pathetic object despite his pleas to be left alone, Edgar forces him to relive his past and thus initiates the repetition of a bizarre psychotic breakdown. And in *Wieland* (1798), the selfish pursuit of amusement by its untouchably placid protagonists is suspect from the start: they appreciate the calamity of war for "agitating our minds with curiosity"; Clara is unsaddened at thoughts of her father's mysterious death because of its stimulating and thrilling aspect; and she is well pleased that her friend is grief stricken at the death of his lover because it secures him as a more steady and sober companion (*W*, 43, 45). By novel's close, however, they are brutally punished, made victims of the curiosity of Carwin the ventriloquist, who (as reader) spies upon their private gatherings and (as author) manipulates their actions to disastrous consequence by inventing dramatic dialogues. Carwin is Brown's guilty double, the sign of an authorial culpability to match the reader's. Who else but an author could know the pleasure, as Carwin puts it, of "scattering around me amazement and fear" (*W*, 193)? Later in his life, Brown would express extreme regret for having written his novels.[32]

Is our curiosity suspect? Do fictional characters have a right to privacy? Is it cruel to subject them to pain? Brown's peculiar sense of guilt points up the disturbing way fictions can acquire a psychological reality that rivals the material world. One of the most astonishing background facts of human existence is that we are capable of forming a deep emotional intimacy with fictions. We *live with* our characters—we form complex attachments to them. As Brown recounted of his own life, the "barrier" separating us from the world of illusion and the touch of nonentities is frail ("BLW," 61). I grieve for Milly Theale not because she resembles nonfictional persons I know and care for, nor because I empathize with nonfictional persons who must have suffered as she has, but because over time, Milly has become part of my life. Not only can we yearn for the realization of Gatsby's dreams, we can also feel anger at Fitzgerald for relentlessly dashing them. In working through the ontology of fictional persons (and, eventually, offering a theory for how these strange facts can be), I will stay with fear as the most salient emotional example of how the planes of material reality and imagination can intersect.

Fear is a clarifying example for two reasons. First, the physicality of its symptoms, even more radically than grief, reveals how involuntary, how coercive, the fictional experience can become.[33] Readers push books away as if they possess a force to be resisted; Edith Wharton, for instance, reports how reading a horror story brought on a relapse of typhoid fever when she was a child, and how even as an adult she "could not sleep in the room with a book containing a ghost story."[34] Writes Burke: "No passion so effectively robs the mind of all its powers of acting and reasoning as fear."[35] Second, fear is notable among emotions for its thin border between self and other. Scant attachment is required for fear to be triggered in its empathetic modality (consider the ease with which we can be made to fear for inadequately realized characters in slasher films), and little more is required for the empathetic to become assimilative. The latter cannot be said for, say, grief. We may feel sad for Frederic or Catherine when Catherine dies; indeed, we may feel as though we ourselves have experienced a personal loss, the loss of a friend. But we typically remain external to Frederic and Catherine; we are, as readers, different from the fictional friends we grieve for or the fictional friends we lose. Even empathy ("if I were that person") does not fully threaten that distinction. We experience non-fear emotions generated by the situations of fictional beings because of the imagined consequences of events in the narrative *for them* or because of similar projected consequences for our hypothetical selves—but not even the most empathetic reader will feel compelled by *A Farewell to Arms* to check that his own partner is still alive.

However, with fear, and with emotions like embarrassment that are invested with fear, the consequences are quite often for our present selves *as* the character. If I flinch self-protectively when a fictional being like Clara is in danger, if I look under my bed or check my closet, I am not doing so because I perceive that the consequences of physical harm to Clara will be bad for her or because they would be bad for an imagined future me that I pity. We experience fear "from the inside," not analogically or by comparison. Fear is self-oriented, the closest of all emotions to such physical reflexes as shock or visceral disgust. I can feel anxiety for Clara and have a deep aversion to her anticipated suffering, but when I am frightened, it is because *I* am in danger. And fictions can put me in danger. We live in an obscure bowl of space surrounding fictional protagonists, a bowl of space contiguous to their perils, close enough for touch, penetration, and contagion. Certain threats to them can afflict us as well. Indeed, it is as if the nonphysicality of fictional persons makes them permeable in a way resistantly material human beings are not: we can, for a moment, possess their bodies. I can experience a predominantly ego-centered fright when witnessing Clara's danger in a way I can never do when witnessing yours. Your reality prevents altruism (empathy) from becoming egoism (fear); but Clara cannot prevent this, and the consequences for the reader can be as physically coercive as the famous headache of Hawthorne's wife.

■ ■ ■

But can I really be afraid of a fiction? Peter Lamarque puts the question this way:

> On the one hand, it is assumed that as reasonably sophisticated adults, we are not *taken in* by fiction. . . . No one is in fact murdered in the performance of *Othello*, just as no one is in fact jealous or innocent. And we know that. On the other hand, we respond often enough with a range of emotions, including fear and pity, that seem to be explicable only on the assumption that we do after all believe there to be real suffering or real danger. For how can we feel fear when we do not believe there to be any danger? How can we feel pity when we do not believe there to be any suffering?[36]

If as many philosophers have asserted, emotions are "belief-dependent, judgmental mental states,"[37] and if fear of an object "necessarily involves a belief or judgment that the feared object poses a threat,"[38] then my claim that I'm afraid of a fiction translates into the statement, I believe that I'm in danger when I don't believe that I'm in danger.

Philosophers have tried to resolve this paradox in three ways, each of which I shall discuss in the pages that follow: first, and most familiarly, by arguing that the belief-requirement of emotions is not violated in my fictional experience; second, by arguing that emotions do not have belief-requirements; and third, by arguing that my self-described feeling of fear is not in fact an emotion. The most influential instance of the first response is the pretheoretical notion that we somehow suspend our disbelief when we are transported into fictional worlds. By this Coleridgean argument, we neither believe nor disbelieve in fictions. In other words, we can be afraid because we don't believe we aren't in danger. But as this tortured grammar reveals, it is unclear what we are left with when we suspend our disbelief. It might be implied that we are neutral with respect to the differences between fictional and real-world propositions; however, because we are, as readers, engaged rather than detached, this position amounts to a state of universal acceptance: we believe, on some level.

This idea was taken seriously by Brown, who depended upon such belief for the popularity of his novels. "The tales of apparitions and enchantments," explains Clara Wieland in a negation that reveals the basis of fictional successes, "did not possess that power over my belief which could even render them interesting" (*W*, 42). A contemporary reviewer of Brown put it more directly: "A spell is cast over our imaginations, and our belief is at least strong enough for sympathy." And again: there is little "so monstrous and unusual that he has not been able to recommend it sufficiently to our belief for all his purposes" ("BLW," 69, 70). *Wieland*, a novel that mischievously presents itself as an allegory of its own reading, offers up a series of characters whose inability to disbelieve mockingly models Brown's image of our own readerly credulity. The "narrations" of Carwin—The Baroness de Stolberg is dead! You will die if you approach this chasm! Be afraid! Believe! (*W*, 42, 59)—are never discarded as trickery or mere illusion but are, rather, immediately integrated into the protagonists' realities with blinkless unresistance. The "readers" in this tale universally and immediately obey all instructions to accept and to emote, consequently losing their ability to distinguish between reality and illusion: "I could do nothing but obey"; "So flexible, and yet so stubborn, is the human mind. So obedient to impulses the most transient and brief, and yet so unalterably observant of the direction which is given to it!"; Carwin's voice "imparted to me an emotion altogether involuntary and incontroulable"; "Images so terrific and forcible disabled me, for a time, from distinguishing between sleep and wakefulness, and withheld from me the knowledge of my actual condition" (*W*, 32, 50, 48, 58).

The protagonists of *Wieland* are susceptible to "wonder and panic" as a *first* response (*W*, 32). It is as if the mind were programmed to believe all new data, and could only achieve and maintain disbelief through special effort. Unsurprising is the protagonists' recreational focus on oratory rather than fictional theater—indeed, the one play they intend to stage never takes place, as if they cannot finally enter the realm of fictions acknowledged as fictions. Brown's heroes here are like the canal boatman who threatened the actor playing Iago during a nineteenth-century production of *Othello* in New York: "You damned-lying scoundrel, I would like to get hold of you after the show and wring your infernal neck."[39]

This possibility of anomalous belief is taken seriously by few in the philosophical tradition. Surely if we suspend our disbelief, philosophers argue, we are not left with belief, not even belief *on some level*. If we believed we were in danger, we would take action to protect ourselves, and as Kendall Walton has lucidly demonstrated, we never do that. Experiencing fear during a slime-monster movie, Charles never considers fleeing to call the police or warn the town. Nor is it possible that we are left with half-belief: Charles does not act anxiously suspicious of the slime; he acts afraid. "Charles's heart pounds violently; he gasps for breath; he grasps the chair until his knuckles are white. This is not the behavior of a man who basically realizes that he is safe but suffers flickers of doubt." And we do not, finally, *momentarily* believe. Charles is not simply startled; he is afraid, and his fear endures for long strips of time. His "grip on reality," however, is never threatened. With frightening fictions, we never believe we are in danger, on *any* level; we *always* disbelieve. And yet, somehow, we are afraid. We are not rescued from the paradox (*M*, 196–98). The Coleridgean thesis, as currently formulated, should not convince.

Some have therefore attacked the problem with the second approach described earlier: namely, by trying to pry apart emotion and belief. We are pulled as emotional participants into the reality of fictional worlds through sometimes preconscious cognitive reflexes that bracket as *irrelevant* the question of belief-worthiness. For instance, encountering a partially built fiction, we automatically begin establishing the implicit backgrounds necessary for a complete and coherent world (without thinking, we fill Arthur's Philadelphia, for instance, with all the unnarrated features of its real-world counterpart); and processing information according to the schedule of a suspense narrative, our cognitive structures oriented to problem-solving instantly begin to entertain both optimizing and aversive counterfactuals (If they look they will live! If they keep walking they will die!).[40] We can generate in ourselves commitments to or interests in states of affairs without triggering questions of belief. We can, indeed, experience deep emotions even when belief has been negated. You do not believe you are in danger when you give public talks—you know you will do just fine— but nonetheless you experience all the sensations of fright just before speaking. You do not *really* think bugs are dangerous, but when you see a bug in your basement you are nonetheless overwhelmed by fear. These are surely instances of emotions, instances of fear, and yet the belief requirement has not been fulfilled in either case.[41] Perhaps fictions operate in the same way.

Arguing that there is a disanalogy here to fictional experience, how-ever, Walton contends that what's important about the idea of believ-ing you are in danger is that beliefs make you do something appro-priate; they carry a motivational component (*M*, 198). In both of the phobia cases I've just cited, there is a motivational force pushing you; you take deliberate actions to avoid the perceived threat (staying out of your basement, skipping conferences). It can therefore be inferred that you can and in fact do believe two opposed things at once: that there are no real risks, but also that there are real risks. With fic-tions, however, you *never* believe there are any risks; and in sharper contrast, you inappropriately seek out rather than avoid threatening fictions precisely *because* of the sensations of fear they provide. In a gothic novel, fear is what you want; with a phobia, fear stops you from doing what you want. But while there are surely few cases where we seek out phobic triggers, as Walton would require, it is quite pos-sible that there are many instances of phobias and resurgent trau-mas that involve no element of belief rather than two simultaneous contradictory beliefs. A bug phobia might, for instance, have noth-ing to do with the fear (and hence the belief) that bugs are danger-ous; it might rather involve the desire to avoid objects that trigger a conditioned (belief-free) fearful emotion that is both predictable and unpleasant. Motivational disanalogies aside, then, phobias (fears with-out beliefs) might reveal something about the possibilities of our emo-tional makeup that change how we think about the seeming paradox of fictional fear. Perhaps, as Colin Radford argues, there is a brute irratio-nality to our emotional lives: fear of fictions and phobias both involve an inconsistency much like that displayed in the behavior of the ten-nis player who does not believe that hopping can raise balls physically distant from her but nonetheless hops upward to raise her failing shots above the net.[42]

But I do not think we can sever the connection between emotion and cognition based solely on the example of phobias. Whatever the mechanism of phobic reactions, it is surely different from both our quotidian emotional responses and our responses to fiction. More steps in the argument are needed to displace the cognitive theory of emotions as it relates to fiction, including evidence from readers' responses. At least for now, then, it seems advisable to stay with the thesis that emotion, as we typically experience it, and belief, in its motivational aspect, are linked, as even the Coleridgian thesis would suggest. The hop of the tennis player, after all, is not an emotion: no one ever asserted that belief was required for a gesture of desire. "Cognition," writes psychologist Richard Lazarus, summarizing the view that higher-thought processes are determinative of our emotional lives, "is both a necessary and sufficient condition of emotion."[43] Or as anthropologist Robert Solomon puts it, defending the relativity of cultures from what he sees as universalizing biological theories: "An emotion is not a feeling (or a set of feelings) but an *interpretation*."[44]

Brown, as we have noted, seems to agree. At the very center of part 1 of *Arthur Mervyn*, the protagonist is left alone in a mysterious cellar with a murdered corpse. It is a fearful situation, but once Arthur comes to the belief that he is not in danger, his fear response is disabled. "I was not, on ordinary occasions, destitute of equanimity," he explains:

> But, perhaps the imagination of man is naturally abhorrent of death, until tutored into indifference by habit. Every circumstance combined to fill me with shuddering and panick. For a while, I was enabled to endure my situation by the exertions of my reason. That the lifeless remains of an human being are powerless to injure or benefit, I was thoroughly persuaded. I summoned this belief to my aid, and was able, if not to subdue, yet to curb my fears. (*W*, 329)

This example is especially illuminating because of the temporal gap that appears between cognition and emotion. Finding analyzable instances of a belief-feeling articulation in Brown's fiction—or any fiction—is often difficult precisely because the two are so closely conjoined that they are sometimes difficult to separate. When Arthur weeps over the fate of plague victims, does his compassion follow a cognitive movement toward belief in their suffering and their worthiness? Does his belief that such suffering is terrible follow obediently on the heels of his instant, reflex-like emotional reaction to the harsh revelation of their demise? Or do the two happen as a psychological pair: belief-and-emotion? Emotion and belief seem almost inexplicable unless taken together as a unit—and yet surely this cannot be so, as we have all had beliefs that entail no emotions. Perhaps it is best to say that Arthur cries because he believes and he believes because he cries. But Brown thinks this is not so, and shows it with the terrors of the corpse. Here, emotion follows the lead of belief.

We should, however, be suspicious of any account of personality in Brown that takes reasoned beliefs as the normative basis for emotionally experiencing the world. After all, it is Clara Wieland at her most poignant—when she fears there is a murderer in her closet and her jeopardy forces us beyond sympathy to possession and identification—who displays emotions *independent* of reasoned beliefs, a "war" between "actions and persuasions": "Had not the belief, that evil lurked in the closet, gained admittance, and had not my actions betokened an unwarrantable security?" (*W*, 81). And it is her pathological and finally murderous brother Theodore who insists most strenuously upon demoting emotion and maintaining a symmetry of belief, motivation, and action (*W*, 22). For Brown, Theodore's rational establishment of a gapless relation between belief and its subordinate, emotion, ultimately allows for inhuman reversals: certain powerful emotional triggers can not only overwhelm but also force the realignment of established belief structures, thereby producing coolly relentless and inhuman conduct. In the world of the American gothic, in other words, it is the unreasonableness of human emotional lives, the irrational slack and mismatch between our emotions and beliefs, that ultimately keeps us human.

Just so with Arthur and the corpse. For upon looking closely at the scene, we see a marginalization of the role of reason and belief— the original emotion of terror arose in Arthur *without* a foundational belief—that makes him ever more familiarly and endearingly human (even as elsewhere, delighting in shaking apart our own beliefs and emotions, Brown gives us ever more evidence to suspect he is a moral monster). It is not the case that Arthur believes there is a danger with the corpse, feels fear, and then remembers that there is not a danger as a precursor to regaining equanimity. He feels fear, his fear endures, and in a classic reason-passion dualism, he pulls belief from *somewhere else* to compete with his autonomous and fully embodied emotion. His fear is "curbed," which is quotidian as a matter of probability (a person who fears contracting mad-cow disease may find her fears curbed when she sees the statistics) but inexplicable as a matter of belief (a person who suddenly feels the tickle of spider legs crawling up his neck experiences an erasure of fear, not a curbing, when he realizes somebody is playing a joke on him). Arthur's "curbed" terror is an experience nearly as astonishing as tears for a nonexistent Anna Karenina. Brown has returned to the problem of fear and the counterfactual, as he had explored it with Baxter in "The Man at

Home"—the case with which we began—but now our intuitions are given another perverse turn. Baxter, however peculiar, is nonetheless explicable: there, beliefs (I've been exposed to disease) cause emotions (fear, anxiety), and these together, through some occult mechanism, influence physiology. But here, even though Arthur believes in belief as a necessary condition for emotion and its physiology (piloerection, pulse acceleration, contraction of arterial walls, increased blood pressure), the unsteadiness of his belief-achieved composure suggests he is wrong. The question "How can an event exert physiological force when we believe it but it is not real?" has become "How can an event exert physiological force when it is not real and we do *not* believe it?"

Arthur Mervyn is structured as a whole according to this uncertain play of the cognition-emotion pairing. Dr. Stevens is moved by Arthur's tale, especially by his performance of it. Belief is compelled, Stevens notes, by the emotions Arthur displays and elicits in the telling (*AM*, 436), as if, in the peculiar Jamesian logic I will return to later, we end up with our beliefs upon discovering our emotions. On the other hand, when Stevens is given cause to suspect Arthur of lying, his emotions are cognitively bracketed: until "belief" can be resolved, emotions cannot be determined; they can neither be endorsed nor dismissed. Brown is forcing us to ask: What is the status or experience of an emotion that is in between beliefs? Must an emotion cease with the realization that it depends upon belief in a "fiction"? Can it? The disquieted state of Stevens and the reader-in-the-fiction—full with emotions that may lack a real referent (real for Stevens, and fictionally real for the reader-in-the-fiction)—refigures the puzzle of reading Brown's fiction generally. Brown offers an account of events that he claims actually "happened" (*AM*, 232) and the reader-of-the-fiction responds with the emotions appropriate to belief, even while belief surely must be at best bracketed here. The reader-of-the-fiction is not disquieted—his emotions are not bracketed symmetrically with his beliefs—even though the emotions of Stevens and the reader-*in*-the-fiction are.

Perhaps, then, the only way to make sense of this situation is to endorse the third solution to the original paradox: our fear (or empathy, or anxiety) is not an emotion. This possibility is highlighted in Brown's own writings. Depicting his first experience of romantic love as a young man as a movement from imaginative experience to intersubjective bodily experience, from fictional worlds to real worlds,

Brown writes: "[Previously] the want of opportunities, of experience, and the consciousness of my obscurity and of the meanness of my situation confined me to the region of fiction, and the only source of entertainment from my powers consisted in my own reflection, but in a short time I discovered with rapture and astonishment that those emotions which I had hitherto delighted to feign had suddenly become real, that I was actually enamored of an object that visibly and indisputably existed."[45] Such "feigned" emotions, so central to Brown's vision of youth, can be utterly engrossing, as he recounts in *The Rhapsodist*—as engrossing as the emotions experienced by a child involved in a game of make-believe. For Walton, such feigned emotions are indeed the basis for all representational-artistic experience. Walton sees books and films as props in games of make-believe that fill us with pseudodelight and pseudoterror. We shrink from the myriad horrors of *The Exorcist* just as a child shrieks when the person assigned to be Monster in the game A Monster Is Chasing Me approaches. But in neither case is anyone really afraid, and the physiological response that each would identify as fear is in fact only feigned or quasi fear. We (really) believe that we are (make-believedly) in danger and have the appropriate (make-believe) emotional response.[46] Walton's account is detailed and persuasive, but it leaves important gaps. As he himself puts it, "Why does the realization that fictionally one is in danger produce quasi fear when it does? Why does it bring about a state similar to one of real fear, even if the person knows he is not really in danger?" (*M*, 245). With a theory of make-believe, we may preserve the coherence of a belief-motivation complex, but we are no closer to understanding how it is that the physiological aspect of emotion or quasi emotion is generated in the first place. Our fear may not be a real emotion, but the physiology of a non-incoherent quasi fear is as mystifying as the physiology of an incoherent fear. As we shall see, Walton's stopping point is determined by the blindnesses and biases internal to philosophy as a discipline: namely, an overestimation of the importance of both consciousness and reality. To move beyond its useful but partial answers, we must switch disciplines.

■ ■ ■

Does Charles flee from the green slime because he is afraid, or is he afraid because he flees from the green slime? Developing a theory that would prove crucial for contemporary neurobiology, William James argued that Charles is afraid because he flees. Giving fear a primary focus in his discourse on emotions generally (like so many other investigators), James writes: "If we abruptly see a dark moving form in the woods, our heart stops beating, and we catch our breath instantly and before any articulate idea of danger can arise." In other words, emotions are our experience of precognitive bodily reactions to stimuli. Typically we believe that "we cry, strike, or tremble because we are sorry, angry, or fearful," but in fact, James argues, "we feel sorry because we cry, angry because we strike, afraid because we tremble."[47] This view (known now as the James-Lange theory) was dismissed for many years and remains neglected in cultural and literary criticism and theories of readers' responses.[48] As Noël Carroll puts it, James's idea is "insupportable." Echoing an argument from Walter Cannon, Carroll notes that the same emotion often has very different physiological manifestations, and different persons have different physical manifestations of emotions. Hence, no particular emotion can be experientially derived simply by reading one's bodily reactions.[49] These objections notwithstanding, models of emotions that take James's insights as a cornerstone now represent a dominant approach in contemporary neural science. In one study by Paul Ekman, for instance, subjects were instructed to move their facial muscles in ways that, unbeknownst to them, approximated "happy" and "angry" expressions. In subsequent evaluation exercises, their moods were revealed to be influenced by their assigned expressions.[50] It has been observed in a similar false-feedback structure that panic attacks can be induced in patients suffering from anxiety by providing them misleading information about the rate at which their hearts are beating, "making the patient believe that heightened bodily arousal is occurring when it is not" (*EB*, 258). This conception of the body as a read text or a cue for consciousness (recall Baxter), and, in the Ekman experiment, the decoupling of emotion and cognition it entails, is part of Antonio Damasio's definitional structure of our complete emotional lives. That is, "feelings" are conscious awareness of sometimes nonconscious mental representations of the physiological changes that constitute emotions.[51]

For further evidence of a cognition-emotion split, researchers point to the discovery of learned, durable, nonconscious emotive preferences in people with forms of brain damage that prevent them from learning any new facts, hence revealing that emotions and behavior stimulated by emotions can occur in the absence of any biological capacity for belief (one patient pricked by a tack when shaking hands with her doctor found herself unwilling to shake hands with her doctor);[52] to experiments with split-brain patients who can identify with their left hemispheres the emotional value of stimuli perceived by their right hemispheres, without having any conscious left-hemisphere knowledge of what those stimuli are (one patient, when the word "Mom" was presented to his right hemisphere, was able to say with his left hemisphere that he did not know what the stimulus was but that he knew it was "good" [EB, 14]); and to a host of studies in normal-brain patients revealing emotional reactions to stimuli received without conscious awareness (EB, 53–55, 59, 238). Consciousness is only one section of our emotional lives; a great deal of stimulus-processing occurs in a preconscious state, which can endure over time. As Brown writes in "Somnambulism," we are all "at times, influenced by inexplicable sentiments"; emotions "come and go when they will, and not at the command of reason."[53] Just as we can know and not feel, then, we can feel and not know. Joseph LeDoux summarizes: "Fear feelings and pounding hearts are both effects caused by the activity of this system [that detects danger], which does its job unconsciously—literally, before we actually know we are in danger" (EB, 18). Explaining the concept of "perceptual defense," LeDoux describes a typical language experiment:

> Subjects were shown words on a screen. By varying the amount of time that the words were shown, it was possible to determine the amount of time a particular subject needed to recognize a given word. It was discovered that the exposure time required for "taboo" words . . . was longer than for words lacking taboo connotations. The results were interpreted in terms of Freudian defense mechanisms, particularly repression: the taboo words were perceived subconsciously and censured (prevented from entering consciousness) because their appearance in consciousness would have elicited anxiety. (EB, 56)

The action of knowing can be as coercive as automatic bodily processes. Reading is, on one level, a symbol of thought and will, but it is also something that happens to us, as the remarkable Stroop effect has revealed. If we attempt to identify orally the print-color of color-words (for example, that the word "red" is printed in green ink) after doing the same for nonsense words (for example, that the word *jerfl* is printed in green ink), we often find we are unable to do so without strain (we find ourselves saying "red" instead of "green"). We cannot *not* read, however much we may will ourselves to perform other cognitive activities. Just so, the movement from read-sign to integrated-knowledge is as automatic as the development of infection, and as the experiment with taboo words reveals, it is not a substantively neutral operation. Film and literature, then, like obscenity, or corpses, can indeed function as props—but not props in games of make-believe. They are, rather, props for presenting stimuli to trigger actions and emotions that we wish to experience or cause others to experience (*EB*, 19).

In many philosophical models of emotion and cognition, mind is depicted as a form of metaphysical willing; in these neurobiological cases, mind is depicted as body. If the latter is persuasive, it should not be surprising that emotions can overwhelm cognition, can make belief irrelevant. We can will our emotions and cognition no more effectively than we can will away the sensation of itching. This is so for good reason, particularly in the case of fear. It seems plausible that we should have evolved into creatures that have the capacity to react to stimuli faster than we can cognitively process them (increasing our chances of escape) and that we can find ourselves coerced, against our more reasoned assessments, into avoiding situations previously marked dangerous (decreasing our ambient risks).[54] Our postulated phobic fear of public speaking or of bugs should thus not be construed as the conflict between two opposing beliefs. Phobic fear is instead a coercive corporeal reaction (in the "universal nonverbal vocabulary of bodily signals"[55]) that alters our cognition and action in the *absence* of belief. If this assertion is true, philosophical cognitivism cannot provide an adequate account of emotions.

Psychologists Paul Rozin, Linda Millman, and Carol Nemeroff, using fear and disgust as models—that is, taking anxiety over bodily contamination, like Brown, as the basic illuminating model for our emotional lives—conducted a series of experiments that reveal the wide variety of our quotidian, belief-free emotions or, rather, our cognitively impenetrable emotions (*ENW*, 184–87). They explain the reluctance of subjects to eat fudge molded into the shape of dog feces or to drink juice from a glass in which a sterilized cockroach has been dipped, for instance, by using classical conditioning models that argue we can overlearn emotional associations between particular stimuli and our own defensive responses. But even unlearned or underlearned fears can trump our beliefs. In one ingenious study, subjects expressed anxiety over drinking water from what they knew to be new, clean, untainted glasses after they had been instructed to apply "sodium cyanide" labels to the glasses. As Charles Darwin writes, explaining his inability to *not* leap away from a striking glassed-in snake, "[M]y will and reason were powerless against the imagination of a danger which had never been experienced."[56] The emotions of Constantia Davis in Brown's "Somnambulism," who experiences fright even as she anticipates she will be frightened by a harmless prankster, reproduces the anomalous fear of Darwin and of Rozin's subjects, and these reproduce the suspense of Brown's reader, who experiences suspense and anxiety for Constantia Davis despite the fact that "Somnambulism" has announced from the beginning what its ending will be.

Brown produced texts that were deeply versed in and critically engaged with the sensationalist psychology of the late Enlightenment but that also anticipated, like the work of William James, many of the experiential principles of human emotion that would find empirical confirmation in the contemporary lexicons of the cognitive sciences. Brown's "Somnambulism" is a particularly instructive example. It is both an allegory of reading and the first U.S. detective story. Here, the actions of father and daughter, who are coerced by instinct into reading the clues of their environment by the threat of danger, double the actions of the narrator, who is coerced by the blank space of sleepwalking (significantly, a "disease of the mind" in the medical vocabulary of the time),[57] and the crime it generates into laboriously rereading the body of history in his search for a coherent narrative. As in *Wieland*, Brown is making assertions about what happens to us when we read: we become hypochondriacs like Baxter, realizing the fantasies we read in our bodies; we become sleepwalkers, actors without will like Edgar Huntly, who "catches" the disease of sleepwalking from his too-close-reading of the somnambulist Clithero. Richard Gerrig's review of contemporary studies on reading and suspense resonates with Brown's more latent models. Gerrig argues that subjects do not simply lose their hold on precognitive emotions when reading; rather, they lose their hold upon reality. It is not just that fiction reveals how emotion and cognition can decouple, or how emotion can overwhelm cognition. Our deep cognitive structures do not operate the way we once believed. In repeated experiments, Gerrig found that readers had more difficulty confirming the truth of "real-world outcomes" when reading suspense stories (*ENW*, 164). Increased verification latencies were also discovered with experiments that exposed subjects to clearly identified fantasy facts (for example, George Washington wrote *Tom Sawyer*) alongside clearly identifiable real-world facts. These experiments, according to Gerrig, point to the "integration of the fantasy facts into preexisting memory structures" (*ENW*, 227–29). And the experience of anomalous suspense (that is, the readerly experience of anxiety or surprise in texts already read) points irresistibly, he concludes, to the thesis that "readers who are transported to narrative worlds lose access to the details of the real world" (*ENW*, 209). Indeed, in one particularly inventive experiment, D. T. Gilbert postulates that human cognition operates under a universal belief principle; that is, acceptance or rejection of ideas does not require conscious activity, as previously believed, but occurs automatically: acceptance is our default cognitive response. In this experiment, subjects whose cognitive processes were interrupted when absorbing information consistently erred, when determining the truth-value of these statements, in favor of universal acceptance. As Gerrig summarizes it, there is a "special effort to unaccept false information," and fictional information is not automatically tagged as such in mental representations (*ENW*, 173):

> . . . *fictional information* in fact fails to refer to a category that has any a priori psychological coherence. Information becomes tagged as fictional only as a function of readers' conscious scrutiny. Even then, "fictional" information is unlikely to be represented in memory in a fashion different from any other sort of information readers have worked at disbelieving. The account I am advocating, therefore, replaces a "willing suspension of disbelief" with a "willing construction of disbelief." The net difference is that we cannot possibly be surprised that information from fictional narratives has a real-world effect. (*ENW*, 230)

The inability of the protagonists of *Wieland* to disbelieve is, then, an emblem of our own readerly consciousness. But if these characters always believe, they also act, unlike Charles when facing the green slime—and here Walton would argue that the failure to act in response to fictions is precisely the evidence that signifies our failure to believe, that signifies, at best, our make-believing. Gerrig counters that we experience behavioral inhibition with true and really-believed information all the time. A documentary film on a green slime terrorizing a town, even when taken as fact, will nonetheless provoke no fight-or-flight reaction in Charles (*ENW*, 188–91). It could also be argued that the decision to act (to flee, to call the police) is a higher-level cognitive process that is separable both from emotional response and from low-level cognitive acceptance. In any case, there are a variety of ways we can understand and be moved by the real world without finding ourselves personally committed to action. For Gerrig's argument to succeed, though, it would still be necessary to explain how it is that we experience full, durable, and vivid emotion *after* we have constructed our disbelief (Don't be afraid: it's only a movie, it's only a movie, it's only a movie). We would still have to provide some model of preconsciously triggered emotions that can survive alongside the emotions or emotional inhibitions typically generated by conscious, higher-level disbelief. With models of belief and emotion appropriately modified by the preceding cognitive scientific accounts, however, this should not be difficult. One might hypothesize that in narrative encounters, continual preconscious acceptances compete with continual constructions of disbelief to create the semblance of a continuous (or quasi) emotion. One might also argue that emotions are triggered and endure as physical processes for some time, quite independently of the cognitive work of belief formation and revision; heart rate readjusts itself quickly, for instance, but emotion-generating hormonal or chemical secretions in the bloodstream (and our reading of these stimuli as feelings) do not. In other words, a hybrid of the three replies to the paradox of fictional fear may end up being the best description of a frightened reader's response: (1) we do in fact fail to achieve disbelief at a basic level of awareness; (2) higher mental evaluations (for instance, in the form of reasoned beliefs) can be an aspect of our emotional lives but should not be viewed as primary, normative, or even causal as opposed to caused: emotions and beliefs are competitive and mutually causal, and while clearly intertwined they might most usefully be considered semi-autonomous aspects of consciousness (as the case of phobias revealed); and (3) feelings we experience as coercive, automatic, or physically overpowering can nonetheless be understood as willed, directed, or sustained through the narrative frames we provide ourselves—as with a game of make-believe or the ruminations of a hypochondriac.

Like Tolstoy, who saw "infectiousness" as the primary quality of art, Brown found a model for the experience of reading in illness and contagion. Sickness, and the unique form of knowing it brings, was after all the central fact of Brown's life. Brown was a sickly child; he was infected with the yellow fever as an adult during an outbreak of the plague in New York (he survived, but lost his intimate friend Dr. Elihu Hubbard Smith to the disease); and he died young of consumption, which had afflicted him since early boyhood. "When have I known," writes Brown in a letter to a friend, "that lightness and vivacity of mind, which the divine flow of health, even in calamity, produces in some men! Never—scarcely ever. Not longer than half an hour at a time, since I have called myself man."[58] For Brown, illness was a worldview, but reading and illness were specially conjoined. Putting aside his books, indeed, was taken as an important first step in recovering his strength ("BLW," 60). Reading, like disease, was an experience that blended will and coercion; disease, like reading, progressed according to a plot delivered in signs. Disease transformed the body into a sign not only readable (if you have tuberculosis you will minutely observe the progress of your body to determine how you should feel about your state) but also, as the hypochondriacal Baxter showed and Brown almost certainly experienced, writable. Willing entry into a narrative world meant surrender to whatever story one constructed (I Am Ill, A Monster Is Chasing Me). To put it another way, disease showed Brown both how we can be physically changed by the things we read and how we read our bodies to know what to feel. In Baxter, Arthur, Clara, and Constantia, then, Brown found a model not only for the feeling of reading but also for our emotional lives more generally. With a book, as with a disease, as with the frights or desires we take upon ourselves each day, we experience what our body does as the result of things we have not realized we believe.

And this returns us to the question of why—why read horror? why seek aversive stimuli?—because part of what gothic art demonstrates is that we have discovered this oddity in our programming, this structural stutter-step in cognition, and that we have learned how to manipulate it for amusement. We discover ourselves to be creatures with certain properties, properties that can be manipulated, in full knowledge of their manipulation, in order to produce an expected coercive result. Why do we love the coercion of art-fear? Just as a child, having learned so recently to accept as a given that the gross movements of her body are an extension of her consciousness, watches her body reacting in reflex (If you hit your knee here, it will kick!) and experiences the sudden but safe reversal of expectations that characterizes both comedy and small wonder, so do we, having learned so thoroughly to treat our thinking as coterminous with being, watch our belief-implying emotions sweep over us in sudden violation of all our most reasoned background assumptions (but safely, since we have willed the circumstances that predictably produce this violation) and thus experience the wondrous and absurd revelation that we are, in conscious thought, only dancing on the surface of what we truly are.

What are Brown's gothic tales to us then? An emotionally wrenching novel in some ways functions much like, say, a nicely painted room or mint-scented shampoo—with each we are manipulating our emotional susceptibility to props to trigger beliefs and reactions that we know we have no reason to have. Are tears for Anna Karenina, after all, any more mystifying than the fact that your ambient sense of life-satisfaction can change radically without the conditions of your life changing (depending on factors as irrelevant as the intensity of light and color in a room)? Is it not even more odd that you should swoon at the smell of mint in your lover's hair, as if you believed the implicit claim the shampoo's residue puts to you: namely, that you have discovered to your great fortune a partner that smells like mint, that the mint is part of what constitutes your partner? With all such props, from Arthur's pestilence and Charles's green slime to your partner's shampoo, we have discovered that we are a very peculiar type of animal. We have discovered, in essence, that we will believe anything we tell ourselves.

Macalester College

Notes

1   Rei Terada describes "a surge in the academic study of feeling" and "criticism's newfound thematization of emotion" (*Feeling in Theory: Emotion after the "Death of the Subject"* [Cambridge: Harvard Univ. Press, 2001], 14–15). Signal titles representing this broad shift in focus range from Wendy Steiner's *The Scandal of Pleasure* (Chicago: Univ. of Chicago

Press, 1995) and Elaine Scarry's *On Beauty and Being Just* (Princeton, N.J.: Princeton Univ. Press, 1999) to Eve Sedgwick's *Touching Feeling* (Durham, N.C.: Duke Univ. Press, 2003), Philip Fisher's *The Vehement Passions* (Princeton, N.J.: Princeton Univ. Press, 2002), and "Representing the Passions," the Getty Research Institute's scholars-in-residence program (1997–98, 1998–99).

2   See, for instance, Evelyne Keitel, *Reading Psychosis*, trans. Anthea Bell (Oxford, Eng.: Basil Blackwell, 1989), 10. Jonathan Culler writes that the experiences "reader-oriented critics invoke are generally cognitive rather than affective: not feeling shivers along the spine . . . [but] struggling with an irresolvable ambiguity, or questioning the assumptions on which one had relied" (*On Deconstruction* [Ithaca, N.Y.: Cornell Univ. Press, 1982], 39).

3   See Julie Ellison's insightful *Cato's Tears and the Making of Anglo-American Emotion* (Chicago: Univ. of Chicago Press, 1999), 4–9. See also Julia Stern, *The Plight of Feeling: Sympathy and Dissent in the Early American Novel* (Chicago: Univ. of Chicago Press, 1997); and Shirley Samuels, ed., *The Culture of Sentiment: Race, Gender, and Sentimentality in Nineteenth-Century America* (New York: Oxford Univ. Press, 1992).

4   See William K. Wimsatt and Monroe Beardsley, *The Verbal Icon: Studies in the Meaning of Poetry* ([Lexington]: Univ. of Kentucky Press, 1954), 34.

5   The peculiarities of Brown's manner—unreliable narrators, self-referentiality, narrative inconsistencies, moral ambiguity, loose ends—have made his work a preferred site for the reader-oriented criticism that Culler describes in *On Deconstruction*; see also William Scheick, "The Problem of Origination in Brown's *Ormond*," in *Critical Essays on Charles Brockden Brown*, ed. Bernard Rosenthal (Boston: G. K. Hall, 1981), 126–41. When emotion or readerly affect in Brown has been critically addressed, it has been treated as a starting point for cultural analysis rather than as an endpoint in itself; see Ellison, *Cato's Tears*; and Stern, *The Plight of Feeling*.

6   Charles Brockden Brown, "The Man at Home," in *"The Rhapsodist" and Other Uncollected Writings*, ed. Harry Warfel (New York: Scholars' Facsimiles and Reprints, 1943), 56.

7   See D. A. Miller, *The Novel and the Police* (Berkeley and Los Angeles: Univ. of California Press, 1988); see also Dana Luciano, "'Perverse Nature': *Edgar Huntly* and the Novel's Reproductive Disorders," *American Literature* 70 (March 1998): 1–27.

8   "Brown's Life and Writings," in *North American Review and Miscellaneous Journal* 9 (1819): 73, 64. Further references will be cited parenthetically in the text as "BLW."

9   "American Literature," in vol. 9 of *The Retrospective Review* (London: Charles Baldwyn, 1824), 317–18.

10   Charles Brockden Brown, *Wieland*, in *Three Gothic Novels* (New York:

Library of America, 1998), 17, 19, 52, 79. Further references are to this edition and will be cited parenthetically as *W*.

11 For a review of work combining literary studies and cognitive science, see Mary Thomas Crane and Alan Richardson, "Literary Studies and Cognitive Science: Toward a New Interdisciplinarity," *Mosaic* 32 (June 1999): 123–40. For exemplary work on perception in literary experience, see Elaine Scarry, *Dreaming by the Book* (New York: Farrar, Straus, and Giroux, 1999); on a certain construal of narrative as a substratum for cognition, see Mark Turner, *The Literary Mind* (New York: Oxford Univ. Press, 1996); and on metaphor as a basic procedure of cognition, see Raymond Gibbs, *The Poetics of Mind: Figurative Thought, Language, and Understanding* (New York: Cambridge Univ. Press, 1994).

12 Charles Brockden Brown, *Arthur Mervyn*, in *Three Gothic Novels* (New York: Library of America, 1998), 379. Further references are to this edition and will be cited parenthetically as *AM*.

13 Brown to James Brown, 25 October 1796, in David Lee Clark, *Charles Brockden Brown: Pioneer Voice of America* (Durham, N.C.: Duke Univ. Press, 1952), 156.

14 See Brown, "The Rhapsodist," in *"The Rhapsodist" and Other Uncollected Writings*, 21, 23.

15 Leo Tolstoy, *What is Art?*, in *Critical Theory since Plato*, ed. Hazard Adams (New York: Harcourt Brace Jovanovich, 1971), 710, 714. The words translated under the category of infection correspond to the Russian "*zarazitel'nost'*."

16 Brown, "The Man at Home," in *"The Rhapsodist" and Other Uncollected Writings*, 81.

17 Daniel Webster, quoted in Karen Halttunen, *Murder Most Foul: The Killer and the American Gothic Imagination* (Cambridge: Harvard Univ. Press, 1998), 61.

18 Matthew Carey, *A Short Account of the Malignant Fever Lately Prevalent in Philadelphia*, 4th ed. (Philadelphia: published by the author, 1794), 13, 16, 25, 23.

19 David Hume, "Of Tragedy," in *"Of the Standard of Taste" and Other Essays*, ed. John W. Lenz (1757; reprint, Indianapolis: Bobbs-Merrill, 1965), 32.

20 See Norman Holland, *The Dynamics of Literary Response* (New York: Oxford Univ. Press, 1968), 281–307.

21 See Noël Carroll, *The Philosophy of Horror: Paradoxes of the Heart* (New York: Routledge, 1990), 193.

22 Edmund Burke, *A Philosophical Enquiry into the Origin of Our Ideas of the Sublime and Beautiful* (1757; reprint, New York: Oxford Univ. Press, 1990), 122–23.

23 Marvin Zuckerman, *Behavioral Expressions and Biosocial Bases of Sensation Seeking* (Cambridge, Eng.: Cambridge Univ. Press, 1994).

24 William Brewer, "The Nature of Narrative Suspense and the Problem

of Rereading," in *Suspense: Conceptualizations, Theoretical Analyses, and Empirical Exploration*, ed. Peter Vorderer et al. (Mahwah, N.J.: Lawrence Erlbaum, 1996), 108.

25 Paul Hernadi, "Why Is Literature: A Coevolutionary Perspective on Imaginative Worldmaking," *Poetics Today* 23 (spring 2002): 33.

26 See, for instance, David Stewart, "Cultural Work, City Crime, Reading, Pleasure," *American Literary History* 9 (winter 1997): 676–701.

27 John Mitchell Mason, *Mercy Remembered in Wrath* (New York: Buel, 1795), 6. See also Carroll, *The Philosophy of Horror*, 199.

28 See Halttunen, *Murder Most Foul*, 63.

29 [Charles Brockden Brown], "On the Cause of the Popularity of Novels," *(Philadelphia) Literary Magazine and American Register* 7 (June 1807): 410–12; see also Hume, "Of Tragedy," 29–30.

30 Brown to Henrietta G. (full name unknown), n.d.; quoted in Clark, *Charles Brockden Brown*, 70.

31 Charles Brockden Brown, *Edgar Huntly or, Memoirs of a Sleep-Walker*, in *Three Gothic Novels*, 848.

32 See Charles Brockden Brown, "The Editor's Address to the Public," *Literary Magazine and American Register*, October 1803, 5; cited in Luciano, "'Perverse Nature,'" 3.

33 On the uniqueness of fear as an illuminating human emotion, see Joseph LeDoux, *The Emotional Brain: The Mysterious Underpinnings of Emotional Life* (New York: Touchstone, 1998), 128–34, 204–5, 252. Further references to this source will be cited parenthetically in the text as *EB*.

34 Edith Wharton, "An Autobiographical Postcript," *The Ghost Stories of Edith Wharton* (New York: Scribner, 1997), 303.

35 Burke, *A Philosophical Enquiry*, 53.

36 Peter Lamarque, "How Can We Fear and Pity Fictions?" *British Journal of Aesthetics* 21 (autumn 1981): 291.

37 Bijoy Boruah, *Fiction and Emotion: A Study in Aesthetics and the Philosophy of Mind* (New York: Oxford Univ. Press, 1988), 10.

38 Kendall L. Walton, *Mimesis as Make-Believe: On the Foundations of the Representational Arts* (Cambridge: Harvard Univ. Press, 1990), 197. Further references will be cited parenthetically as *M*.

39 See Lawrence W. Levine, *Highbrow/Lowbrow: The Emergence of Cultural Hierarchy in America* (Cambridge: Harvard Univ. Press, 1988), 30.

40 Richard J. Gerrig, *Experiencing Narrative Worlds: On the Psychological Activities of Reading* (New Haven: Westview, 1993), 26–29, 84–178; and Walton, *Mimesis as Make-Believe*, 16–17. Further references to *Experiencing Narrative Worlds* will be cited parenthetically as *ENW*.

41 See John Morreal, "Fear without Belief," *Journal of Philosophy*, 90 (July 1993): 359–66.

42 Colin Radford, "How Can We Be Moved by the Fate of Anna Karenina?" *Proceedings of the Aristotelian Society* 69 (supplementary vol.): 67–80.

43 R. S. Lazarus, "Cognition and Motivation in Emotion," *American Psychologist* 46, no. 4 (1991): 352–67; quoted in LeDoux, *Emotional Brain*, 51.

44 Robert Solomon, "Getting Angry: The Jamesian Theory of Emotion in Anthropology," in *Culture Theory*, ed. Richard Shweder and Robert LeVine (Cambridge, Eng.: Cambridge Univ. Press, 1984), 248.

45 Brown, quoted in Clark, *Charles Brockden Brown*, 105.

46 It could be argued, against Walton, that the greatest evidence that we experience fear is our statement that we are experiencing it. Many studies, however, have revealed that we are often the worst evaluators of our feelings and reasons for actions, in large part because of our strong tendency to retroactively narrate ourselves into coherence. LeDoux writes that "people normally do all sorts of things for reasons they are not consciously aware of (because the behavior is produced by brain systems that operate unconsciously) and that one of the main jobs of consciousness is to keep our life tied together into a coherent story, a self-concept" (*Emotional Brain*, 32–33).

47 William James, *Psychology: Briefer Course*, in *Writings, 1878–1899* (New York: Library of America, 1992), 353, 352.

48 See Solomon, "Getting Angry," 238–54.

49 Carroll, *The Philosophy of Horror*, 25.

50 See Antonio Damasio, *Descartes' Error: Emotion, Reason, and the Human Brain* (New York: Avon, 1994), 148. See also Burke, *A Philosophical Enquiry*, 120.

51 Antonio Damasio, *The Feeling of What Happens: Body and Emotion in the Making of Consciousness* (San Diego: Harvest Books, 1999), 280, 36.

52 Ibid., 45. See also LeDoux, *Emotional Brain*, 180–81.

53 Charles Brockden Brown, "Somnambulism. A Fragment," *"Somnambulism" and Other Stories*, ed. Alfred Weber (Frankfurt: Peter Lang, 1987), 8, 14.

54 See LeDoux, *Emotional Brain*, 204, 252; and Morreal, "Fear without Belief," 361–62.

55 Damasio, *The Feeling of What Happens*, 31.

56 Charles Darwin, *The Expression of the Emotions in Man and Animals* (London: HarperCollins, 1998), 43–44.

57 Brown, introduction to *"Somnambulism" and Other Stories*, xiv.

58 Brown to "a friend," in Evert Duyckinck, *Cyclopaedia of American Literature*, 2 vols. (Philadelphia: W. M. Rutter, 1854), 1:611.

Paul Gilmore

Romantic Electricity, or the Materiality of Aesthetics

Perhaps the central problem for contemporary critics who address aesthetics is defining exactly what we mean by the term. In addition to the abundance of historically specific ideas about aesthetics, various topics can be crowded under its aegis: aesthetic objects, aesthetic judgments (or values), aesthetic theories, aesthetic experience, aesthetic attitude (or function), aesthetic practice. In the past two decades, American literary criticism has tended to dismiss aesthetics in toto by identifying it almost exclusively with New Criticism's formal judgments about specific aesthetic objects. This dismissal has consisted of debunking New Criticism's idea of a transhistoric aesthetic object by revealing the sociopolitical interestedness of aesthetic judgments supposedly based on objective formal properties. Yet as Winfried Fluck has argued, "[T]he new revisionism has systematically misunderstood and misrepresented the issue of aesthetics, because it has conflated the New Critical version of aesthetic value with the issue of aesthetics in general. . . . [in part] . . . to justify their own project of an historical and political criticism." Such a conflation of aesthetics with a formal focus on "an inherent quality, structure, or *gestalt*," Fluck contends, "is by no means plausible" and, in fact, is "ahistorical."[1] Instead of continuing to dismiss aesthetics or retreating into the defense of a transcendent canon, American literary criticism needs to explore how historically specific ideas about aesthetics and the aesthetic practices they engendered gave rise to something we might call aesthetic experience.

The earliest uses of the term *aesthetic* in nineteenth-century American criticism reveal the anachronism of identifying aesthetics with

American Literature, Volume 76, Number 3, September 2004. Copyright © 2004 by Duke University Press.

formalism, as these references to *aesthetic* display less interest in distinguishing aesthetic objects from other things or in defining objective aesthetic values than in identifying a certain kind of experience of or attitude toward the world. In fact, as an article from the *American Whig Review* in 1846 reveals, the aesthetic approach of American romantics like Margaret Fuller was regularly attacked for its lack of attention to such formal features as "counter-point, or chiaro-oscuro, subject or composition, style or choice of words."[2] In her introduction to *Aesthetic Papers* (1849), one of the first American volumes with "aesthetic" in its title, Elizabeth Peabody explicitly states: "The 'aesthetic element,' then, is in our view neither a theory of the beautiful, nor a philosophy of art, but a component and indivisible part in all human creations which are not mere works of necessity; in other words, which are based on idea, as distinguished from appetite."[3] It is clear in her prospectus to the volume that Peabody sees the aesthetic as transcending partisan political disputes: "The Editor [of this volume] wishes to assemble, upon the high aesthetic ground (away from the regions of strife, in any bad sense), writers of different schools."[4] Yet Peabody's selection of essays and sketches—including Emerson's "War," Thoreau's "Resistance to Civil Government," and Hawthorne's "Main-Street"—indicates that she views the aesthetic not as a withdrawal into consciousness and form but as a particular kind of engagement with the world. She describes this engagement as "the unpersonal," a kind of experience that "sinks and subordinates the observer to the object,—which, by putting my personality aside, enables me to see the object in pure uncolored light." For nineteenth-century American romantics, then, aesthetic considerations were linked by their "having a reference to the central fact of the constant relation of the individual to the universal, and of their equally constant separation."[5] Rather than a code of formal laws or a canon of transcendent works of art, the aesthetic comprised attempts to bridge the gap between individual experience and universal law or truth, by turning away from the notion of a self-interested individual, driven by material necessity, toward an ideal sphere.

While new historicists have frequently used their rejection of New Critical formal aesthetics to dismiss the aesthetic as a category of analysis, more historically nuanced criticism influenced by cultural materialism has tended to focus on the idealist element suggested in Peabody's distinction between idea and appetite. Most influentially, perhaps, Terry Eagleton's *The Ideology of the Aesthetic* (1990) argues that the aesthetic developed as a modern discourse in the late-eighteenth- and early-nineteenth centuries in response to the rise of capitalism and individuals' alienation from both the products of their labor and from society itself. Taking care to distinguish himself from the "drastically undialectical thought of a vulgar Marxist or 'post-Marxist' trend of thought" that would condemn "the aesthetic [as] simply 'bourgeois ideology,'" Eagleton contends that the aesthetic, as developed in Britain and Germany, actually provides "the first stirrings of a primitive materialism," because it "mediates between the generalities of reason and the particulars of sense," between the individual's specific sensual experience and universal truths accessed through reason.[6] In Eagleton's conception, aesthetic thought not only "provides the middle class with just the ideological model of subjectivity it requires for its material operations" but also engenders "a vision of human energies as radical ends in themselves which is the implacable enemy of all dominative or instrumentalist thought" (*IA*, 9). From his Marxist perspective, Eagleton suggests that "the implicit materialism of the aesthetic might still be redeemable . . . if it can be retrieved from the burden of idealism which weighs it down . . . [through] a revolution in thought which takes its starting-point from the body itself, rather than from a reason which struggles to make room for it" (*IA*, 196–97). Yet in the overarching picture Eagleton paints, the attempt to build on the specific sensual experience of the individual to create a larger, coherent social collectivity most often becomes a model of consensual discipline for integrating the particular into a hegemonic whole that abandons its grounding in the socially enmeshed, historical body for some transhistoric, idealist conception of "pure form" (*IA*, 196).[7] Despite Eagleton's attempts to portray the aesthetic as more than ideology, he seems to see the idealism of the aesthetic as primarily promoting the reconciliation of capitalism's contradictions in an ideal sphere fully detached from the material structures of the production of social life, and thus merely reiterating structures of domination.[8]

Such critiques of modern aesthetics often carefully document the conservative historical uses of aesthetic ideologies and idealist aesthetic practices. But in cataloging how theories of the aesthetic and their attempts to develop abstract accounts of sensual, aesthetic experience seem inevitably to lead to an individualistic idealism, critiques like Eagleton's neglect or dismiss that experience itself in favor of certain dominant accounts of it. In other words, materialist-political critiques of the aesthetic have tended, paradoxically, to eschew the material experience that aesthetic theories attempt to understand, focusing instead on the theories themselves. In place of an attention to the sensual experience and material existence that might give rise to notions of the aesthetic, we get a critique of aesthetic ideology as ideology and an unveiling of its underlying power structures.

In the past decade, however, a number of critics working within a cultural materialist tradition, including Fluck, Ian Hunter, Isobel Armstrong, and Michèle Barrett, have argued for attending to both the material experiences we could call aesthetic and the socially determined institutions and objects that foster such experiences. Rather than dismissing the aesthetic as "a knowledge or practice of cultivation segregated from the driving forces of human development—labor and politics—and retarding further development by diverting culture into the ideal realm of ethics and taste," these critics have interpreted the aesthetic as a material practice or materially produced state of consciousness.[9] These interpretations recognize, as Jan Mukarovský notes, that the aesthetic "manifests itself only under certain conditions, i.e. in a certain social context."[10] It follows, then, that a renewed attention to aesthetics must continue in the interdisciplinary vein of cultural studies, paying particular attention to the confluence of political, economic, and cultural forces that enable certain manifestations of an experience imagined to transcend, suspend, or displace those very forces.

Whether some sort of aesthetic experience is transhistorically and transculturally human, as Fluck and Mukarovský seem to suggest, we can at least conclude that a wide variety of individuals in the modern West have claimed such experience. Produced by diverse objects and states of consciousness, the experience allows one to achieve a kind of "non-identity" ("ACS," 90), what Peabody calls a sense of "the unpersonal," through the momentary disruption of dominant notions of material, political, and social interests and the related conception of the atomistic self in relation to an instrumentalized objective world. Aesthetic experience is the sensual and conscious suspension and ecstatic transcendence of the interested self through an encounter with a stimulus, whether a designated art object or not. As the product of material sensations registered on the individual body that give rise to a sense of the limitations and fluid boundaries of the self, the aesthetic moment is inherently paradoxical, blurring distinctions between self and community, sensual and ideal.

While Fluck notes that aesthetic experience never "allows us to escape, if only temporarily, from reality," its "temporary bracketing of reference" to economic, social, and political ends is useful: "it opens up the possibility of a new perspective on the object and, by implication, on reality," including the social world ("ACS," 88). Reexamining accounts of such experience might then lead to our viewing the connection between politics and aesthetics as potentially more than ideological delusion. Aesthetics, located on the level of an individual body but imagined to connect that body with some universally accessible experience, might provide a needed supplement to identity politics. In other words, the aesthetic moment's potential political power derives from its ability to engender an imagined community that, unlike the one described by Benedict Anderson, transcends racial, social, and national boundaries.[11] It is only through the individual, racial, gendered, nationalized body that the aesthetic can be experienced. Yet that very experience creates a sense of shared humanity, defined not by economic or political interest, as with class or nation, but by the possession of a sensorial body. Further, because the aesthetic moment constitutes a universalizable, yet individualized, experience, it fosters the imagination of a collectivity based in, yet transcending, particular gendered, sexed, and racialized identities. Producing a sense of community while both acknowledging and disavowing the power of particularized interests and bodies, aesthetics potentially reorients our thinking about how and why we identify with certain groups or identities.

Critical practice in past decades has demonstrated how aesthetics has been used to reinforce social, economic, and political distinctions by placing certain groups outside the universal humanity that aesthetic claims involve. And in attending to the material bases that give rise to aesthetic experience, we need to recognize that despite its transcendent claims, aesthetic experience is only potentially, not equally, accessible to all (as my canonical white, male, economically secure examples demonstrate). But as my reconstruction of a strain of romantic thought will show, the aesthetic, considered as a type of universal experience imagined to permeate "all human creations which are not mere works of necessity," is consistently imagined as open to any person with any kind of history, regardless of subject position. Because the aesthetic is described as a material experience that transcends formal definitions of art, it provides the possibility of connecting different groups of people through shared sensual experience rather than common economic or political interests. The aesthetic's universalizing claims imply a kind of egalitarianism that might be translated to the political sphere, where it can offer a starting point for building coalitions and communities across the lines of race, class, and gender reified by identity politics.

Because the aesthetic moment is transient, and the imagined community it fosters is located outside any recognizable public sphere, aesthetics alone cannot substitute for politics, because it does not directly address the political, economic, or social distribution of power. Yet any progressive cultural critique that dismisses the power of the aesthetic moment altogether abandons its latent possibilities. Disrupting an instrumentalizing logic for understanding the relationship between the self and the world, aesthetic experience could become a precondition to greater political and social freedom and equality by imagining a universally shared terrain in place of the delimited ground of identity politics.[12] Contemporary American literary criticism, that is to say, needs to reexamine what Ernst Bloch calls the utopian function of art in order to supplement the work on the limiting and determining power of identity in culture and politics.[13] Moving beyond notions of the aesthetic as form, as canonized (and thereby fossilized) thought and practice, as secular sacralization, to consider aesthetic experience as recorded and inculcated by certain literary practices within specific historical situations would constitute the next step in, rather than a retreat from, cultural and historical approaches to the literary sphere.

■ ■ ■

I want to begin developing one direction such historical attention to aesthetic experience might take by examining how American romantics frequently invoke metaphors of and hypotheses about electricity to describe the aesthetic's potential to transform the world. Such metaphors suffuse the works of British and American romantic poets and thinkers, often figuring either an intense, nearly physical emotion or an ecstatic, shocking sense of sympathy or transcendence. By the mid-nineteenth century, in fact, the idea that an "electric spirit and mysterious principle . . . distinguish the off-spring of genius from that of talent and industry" appeared frequently in American literary criticism and popular discourse.[14] While Walt Whitman's body electric is perhaps best known, Emerson speaks of the poet drawing on "a power transcending all limit and privacy, and by virtue of which a man is the conductor of the whole river of electricity." Margaret Fuller, repeatedly equating the lyrical and the electric, refers to "the especial genius of woman" as "electrical in movement, intuitive in function, spiritual in tendency"; and Poe describes those "moods of keenest appetency, when the film from the mental vision departs" as occurring when "the intellect, electrified, surpasses . . . its every-day condition."[15] The electric, in these examples, seems to refer to some intensified level of consciousness connected to the insights of poetic genius. And such a connotation seems, at best, to locate the electric in some ideal sphere, a product of consciousness, imagination, or affective sympathy detached from the material world.

But metaphors of aesthetic electricity, I will contend, were outgrowths of residual and emergent literary, popular, and scientific understandings of electricity. These sources for aesthetic electricity point to frequent attempts to imagine aesthetics as a sensual experience of the individual body, embedded in specific social situations, that somehow leads to the individual's momentary suspension in a sense of a larger whole. In other words, to understand how these figures of electricity work, we need to attend to the various discursive uses of electricity as well as the material developments and economic structures within which they were conceived. Such attention follows from the definition of the aesthetic as a kind of experience not confined to art but produced by all sorts of human activities. Further, it means moving beyond national borders, not only because an international perspective provides a broader context for understanding the aesthetic's manifestations but also because aesthetics, despite recent accounts of romantic nationalism, was imagined to transcend national boundaries. In keeping with the notion of aesthetics as bracketing or delimiting the differentiated self, romantic electricity works counter to the nationalizing tendency—the idea of culture as creating or voicing a particularized national self, often espoused by the same thinkers. Thus, unlike the mechanical metaphors of the associationist tradition (running from Hobbes to Hartley to Blair and his American followers), which provided the main basis for imagining a distinctly American literature, the electric strain of romantic aesthetics attempted to imagine some sort of collective beyond the nation.[16] Methodologically, then, reconstructing nineteenth-century definitions of the aesthetic in terms of "the unpersonal" requires both an interdisciplinary and international approach.

By the mid-eighteenth century, electricity functioned as a powerful metaphor of emotional connection, bodily excitement, and artistic power, connotations that were given further impetus as American romantics built on developments in electrical science and technology as well as earlier aesthetic uses of electricity by German and British romantics.[17] The era of literary romanticism witnessed some of the key breakthroughs in the development of electromagnetism, culminating in the 1830s with Michael Faraday's experimental confirmation of electromagnetic induction and Samuel F. B. Morse's invention of the telegraph. As a standard progressive history of electrical science frames it, "[t]hree events provided the stable base of modern electrical science: the discovery of a constant-current source of electricity by Volta, the magnetic influence of an electric current by Oersted and, finally, the generation of an electric current from magnetism by Faraday."[18] That base, however, was far from stable in the late-eighteenth and early-nineteenth centuries. Electricity proved a puzzling problem for Newtonian science, for its actions could not be easily reconciled with a world conceived in terms of solid atoms acting directly and mechanically upon one another. The experiments and findings of men like Galvani, Volta, Davy, Oersted, and Ampère in the late 1700s and early 1800s produced not one accepted understanding of electricity but, as Iwan Morus has argued, a "heterogeneity of electricity" with "a variety of different uses. It could explain the movements of the planets, the structure of the earth, the development of plants, and the organization of the human brain."[19]

By challenging a Newtonian notion of solid particles in motion, a clockmaker God, and, concomitantly, a poetics of static form, imitation, and mimesis, the electric sciences provided a potential font of images and ideas for romantic thought, for reimagining the relationships among society, art, the individual consciousness, and some larger social whole. And in turn, romantic theories imagining the universe as a unified, organic whole provided a key theoretical model for those conducting electrical experiments.[20] As Maria Tatar has explained, electricity, understood as not just the "animating agent of organic life" but "the very 'soul of the universe'" became central to German *naturphilosophie* and its main tenets, which included "the concept of nature as an organic whole, the identity between nature and the human mind, the notion of a tripartite rhythm in the history of human consciousness, and the principle of polarity—[which] came to serve as the very foundations of Romantic poetry."[21] The older, conservative Coleridge, for example, while explicitly rejecting the idea of electricity as a vital force or the materialization of thought, continued to regard it as an important phenomenon revealing an ideal, transcendent truth: "the idea of *two—opposite—forces*, tending to rest by equilibrium."[22] The idealist orientation of organicist romantic aesthetics, which views natural phenomena as indicators of sublime, transcendent truths, emerges as the material world (whether manifested in electric science, poetry, or social structures) comes to function primarily as a reflection or outgrowth of an ideal, defining system of laws. While electricity itself may appear volatile, fluid, uncontainable, the truth it reveals is impervious to time, change, and society.

Yet this organic, idealist understanding of electricity was not the only use of electricity in romantic literature. In fact, its most famous evocation, in Mary Shelley's *Frankenstein* (1818), depends on a much more materialist understanding of electricity, as it draws on the scientific possibility that electricity might represent the life force itself, which in turn symbolizes the powers and dangers of the romantic imagination. The possible erasure of the distinction between material experience or substance and immaterial thought or spirit permeated the scientific debates over electricity that would influence romantic thinkers; and as both Chris Baldick and Mark Kipperman have noted, the implications of these debates had far-reaching political and philosophical consequences.[23] If electricity were indeed the life force and medium of thought, and if humans could produce and manipulate it, then a materialist view of the world and of human existence would seem to follow, leaving little room for a deity or a soul. Radical thought in the 1790s, as developed in the theories of Joseph Priestley and others, imagined new discoveries in electricity promoting a new conceptualization of the social world opposed to the hierarchical organization often connected to Newtonian thought.

The earliest uses of electricity in English romantic poetry reflect this line of thought. The *Oxford English Dictionary* cites Coleridge's "Songs of Pixies" (1793) as the first figurative use of *electric* to refer to "the thrilling effect of the electric shock." In his radical youth in the 1790s and early 1800s, Coleridge was friends with Sir Humphrey Davy, the leading English scientist of electricity. The political sense of electricity is exemplified in Coleridge's "Sonnet: To William Godwin" (1795), where he describes Godwin as "form'd t' illume a sunless world forlorn, / As o'er the chill and dusky brow of Night, / In Finland's wintry skies, the Mimic Morn / Electric pours a stream of rosy light." Just as the aurora borealis pours electric light onto the winter of Scandinavia (the Northern Lights were one of many phenomena understood in terms of electricity in the eighteenth century), so Godwin's revolutionary political thought enlightens a "forlorn" world, and makes "OPPRESSION, terror-pale, / Since, thro' the windings of her dark machine, / Thy steady eye has shot its glances keen."[24] Setting the machinations of oppression (and, implicitly perhaps, a mechanical understanding of the world) in opposition to the enlightening energy of radical thought, Coleridge associates electricity with political freedom and revolution as well as aesthetics. As Kipperman verifies, Coleridge's move away from the implications of Davy's science paralleled his retreat from his earlier radical politics, as he replaced his focus on dynamic, fluid process with an interest in organic wholeness and formal idealism (with a strict distinction between an immaterial consciousness and a material world).[25] Thus, in romantic poetry, electricity begins as aesthetic and experiential—as sensual and registered on the body, as shocks, or as a fluid moving through the material body, influencing and changing it and, in turn, potentially changing existing social structures. But it ends up as simply a vehicle to a kind of anaesthetic contemplation of the ideal, a balanced and static structuring of the universe and political society, a move that mirrors the trend that Eagleton describes as plaguing aesthetic theory in general.

An alternative view of aesthetic electricity in English romanticism is suggested most fully by Percy Bysshe Shelley. While sharing Coleridge's interest in science and his commitment to the centrality of human consciousness, Shelley maintained a more dialectical understanding of the relationship between immaterial thought and the material world, an understanding at the base of his political radicalism.[26] Shelley invokes the metaphor of electricity most prominently in his "A Defence of Poetry," describing poetry as "a sword of lightning," in which "electric life . . . burns."[27] Elsewhere, Shelley's comments on electricity suggest that this metaphoric use is grounded in both a materialist understanding of electricity as perhaps the very medium of thought and a utopian dream of technological improvement. This materialist impulse is reflected in "A Refutation of Deism" (1814), in which Shelley draws on the idea of electricity as an imponderable, material force analogous to, if not identical with, thought itself, rejecting the idea of a divine watchmaker behind the creation of animated life. To speak of matter as "inert," Shelley claims, makes no sense: "It is infinitely active and subtle. Light, electricity and magnetism are fluids not surpassed by thought itself in tenuity and activity; like thought they are sometimes the cause and sometimes the effect of motion; and, distinct as they are from every other class of substances, with which we are acquainted, seem to possess equal claims with thought to the unmeaning distinction of immateriality."[28] Electricity embodies the inability to distinguish fully between matter and immateriality, as thought becomes as material as electricity and the material world becomes as "active and subtle" as thought. Poetry, thus, is electric in its ability to blur the line between body and mind, to affect us on both a sensual and a conscious level.

This erosion of the distinction between materiality and immateriality further implies the disintegration of discrete individuals. Shelley is not as explicit about "the unpersonal" nature of the electric-aesthetic self as Byron, whose figurative uses of electricity suggest the implications of this materialist understanding of thought and idealist conception of matter for the idea of the self. In Byron's poetry, electricity repeatedly evokes experiences involving fluid personal boundaries, either in terms of unconscious thought, sympathetic identification, or the porousness of the sensual, material self.[29] It is in this way, then, that understandings of electricity as a kind of universal fluid conveying thought, if not life itself, become a dangerous threat to "the inward sanctuary of organic human authenticity" for conservatives like the later Coleridge and Thomas Carlyle.[30] Shelley's idea of the poet as an unacknowledged legislator wielding a sword of lightning is not based simply on a reconception of thought as material or a notion of the self as fluid; rather, Shelley links the poet's ability to overcome political and economic inequality to technological improvements, including those involving electricity. As Thomas Jefferson Hogg recalls in his remembrance of Shelley at Oxford, Shelley contended that "[t]he galvanic battery is a new engine; it has been used hitherto to an insignificant extent, yet has it wrought wonders already;

what will not . . . a well-arranged system of hundreds of metallic plates, effect?" Linking voltaic electricity to the balloon, Shelley concludes, according to Hogg, that such inventions "would virtually emancipate every slave, and would annihilate slavery for ever."[31]

For Shelley, the human imagination, physically embodied in electric current and manifested in technological improvements involving electricity, becomes both the medium where the mental and physical meet and the source of intellectual and physical freedom. And as potentially the material form of thought itself, electricity challenges not just the distinction between the material and the immaterial but also the notion of the individual atomistic self by making the mind the porous receiver and transmitter of a stimulating substance not fully under its control. That substance, in the case of poetry, consists of words, as words themselves become, like electricity, the materialization of thought, which suggests the social nature of language. Shelley indicates that it is poetry's embeddedness in what we might now call social discourse that gives it "electric life," as that life is "less [the poet's] spirit than the spirit of the age."[32] Aesthetic experience is electric, for as electricity had been shown to pass mysteriously, almost immaterially, from one material body to other bodies, so the aesthetic experience (through language, in the case of poetry) seemed also to temporarily dissolve the distinctions between self and other, mind and body. Poet and reader share words not just idealistically, as their common cultural and educational heritage, but physically as thought itself becomes materialized. That aesthetic experience is not, in itself, political, but it calls into question the idea of a stable self by opening it to new perspectives, new thoughts, new ways of organizing society. The change actually registered on the material body through an understanding of thought as electric opens the door to reconstituting the self and the biological, economic, political, and ideological forces constituting individuals and society.

■ ■ ■

Coleridge and Shelley represent two major trends in romantic appropriations of electrical science that begin to suggest the potential that electricity presented for understanding aesthetic experience in material terms. American literary criticism has, reasonably, tended to identify Coleridgean organic symbolism as a central influence in American romanticism, but American romantics' use of aesthetic electricity, I will argue, comes much closer to Shelley's more materialistic approach, with its focus on the physical body and the possibility of social change.[33] One of the main reasons for this tendency to analogize electricity and aesthetics as material forces was the invention and development of the electromagnetic telegraph. Where early-nineteenth-century romantics could draw on the mysterious, life-giving, but potentially dangerous power of electricity, for the writers of the American Renaissance, electricity, although still mysterious, represented a potential technological and physical force. In American romantic and mainstream thought from the 1830s to the 1850s, long-standing ideas of electricity as related to the nervous impulse—a divine, nearly immaterial spark of life—and to thought itself were reconceived in terms of Morse's telegraph. In turn, through the telegraph, American romantics' conception of aesthetic experience as electric locates that experience even more squarely within a nexus of material forces. With the telegraph, the idea that both thought and language were electric and therefore part of a network linking all of humanity assumed even greater currency, as evinced in an 1848 article in the *United States Democratic Review*, "Influence of the Telegraph upon Literature": "Language is but the medium of thought—which flies as rapidly and acts as instantaneously as the invisible element which flashes along the Telegraphic wire. The more closely, then, that it follows the operation of thought [in a telegraphic manner], the more perfectly does it perform its office."[34] Thought, like telegraphic messages, is electric, and language, at its best, mirrors that electricity, materializing and translating the "invisible element" of electric thought into a form that renders it comprehensible. For American authors, reimagining literature in such terms fostered the notion of a boundaryless, yet embodied, social collective.

Whitman's "body electric" provides the best known, and perhaps most fully developed, use of electricity to suggest the collective materiality of aesthetic experience. Electrical metaphors and allusions appear more frequently in the revisions and additions Whitman made to *Leaves of Grass* after the Civil War, including his addition of the eponymous line "I Sing the Body Electric." But even in the original 1855 edition, Whitman repeatedly mentions electricity, twice alluding to the telegraph. For Whitman, the ecstatic nature of the aesthetic moment becomes, of course, sexualized, and electricity often represents sexual desire, as in "Song of Myself," when he describes the "mystery" of "the procreant urge of the world" as "electrical."[35] Later in "Song of Myself," Whitman develops the implications of this sexual electricity when he imagines his body as electrically charged: "I have instant conductors all over me whether I pass or stop, / They seize every object and lead it harmlessly through me." These conductors seem to prevent exterior stimuli from affecting the self, yet as Whitman continues, he discovers that this current "quiver[s] [him] to a new identity," as his "flesh and blood play out lightning," leaving him "helpless" (*PP*, 55). Sex becomes electric as it leads to the suspension of the self and the creation of a new self through the interconnectedness of the body to all sorts of sensual stimuli. As it loses control of its own boundaries, the self is rendered permeable. Throughout *Leaves of Grass*, Whitman uses the embodied experience of sex to represent the loss of self and sense of communion he hopes his own poetry conjures and to figure what I have been calling aesthetic experience. Electricity helps Whitman draw these connections not only because it was, at that time, imagined as a material force akin to the nervous impulse but also because it continued to represent some sort of ideal, immaterial connection uniting all of creation, even as it was quickly becoming a technological, material force central to social structures. That is, even with the technological advances epitomized by Morse's telegraph, scientific and popular notions of electricity remained in flux.

Telegraphic development led to further considerations of the body as electric and to understandings of the nervous system itself as a telegraphic network; in turn, such understandings encouraged medical explorations of the uses of electricity.[36] Boston physician and inventor William F. Channing suggested this connection between the technological and medical uses of electricity in *Notes on the Medical Application of Electricity* (1849) and in his article "On the Municipal Electric Telegraph" (1852). As Channing suggests, "a revolution has now taken place in favor of [the medical use of] electricity, which, after its wide celebrity at the commencement of the present century, had fallen into disuse."[37] Channing hints at a conceptual source for that revolution in his discussion of the municipal electric telegraph: "The Electric telegraph is to constitute the nervous system of organized societies. . . . [I]ts functions are analogous to the sensitive nerves of the animal system."[38] By the time Whitman was writing *Leaves of Grass*, the telegraph, with its ability to send information across wide distances and to knit together disparate political and social elements, had become the chief reference for reading the body as electric.

Yet even as the telegraph seemed to lend weight to more materialist considerations of human identity, its ability to link widely separated communities spurred considerations of a spiritual electricity—manifested in mesmerism, animal electricity, and atmospheric electricity—that might link all of creation. In these pseudosciences, electricity became an immaterial force, if not a manifestation, of spirit or divinity, circulating through and connecting all of creation. While Whitman may appear to rely primarily on the idea of material electricity flowing through the body as sexual desire, he also clearly wants that electricity to suggest a universal identity or immaterial communion, like the electricity discussed in spiritualism. Leading scientists tended to dismiss or lampoon such ideas, but the desires expressed in these dreams of spiritual integration and communion, I suggest, derived from the material developments of the telegraph in the burgeoning market capitalism of antebellum America. In other words, the hope that electricity might offer a material route to a unity where individual identity would be obliterated grew from the actual social uses of telegraphic technology.

This tendency to conflate technological developments with spiritualist and aesthetic understandings of electricity is parodied, even as its material roots are revealed, in Henry Parker's science fiction short story "Von Blixum's Heroic Experiment" (1846). Published in the *American Whig Review* the same year as the review dismissing "aesthetic" criticism, the story's narrator immediately ties spiritualist, pseudomedical, and technological electricity together with the claim that his friend Von Blixum's scientific achievements are "intimately connected" with "Animal Magnetism, the Water Cure, and the Electro-Magnetic Telegraph."[39] Von Blixum's experiments, we learn, culminate in his discovering a manner of "instantaneous transportation of one's self to any distance, by means of the Electro-Magnetic Telegraph," a discovery that will potentially lead to "complete freedom from the chains and pains of matter; the elevation of the laboring classes, and a general relief from the present faulty construction of society" ("VB," 290). This political fantasy leads to the idea of replacing actual with artificial bodies and, as it becomes possible to transport one soul from body to body, to the idea that "one person might pass directly into another's hollow body, thus intermingling and interchanging thought by silent, immediate *felt* communion" ("VB," 294). Hinting that what Von Blixum achieves is his own dehumanization, the story satirizes the narrator's reaction to Von Blixum's death from a faulty wire that fails to connect with his artificial body: "The daring philosopher had involuntarily escaped beyond recovery; he had perished a sacrifice to science. . . . Reach me a fan, reader, lest I go off into a swoon or a sonnet!" ("VB," 295). Ending with the possibility of "going off" into a sonnet and referring to Von Blixum as speaking in "a highly transcendental and often finely imaginative strain" ("VB," 291), the story marks itself as a satire of transcendental desires of joining aesthetic, technological, and pseudoscientific ideas to escape repressive social structures, individual identity, and matter itself.

In doing so, however, the story also demarcates possible deep connections between actual technological improvements and dreams of a kind of egalitarian techno-aesthetic union. "Von Blixum's Heroic Experiment" reflects the widespread feeling that the telegraph challenged individual boundaries through its ability to detach words from bodies. The story thus gestures to the telegraph's power as a unifying force that tied the country and the world together by apparently materializing thought and contributing to spiritualized understandings of electricity. As the story indicates, spiritualist conceptions of electricity seem far removed from the actual political, economic, and social uses of the telegraph. Yet the story also suggests, through its mocking and mapping of these connections, a material source for such readings. Although the story dismisses Von Blixum's dream that the telegraph would revolutionize political and economic structures through its transformation of conceptions of the individual self, its mockery intimates a real concern about the socially transformative potential of this telegraphic model of the self.

It has long been recognized and recently articulated fully by a number of historians that as the telegraph was developed and then monopolized in the mid-nineteenth-century United States, it became both a key tool of and a representative model for the consolidation of capital. It thus became, theoretically, a route to overcoming human alienation from what the early Karl Marx calls "species-being." Marx and Engels argued in 1848 that through "the rapid improvement of all instruments of production" and "by the immensely facilitated means of communication" (including "steam-navigation, railways, electric telegraphs"), the bourgeoisie "creates a world after its own image." But this "constant revolutionising of production" sweeps away "[a]ll fixed, fast-frozen relations, with their train of ancient and venerable prejudices and opinions" while also giving rise to the means by which consciousness of common exploitation can be created. Thus, "the improved means of communication that are created by modern industry and that place the workers of different localities in contact with one another. . . . [are] needed to centralise the numerous local struggles."[40] In other words, the telegraph served as an instrument for the economic domination of individuals as well as nations, races, and classes. Yet the telegraph's ability to broaden the reach of capital, to deterritorialize the geographic as well as psychic world for capitalist development, served to suggest the permeable boundaries of the individual self and the possibility of previously unimagined communities outdistancing both capitalist exploitation and national borders. The telegraph thus became an instrument that helped to consolidate but also belied bourgeois ideologies of the atomistic, isolated self, as individuals in modernizing U.S. society became more firmly entrenched in networks of commerce, information, and power that counterposed a strictly demarcated self.

Aesthetic uses of electricity thus relied on spiritualist and pseudo-scientific ideas of electric communion while insisting on the materiality of the aesthetic experience. As Russ Castronovo has pointed out, notions of spiritual electricity, as evoked in séances and mesmerism, provided important tropes for some abolitionists to imagine a kind of disembodied, interracial union.[41] Despite their roots in Africanist cultural practices, such spiritualist understandings of electricity tended toward an idealist dream of abandoning the body altogether, a dream based in material transformations of the era, as I have shown, but arguably dependent on a subject who inhabits a privileged body unmarked by regimes of oppression and exploitation. In order to imagine doing away with the body, in other words, one has to have proprietorship of it. Aesthetic electricity, however, tended to acknowledge the material and social forces that might allow an aesthetic, sensual experience of the transcendence of narrow, individual boundaries. This acknowledgment of the material forces behind such an experience appears in both Thoreau and Whitman. Thoreau's ambivalence toward the railroad in the "Sounds" chapter of *Walden* suggests the growing interdependence of railroads and telegraphy when, "astonished at the miracles it has wrought," Thoreau locates "something electrifying in the atmosphere" of the depot. That "electrifying" something, he later indicates, is the railroad's (and by extension, the telegraph's) ability to provide a material vehicle to connect him with the rest of the world, allowing him to "feel more like a citizen of the world."[42] New technologies link Thoreau to an imagined world community in a material fashion, mirroring the transcendent aesthetic experience he desires.

More explicitly, Whitman cites the telegraph in imagining a kind of aesthetic experience of the union of all humankind. In "Years of the Modern" (1865), for example, Whitman proclaims that the average man "colonizes the Pacific, the archipelagoes, / With the steamship, the electric telegraph, the newspaper, the wholesale engines of war, / With these and the world-spreading factories he interlinks all geography, all lands." While such technologies foster an imperialist program, Whitman suggests that they will end in "the solidarity of races": "Are all nations communing? [I]s there going to be but one heart to the globe? / Is humanity forming en-masse?" (*PP*, 597–98). Similarly, in "Passage to India" (1871), Whitman describes "[t]he seas inlaid with eloquent gentle wires" as uniting the world in a nearly bodily, sexual bond: "The earth [is] to be spann'd, connected by network, / The races, neighbors, to marry and be given in marriage, / The oceans to be cross'd, the distant brought near, / The lands to be welded together" (*PP*, 531–32). The sexual and aesthetic connection that Whitman imagines as electric in "Song of Myself" becomes materialized in technologies like the telegraph, and his aesthetic dream becomes rooted in the material and social forces that might actually allow cross-cultural interaction and foster a sense of the self's connection to others.

Because it located a transcendent and transformative experience in a material universe largely determined by social forces beyond the individual's control, aesthetic electricity, at its best, emphasized the irreducibility of bodily existence, simultaneously acknowledging the centrality and possible suspension of socially enforced identities. In that way, aesthetic electricity potentially offered a more viable vehicle than purely spiritualist or sentimental calls of sympathy for generating connections across, in particular, racial lines. Two quick examples will have to suffice. In "I Sing the Body Electric," formulating the body as electric allows Whitman to explore it as a site for sensual experience that leads to a sense of transcendence, what "Von Blixum's Heroic Experiment" mocks as the "intermingling and interchanging thought by silent, immediate *felt* communion" and that Whitman famously renders as "what I assume you shall assume, / For every atom belonging to me as good belongs to you" ("*PP*," 27). The body electric also serves as a material, socially embedded figure for imagining such experience, thus propelling Whitman to address deep social divisions that stand in the way of realizing the material and spiritual interconnectedness of all. Most famously in his back-to-back slave-auction scenes, Whitman calls his readers to leave the comfort of their "parlors" and realize their radical commonality by recognizing the "swells and jets [of] his heart. . . . There all passions and desires . . . all reachings and aspirations" (*PP*, 123). Whitman insists on the slave body's otherness, objectifying it with his gaze and suggesting that his readers cannot fully grasp the slave's experience, even as he attempts to locate some shared essence on the level of blood, of the electric body.

Frederick Douglass uses similar tropes of electric thought and feeling to figure an ineffable, essentially human desire for freedom while emphasizing the particular manifestations of that electric force in the life of a slave.[43] In his antebellum autobiographies, Douglass describes how the "flash" of thought given voice by *The Columbian Orator* and the "flash of energetic freedom" that appears even after he has been broken by Covey are countered by slave owners' "electric conductors."[44] In these descriptions, Douglass taps into a line of aesthetic and techno-utopian thought that he frequently invoked in his newspapers and speeches, most tellingly in his response to Pope's "Essay on Man": "It expressed a sublime truth, it came fresh to the ear every time repeated, and vibrated the soul like the lightning the wire; it was felt as well as thought; it was felt before it was thought."[45] Conjuring images of electric thought and electric feelings, Douglass uses the discourse of aesthetic electricity to build bridges with his audience. Unlike sentimental strategies that call readers to place themselves in the protagonist's position, Douglass repeatedly insists that his readers cannot fully understand his experience, that his feelings "can be understood only by those who have been slaves."[46] At the same time (most notably in his discussion of the slave songs and his apostrophe to the ships on the Chesapeake), Douglass posits a shared sense of individual potential and universal connection, which he figures in terms of electricity. Such moments can only occur to someone in Douglass's position, with his particular history, yet the electricity they create suggests that his sensations might parallel a potentially universal human experience. Reconstructing these events from a more secure position in the North, Douglass reconfigures his experiences in the terms of aesthetic electricity that I've traced. These reconfigurations exemplify what Peabody describes as "the central fact of the constant relation of the individual to the universal, and of their equally constant separation." As such, these moments remain relatively apolitical within the polemical context of Douglass's autobiographies, yet they become essential to his political project of building new types of alliances based less in shared identity or interests than in a universally accessible experience of the individual body. Douglass exemplifies the way that aesthetic experience could serve, even for those without direct access to cultural institutions of power, as a material supplement to a politics based on common interests or sympathy.

None of the writers I have glanced at fully constructed the vision of the aesthetic I have attempted to discern, but through their allusions to electrical science and technology and their hypotheses about the nervous system and thought itself as electric, they point in the direction of imagining an aesthetic moment experienced on a material, bodily level. Through aesthetic electricity, American romantic writers were attempting to think through the connection between material existence and consciousness, to locate the aesthetic experience at the level of both the individual body and communal identification. A distinct line of romantic writers, who imagined ideas, passions, and feelings not as atomized particles in motion or as immaterial entities but as both embodied and ideal forces gestured toward electricity as a model for understanding the material effects of words. Aesthetics, in such a light, emphasizes the tenuousness of the modern atomistic subject in relation to objects and other selves, an emphasis that opens the door to its appropriation by writers and thinkers who, like Douglass, could not depend on reclaiming a privileged body after the aesthetic moment. Recreating the experience of such tenuousness, whether in poetry, novels, or essays, would constitute not an avoidance of the political sphere for an ideal realm but an attempt to foster an embodied experience of the instability of individual identity upon which most modern politics depends. As such, it could be a catalyst for moving beyond impasses caused by narrowly understood political interests and rights.

What remains largely implicit is an account of how the descriptions of aesthetic experience as electric might constitute or be translated into a kind of practice, creating more such experiences among audiences. It would follow that reading or listening or seeing itself would become, as Whitman puts it, a kind of experience "quiver[ing]" the individual to a "new identity" marked by porous boundaries and a deep connection with what is perceived as a universal whole. Such an identity is not sustainable, but practices of evoking or recalling such moments might help to produce, as I think Douglass attempts, new alliances across clearly distinguished identities by momentarily bracketing economic and political concerns and interests. Because aesthetics imagines a boundaryless community, it occupies what Hawthorne might describe as "a neutral territory, somewhere between the real world and fairy-land," so that any purely aesthetic collectivity remains amorphous and undifferentiated.[47] In this way, a focus exclusively on aesthetics will always potentially distract attention from social, political, and economic oppression. Thus, a politics built on aesthetic experience would have to be developed within the world of political, social, and economic realities such experience eschews. Such a politics might be (and has been) used to reerect nearly insurmountable boundaries along the racial, national, and class lines that the experience itself seems to negate. But the utopian tendency of the aesthetic that I have reconstructed, the political potential of romantic electricity, lies in its very negation of those boundaries and its cultivation of a politics of universal inclusion based, finally, in the material (economic) interpenetration of the world. Reconsidering the aesthetic in this moment of globalization, we should not abandon the aesthetic to those who would use its universalizing principles to exclude but, rather, we should reevaluate the ways past writers have attempted to harness such an experience to a progressive politics. For while aesthetics on its own does not create a more just or egalitarian world, any progressive politics shorn of the utopian and sensual experience the aesthetic attempts to capture is bound to be as empty and detached from material lives as the idealist, formalist aesthetics of the New Critics.

California State University, Long Beach

Notes

This essay began with the support of a Barbara Thom Postdoctoral Fellowship at the Huntington Library, San Marino, California. I extend my thanks to Roy Ritchie and the Huntington's research staff. I am also grateful to California State University, Long Beach, for faculty-release time and, as always, to Reid Cottingham for providing insightful readings along the way.

1   Winfried Fluck, "Aesthetics and Cultural Studies," in *Aesthetics in a Multicultural Age*, ed. Emory Elliott, Louis Freitas Caton, and Jeffrey Rhyne (New York: Oxford Univ. Press, 2002), 84–85; further references to this source will be cited parenthetically as "ACS." For an illustration of Fluck's point, see John Carlos Rowe, *At Emerson's Tomb: The Politics of Classic American Literature* (New York: Columbia Univ. Press, 1997), 1–5. Rowe reflects the widespread acceptance of ahistorical accounts of the aesthetic, eliding, for example, the difference between the New Critics and Emersonian romanticism.

2   Review of *Papers on Literature and Art*, by S. Margaret Fuller, *American Whig Review*, November 1846, 515–16.

3   Elizabeth Peabody, "The Word 'Aesthetic,'" *Aesthetic Papers* (Boston: Peabody, 1849), 1.

4   Peabody, prospectus to *Aesthetic Papers*, iii.

5   Peabody, "The Word 'Aesthetic,'" *Aesthetic Papers*, 3, 2.

6   Terry Eagleton, *The Ideology of the Aesthetic* (Oxford, Eng.: Basil Blackwell, 1990), 8, 13, 15; further references to this source will be cited parenthetically as *IA*. Jonathan Hess makes a more specific case for the emergence of the idea of an autonomous aesthetic sphere in late-eighteenth-century Germany. In positing such a realm, thinkers like Kant and Schiller were engaged in a political and social critique of the failures of rationality, constructing the aesthetic as a nonpolitical "supplemental domain of political practice" in reaction to the failure of the Enlightenment's public sphere to account for the gap between individual consciousness and rationalized systems (*Reconstituting the Body Politic: Enlightenment, Public Culture and the Invention of Aesthetic Autonomy* [Detroit: Wayne State Univ. Press, 1999], 26).

7   As Isobel Armstrong contends, Eagleton's theme is thus in the end "[n]othing less than the impossibility of the category of the aesthetic" (*The Radical Aesthetic* [Oxford, Eng.: Basil Blackwell, 2000], 16).

8   In this way, Eagleton echoes a long-standing argument, perhaps best exemplified in Herbert Marcuse's contention that aesthetic culture acts as an alibi for the continued economic exploitation of capitalist structures ("The Affirmative Character of Culture" [1937], in *Negations: Essays in Critical Theory* [London: Free Association Books, 1988], 88–133); for Marcuse's attempt to recuperate aesthetics, see his *The Aesthetic Dimension: Toward a Critique of Marxist Aesthetics*, trans. Herbert Marcuse and Erica Sherover (Boston: Beacon Press, 1978).

9   Ian Hunter, "Aesthetics and Cultural Studies," in *Cultural Studies*, ed. Lawrence Grossberg, Cary Nelson, and Paula A. Treichler (New York: Routledge, 1992), 348. Drawing on the idea of a Weberian ethos or Foucauldian technology of the self, Hunter argues for taking aesthetics as a material practice of the self, a "means by which individuals have come to form themselves as the subjects of various kinds of experience and

action and to endow their lives with particular kinds of significance and shape" (359). A number of recent critics have moved in this direction also; on Wolfgang Iser, see Brook Thomas, "Restaging the Reception of Iser's Early Work; or, Sides Not Taken in Discussions of the Aesthetic," *New Literary History* 31 (winter 2000): 13–43; on Max Raphael, see Michèle Barrett, *Imagination in Theory: Culture, Writing, Words, and Things* (New York: New York Univ. Press, 1999); and on John Dewey, see Isobel Armstrong, *The Radical Aesthetic*. There are, of course, plenty of idealist defenses of the aesthetic that reject the need to treat aesthetic experience as the product of particular sociohistorical conditions; see Martha C. Nussbaum, *Poetic Justice: The Literary Imagination and Public Life* (Boston: Beacon Press, 1995); Mark Edmundson, *Literature against Philosophy, Plato to Derrida: A Defence of Poetry* (Cambridge, Eng.: Cambridge Univ. Press, 1995); Elaine Scarry, *On Beauty and Being Just* (Princeton, N.J.: Princeton Univ. Press, 1999); and the essays in *Revenge of the Aesthetic: The Place of Literature in Theory Today*, ed. Michael P. Clark (Berkeley and Los Angeles: Univ. of California Press, 2000). In returning to the aesthetic, my desire is to build on, rather than reject, the insights of cultural studies and cultural materialism.

10 Jan Mukarovský, *Aesthetic Function, Norm, and Value as Social Facts*, trans. Mark E. Suino (Ann Arbor: Dept. of Slavic Languages and Literature, Univ. of Michigan, 1970), 3.

11 Benedict Anderson writes that the nation is "an imagined political community—and imagined as both inherently limited and sovereign" because "the members of even the smallest nation will never know most of their fellow-members, meet them, or even hear of them, yet in the minds of each lives the image of their communion" (*Imagined Communities: Reflections on the Origin and Spread of Nationalism*, rev. ed. [New York: Verso, 1991], 6). In contrast, the community imagined at the aesthetic moment is neither limited nor sovereign, and rather than a sense of simultaneity in terms of "homogeneous, empty time," members experiencing the aesthetic partake of something more akin, given its ecstatic character and spiritual inclinations, to "Messianic time" (*Imagined Communities*, 24; Anderson borrows these terms from Benjamin, of course).

12 As Friedrich Schiller puts it, "[I]f man is ever to solve that problem of politics in practice he will have to approach it through the problem of the aesthetic, because it is only through Beauty that man makes his way to Freedom" (*On the Aesthetic Education of Man, In a Series of Letters*, ed. and trans. Elizabeth M. Wilkinson and L. A. Willoughby [Oxford, Eng.: Clarendon Press, 1967], 9). Schiller implies that it is only by simultaneously addressing the sensual body and imagining the transcendence of its individual interests—what was supposed to happen in aesthetic experience—that true political freedom can be imagined.

13 Ernst Bloch writes: "Whether, of course, the call for perfection—we

could call it the godless prayer of poetry—becomes practical to some degree and not only remains within aesthetic anticipatory illumination is not for poetry to decide but for society. . . . Wherever art does not play into the hands of illusion, there beauty, even sublimity, is that which mediates a presentiment of future freedom" ("The Artistic Illusion as the Visible Anticipatory Illumination" [1959], in *The Utopian Function of Art and Literature: Selected Essays*, trans. Jack Zipes and Frank Mecklenburg [Cambridge, Mass.: MIT Press, 1988], 148).

14 Henry T. Tuckerman, *Artist-Life; or Sketches by American Painters* (New York: Appleton, 1847); quoted in "The Fine Arts in America," *Southern Quarterly Review*, July 1849, 342.

15 Ralph Waldo Emerson, "The Poet" (1844), in *Essays and Lectures*, ed. Joel Porte (New York: Library of America, 1983), 467; Margaret Fuller, *Woman in the Nineteenth Century* (1845), in *The Portable Margaret Fuller*, ed. Mary Kelley (New York: Penguin, 1994), 293; and Edgar Allan Poe, "The Man of the Crowd" (1840), in *Poetry and Tales*, ed. Patrick F. Quinn (New York: Library of America, 1984), 388.

16 On the importance of associationist thought to American literary nationalism, see Robert E. Streeter, "Association Psychology and Literary Nationalism in the *North American Review*, 1815–1825," *American Literature* 17 (November 1945): 243–54; and William Charvat, *The Origins of American Critical Thought, 1810–1835* (Philadelphia: Univ. of Pennsylvania Press, 1936).

17 Philip C. Ritterbush examines how the notion of electricity as a unifying force, potentially related to the spark of life itself, was deployed throughout the eighteenth century by thinkers interested in finding some immanent force, some proof "that interrelated subtle fluids caused all physical and vital phenomena" (*Overtures to Biology: The Speculations of Eighteenth-Century Naturalists* [New Haven: Yale Univ. Press, 1964], 17).

18 Bern Dibner, *Oersted and the Discovery of Electromagnetism*, 2d ed. (New York: Blaisdell, 1962), 57.

19 Iwan Rhys Morus, *Frankenstein's Children: Electricity, Exhibition, and Experiment in Early-Nineteenth-Century London* (Princeton, N.J.: Princeton Univ. Press, 1998), 9.

20 While the discovery of the voltaic pile and the ability to create electricity at will from metals led many to begin theorizing a connection between magnetism and electricity, such thought did not simply flow into a modern understanding but instead drew on romantic ideas of a unified force. The important turn occurred in 1820 when Hans Christian Oersted demonstrated that "not only could an electric current *influence* a magnet, but it was in itself capable of *producing* magnetism" (Dibner, *Oersted and the Discovery of Electromagnetism*, 38). Oersted's attempt to find some link between electricity and magnetism was influenced, as several recent

studies have suggested, by his grounding in Kant and German romantic *naturphilosophie* as articulated by Schelling and his followers. Oersted's findings would lead directly to Faraday's discovery of electromagnetic induction, a process in which a magnetic field creates an electric current. And Faraday's findings seemed to suggest that electricity was independent of matter, so that, as Barbara Giusti Doran argues, "By the end of the nineteenth century, the mechanical notions of 'atoms in a void' and 'forces acting between material particles' had been replaced by the notions of the electromagnetic field as a nonmaterial, continuous plenum and material atoms as discrete structural-dynamic products of the plenum" ("Origins and Consolidation of Field Theory in Nineteenth Century Britain: From the Mechanical to the Electromagnetic View of Nature," in *Historical Studies in the Physical Sciences*, 6 [1975]: 134).

21   Maria M. Tatar, *Spellbound: Studies on Mesmerism and Literature* (Princeton, N.J.: Princeton Univ. Press, 1978), 58–59, 71. For an overview of the main tenets of *naturphilosophie*, see H. A. M. Snelders, "Romanticism and Naturphilosophie and the Inorganic Natural Sciences, 1797–1840: An Introductory Survey," *Studies in Romanticism* 9 (summer 1970): 193–215.

22   Samuel Taylor Coleridge, "Essays on the Principles of Method" (1818), in *The Friend*, ed. Barbara E. Rooke, volume 4, part 1 of *The Collected Works of Samuel Taylor Coleridge*, ed. Kathleen Coburn et al. (Princeton, N.J.: Princeton Univ. Press, 1969–2001), 478. For Coleridge's rejection of the notion of electricity as the vehicle of thought in his general rejection of all materialist accounts of mental processes, see *Biographia Literaria, or Sketches of My Literary Life and Opinions*, ed. James Engell and W. Jackson Bates, volume 7, part 1 of *Collected Works*, ed. Coburn et al., 101.

23   See Chris Baldick, *In Frankenstein's Shadow: Myth, Monstrosity, and Nineteenth-Century Writing* (New York: Oxford Univ. Press, 1987); and Mark Kipperman, "Coleridge, Shelley, Davy, and Science's Millennium," *Criticism* 40 (summer 1998): 409–36.

24   Coleridge, "Sonnet: To William Godwin," in *Poetical Works*, ed. J. C. C. Mays, vol. 16, part 1 of *Collected Works*, ed. Coburn et al., 166.

25   See Kipperman, "Coleridge, Shelley, Davy."

26   In summarizing the difference between Shelley and Coleridge, Kipperman notes: "Coleridge came to see scientific knowledge, in the fashion of *Naturphilosophie*, as knowledge that implied the reconciliation of material polarities in the ideal absolute. . . . Shelley's is a world of ideal, but essentially *immanent*, forces evolving with an *inner* necessity, an organic purposiveness Coleridge associated with pantheism. Moreover, Shelley's social hopes were linked to such immanent forces, since these unfold in a real time and within a human *history* that progressively comprehends and harnesses them" ("Coleridge, Shelley, Davy," 410).

27   "A Defence of Poetry," in *The Complete Works of Percy Bysshe Shelley*, ed.

Roger Ingpen and Walter E. Peck, 10 vols. (New York: Charles Scribner's Sons, 1926–1930), 7:122, 140.

28 Shelley, "The Refutation of Deism" (1814), in *Complete Works*, ed. Ingpen and Peck, 6:50. On Shelley's interest in science, especially in electricity as a central principle in his attempt to negotiate between his materialist and idealist tendencies, see Kipperman, "Coleridge, Shelley, Davy"; Carl Grabo, *A Newton among Poets: Shelley's Use of Science in "Prometheus Unbound"* (Chapel Hill: Univ. of North Carolina Press, 1930); Alan Richardson, *British Romanticism and the Science of the Mind* (New York: Cambridge Univ. Press, 2001); and Edward S. Reed, *From Soul to Mind: The Emergence of Psychology, from Erasmus Darwin to William James* (New Haven: Yale Univ. Press, 1997).

29 In *Childe Harold*, for example, Byron refers to "the things which bring / Back on the heart the weight which it would fling" as "Striking the electric chain wherewith we are darkly bound" (Canto IV, Sec. 23) and later alludes to "the electric chain" of sympathy (Canto IV, Sec. 172); see *Childe Harold's Pilgrimage*, vol. 2 of *The Complete Poetical Works*, ed. Jerome J. McGann (Oxford, Eng.: Clarendon, 1980). In *Mazeppa* (1819), Byron speaks of "Involuntary sparks of thought, / Which strike from out the heart o'erwrought, / And form a strange intelligence, / Alike mysterious and intense, / Which link the burning chain that binds, / Without their will, young hearts and minds; / Conveying, as the electric wire, / We know not how, the absorbing fire" (lines 236–43); see *Mazeppa*, in *1816–1820*, vol. 4 of *Complete Poetical Works* (1986).

30 Baldick, *Frankenstein's Shadow*, 105.

31 Thomas Jefferson Hogg, *The Life of Percy Bysshe Shelley* (New York: Dutton, 1933), 51, 52.

32 Shelley, "Defence of Poetry," *Complete Works*, 7:140. On Byron's and Shelley's more material understanding of words as things, see William Keach, "'Words Are Things': Romantic Language and the Matter of Poetic Language," in *Aesthetics and Ideology*, ed. George Levine (New Brunswick, N.J.: Rutgers Univ. Press, 1994), 219–39.

33 Eric Wilson's work on Emerson's engagement with electromagnetic science exemplifies this tendency to read American romanticism as following in Coleridge's footsteps at the same time that it broke from that lineage; see *Emerson's Sublime Science* (New York: St. Martin's, 1999), 11. For a different account of electromagnetism and antebellum American literature, see Deandra Little, "'The Body Electric': American Literature and the Culture of Electromagnetism, 1750–1855" (PhD diss., Vanderbilt University, 2001).

34 "Influence of the Telegraph upon Literature," *United States Democratic Review*, May 1848, 411.

35 Walt Whitman, "Song of Myself," *Poetry and Prose*, ed. Justin Kaplan

(New York: Library of America, 1996), 28. Further references to Whitman's poems are to this edition and will be cited parenthetically in the text as *PP*. Whitman mentions the telegraph twice in the 1855 version of *Leaves of Grass* (*Poetry and Prose*, 97, 144).

36 For an account of scientific explorations of the connection between electricity and the nervous system, see John D. Spillane, *The Doctrine of the Nerves: Chapters in the History of Neurology* (New York: Oxford Univ. Press, 1981).

37 William F. Channing, *Notes on the Medical Application of Electricity* (Boston: Daniel Davis Jr., 1849), 1. Channing was the son of the elder William Ellery Channing, the influential Unitarian minister, and the cousin of William Ellery Channing, the transcendentalist poet.

38 William F. Channing, "On the Municipal Electric Telegraph; Especially in Its Application to Fire Alarms," *American Journal of Science and Arts*, 2nd ser., 13 (January 1852): 58–59. Channing echoes Samuel Morse's 1838 prediction that "the whole surface of this country would be channeled for those *nerves* which are to diffuse, with the speed of thought, a knowledge of all that is occurring throughout the land" (*Samuel F. B. Morse: His Letters and Journals*, ed. Edward Lind Morse, 2 vols. [Boston: Houghton Mifflin, 1914], 2:85). From the 1840s through the 1860s, such analogies were prominent in explaining both the telegraph and the body. As a copiously illustrated article in *Harper's* reveals, the human nervous system was conceived as "present[ing] a very curious analogy" to a telegraphic system ("What Are the Nerves?" *Harper's New Monthly Magazine*, May 1862, 758–59).

39 Henry W. Parker, "Von Blixum's Heroic Experiment," *American Whig Review*, March 1846, 290; further references to this source will be cited parenthetically in the text as "VB."

40 Karl Marx and Friedrich Engels, *Manifesto of the Communist Party*, in *The Marx-Engels Reader*, 2nd ed., ed. Robert C. Tucker (New York: Norton, 1978), 477, 476, 481.

41 See Russ Castronovo, "The Antislavery Unconscious: Mesmerism, Vodun, and 'Equality,'" *Mississippi Quarterly* 53 (winter 1999–2000): 41–56; see also my discussion of Thoreau and Whitman in "The Telegraph in Black and White," *ELH* 69 (fall 2002): 805–33.

42 Henry David Thoreau, *Walden*, ed. J. Lyndon Shanley (1854; reprint, Princeton, N.J.: Princeton Univ. Press, 1971), 118, 119.

43 See my "Aesthetic Power: Electric Words and the Example of Frederick Douglass," *ATQ: The American Transcendental Quarterly*, new ser., 16 (December 2002): 291–311.

44 Douglass speaks of flashes of thought at least twice in the original 1845 version of his autobiography (*The Narrative of the Life of Frederick Douglass* [New York: Library of America, 1994], 58). Douglass added "elec-

tric" to describe the slave owners' use of the Christmas holidays in his 1855 *My Bondage and My Freedom* (*Autobiographies* [New York: Library of America, 1994], 291).

45 "The Trials and Triumphs of Self-Made Men: An Address Delivered in Halifax, England, on 4 January 1860," *The Frederick Douglass Papers, Series One: Speeches, Debates, Interviews*, ed. John W. Blassingame, 5 vols. (New Haven: Yale Univ. Press, 1979–1992), 3:292.

46 Douglass, *Narrative* (1845), 95.

47 Nathaniel Hawthorne, *The Scarlet Letter* (Columbus: Ohio State Univ. Press, 1962), 36.

Elizabeth
Maddock
Dillon

Sentimental Aesthetics

In a poem entitled simply "Woman" (1850), Frances Sargent Locke Osgood describes an idealized female figure in terms of her natural beauty:

> She's stolen from Nature all her loveliest spells:
> Upon her cheek morn's blushing splendour dwells,
> The starry midnight kindles in her eyes,
> The gold of sunset on her ringlets lies.[1]

In sentimental fashion, the poem extols woman's aesthetic value and warns that the treasure of feminine grace will be destroyed if placed in "chain" to a masculine world of commerce and politics. The reader is cautioned to preserve woman's unsullied beauty within a hallowed domestic space:

> Not thus forego the poetry of life,
> The sacred names of mother, sister, wife!
> Rob not the household hearth of all its glory,
> Lose not those tones of musical delight.

Yet while the poem locates aesthetic worth in the figure of the sentimentalized, domestic woman, few contemporary critics of literature would find aesthetic value within the formulaic tropes or tripping rhymes of such a poem. Indeed, in the critical tradition of American letters, placing *sentimentalism* and *aesthetics* together constitutes something of an oxymoron. Critical judgments of the sentimental writing of nineteenth-century American writers, particularly the poetry and prose of the "damned mob of scribbling women," has been sum-

American Literature, Volume 76, Number 3, September 2004. Copyright © 2004 by Duke University Press.

mary. Sentimental writing represents "an escape rather than a challenge," according to Herbert Ross Brown. For Ann Douglas, it is language "gone bad"—"rancid writing."[2] These assessments accord, broadly speaking, with the disdain in high modernist thought for both mass culture and the sentimental. As Suzanne Clark argues, "[T]he term sentimental marks a shorthand for everything modernism would exclude, the other of its literary/nonliterary dualism."[3] In the past two decades, a burgeoning field of scholarship has focused on reevaluating sentimental writing, addressing in particular what Jane Tompkins has characterized as the "cultural work" of women's sentimental writing. Shirley Samuels's important collection, *The Culture of Sentiment* (1992), is representative of more recent assessments of sentimental women's writing in the United States that make the case for its cultural rather than aesthetic value.[4] This vital and growing body of scholarship thus might be seen as itself emblematic of a critical divide between the evaluative standards of an aesthetic criticism—in which sentimental literature retains an aura of failure—and the standards of cultural studies—in which, by virtue of its pervasiveness and popularity in the mid-nineteenth century, sentimental literature is a wellspring of cultural meaning and value.

A number of critics have noted the divide between cultural and aesthetic assessments of sentimental writing and have, indeed, called for an aesthetic reassessment of sentimentalism. Joanne Dobson, for instance, argues that modern literary aesthetic approaches miss the mark, failing to understand that a quite different set of values influenced sentimental writers. "Historically, blanket condemnations of sentimentalism's 'unskilled rhetoric' and 'false sentiment' have misunderstood or trivialized its aesthetic purposes and/or focused selectively on exploitative or banal realizations of the tradition," Dobson explains. "With an awareness of the values and literary practices of the sentimental ethos, critical readers can recognize in accomplished writers the inherent effectiveness of sentimentalism's transparent language and the intrinsic thematic richness of its affectional tropes."[5] Dobson thus indicates that a version of cultural relativism is necessary to generate aesthetic understanding and value for sentimental texts. Rather than deploying aesthetic standards ushered in with modernism and New Critical reading strategies, the standards of the period need to be exhumed and placed back into service. With nineteenth-century lenses imposed upon our glasses, we might thus be able to assign aesthetic, literary value to these texts rather than merely see them as examples of dominant (or subversive) cultural formations. Dobson's argument resonates with recent attempts within the broader field of literary studies to rehabilitate the category of the aesthetic in the wake of the "cultural turn" of the discipline. In the introduction to *Aesthetics in a Multicultural Age*, Emory Elliott writes that reevaluating the aesthetic will entail developing alternative standards of value: "For this time, we need to formulate new terms and definitions and perhaps also a new system of analysis for describing the characteristics of art and literature and the feelings and intellectual pleasures they evoke in the particular diversity of the people we are today."[6] Described in this fashion, the category of the aesthetic is something like a measuring stick—primarily an evaluative tool—that, having been discovered to lack universality, needs to be recalibrated to specific cultural and historical moments in order to retain its capacity to produce qualitatively accurate judgments.

Yet this new account of aesthetic value discards the claim to universality that has been central to the development of aesthetics. Precisely in its link to universality, aesthetic judgment has far-reaching political implications, particularly with respect to the development of liberalism. In this essay, I would like to suggest an alternative approach to negotiating the division between cultural studies and aesthetics by offering a more thorough-going account of aesthetics as a political and cultural practice and, in particular, a genealogical account of sentimentalism that points to its close links to the development of aesthetic theory. My aim is not to rehabilitate sentimental writing—to answer the relentless question of whether or not it is any good—but to illuminate the function of aesthetics in relation to literary culture in a way that accounts for both the prominence of sentimentalism in the nineteenth century and its subsequent debased status as an aesthetic form in the twentieth century and today. Rather than viewing aesthetics as an instrument of measurement that might be retooled to fit any cultural or historical moment, I will examine the history of aesthetics in western Europe and the United States as it developed in response to the revolutions of the eighteenth century that ushered in liberal political regimes and societies oriented around (newly) autonomous, self-governing citizen-subjects.

Aesthetic theory in the United States arose primarily from two sources: the Scottish strain of moral philosophy articulated by writers such as Hugh Blair, Archibald Alison, Lord Kames (Henry Home), and Adam Smith; and the German idealism and romanticism of Immanuel Kant, Friedrich Schiller, and Johann Wolfgang Goethe. I will discuss these ideas—particularly Schiller's notion of an aesthetic state—at greater length, but for the moment, I want to underscore the fact that aesthetic theory developed in Europe and the United States in relation to a common political situation: the reconfiguration of social and political structures, which marked a turn from autocratic and monarchical regimes toward liberal and republican ones. Lodging new authority in the individual, in every instance, required developing an account of the individual's right to that authority and the capacity to exercise it with responsibility. Aesthetic theory offered precisely such a description of the "moral law within" the individual, or what Kant would famously call a "conformity to law without a law."[7] Aesthetic judgment ideally produced subjects who enacted their freedom in a moral and lawful manner, thereby creating the ground for a new political community—a community of taste—united by individual consent and judgment rather than by constraint and subordination. Aesthetic theory thus engaged in the project of imagining and giving shape to the autonomous subject who could function in the political world of liberalism.

Sentimentalism in the United States has been seen as divorced from aesthetic theory and the claims to autonomy that define the liberal subject, in part because sentimentalism seems to point to moments of what Jacques Rancière calls "heteronomy" rather than "automony."[8] Critics such as Richard Brodhead and Laura Wexler have demonstrated the link between the discourse of sentimentalism and disciplinary control over women's bodies; Ann Douglas and others, including Gillian Brown and Lori Merish, have linked sentimentalism decisively to the rise and dominance of consumer culture; and still others—Dobson, Marianne Noble, and Mary Louise Kete—have defined sentimentalism in terms of an anti-individualist ethos that emphasizes connective over autonomous relations.[9] Sentimentalism would seem, then, to have little to do with autonomous subjects or the autonomy of the work of art. Yet sentimentalism has its roots in the same concerns with autonomy that define aesthetic theory of the eighteenth century, and as I will argue, it participated in defining the terrain of liberal subjectivity. I will begin my analysis by tracing that alignment before turning to the subsequent fractures that have caused sentimentalism to be regarded as antithetical to autonomy. I aim, then, to trace the historical proximity of sentimentalism and aesthetics—a proximity that has been largely erased by modernist aesthetics and the critical trajectory of the late twentieth century—as well as to reflect more broadly on the vicissitudes of sentimentalism and aesthetics in their relation to the politics of liberalism.

■ ■ ■

In *Keywords*, Raymond Williams defines aesthetics as "a key formation in a group of meanings which at once emphasized and isolated subjective sense-activity as the basis of art and beauty as distinct, for example, from social or cultural interpretations."[10] Williams's definition touches on three important elements united in the term *aesthetic*: subjective sense-activity, a concern with the beautiful, and a relation to autonomy. Etymologically, the word derives from the Greek term, *aesthetikos*, referring to "things perceptible by the senses, things material."[11] Yet its contemporary usage dates only to the mid-eighteenth century when it was first employed by Alexander Baumgarten to refer to the criticism of taste. In the wake of Baumgarten, however, Kant argued for understanding the term in a sense closer to its Greek derivation, defining aesthetics as "the science which treats of the conditions of sensuous perception."[12] Thus, while contemporary usage tends to emphasize the criteria of taste and an intellectual concern with beauty, we might note that from its inception, aesthetics has been focused on *bodily sensation*.[13] It is worth emphasizing the historical and etymological link between aesthetics and corporeality, given that aesthetics is often taken as a discourse of form rather than matter, as a philosophical calculus aimed at abstraction rather than embodiment. While it is indeed the case that aesthetic theorists such as Kant and Schiller aim to explain the meaning and value of what we might call the "formal feeling" produced by aesthetic experience, the sensate, *felt* aspect of aesthetic form is nonetheless resolutely tied to the subjective experience of bodily sensation.

Emphasizing the corporeal dimension of aesthetic discourse indicates, for my purposes, a significant point of connection with sentimentalism. Often characterized in terms of a capacity to produce or convey emotion, sentimental writing aims to generate sensation defined in quite material terms. "Reading [it] is a bodily act," explains Karen Sánchez-Eppler. Sentimental writing "radically contracts the distance between narrated events and the moment of their reading, as the feelings in the story are made tangibly present in the flesh of the reader."[14] As Sánchez-Eppler points out, the tears that sentimental writing seeks to evoke from the sympathetic reader register the physical nature of sentimental discourse. In related terms, Noble argues that sentimental writing aims to promote the voice of "embodied, affective personhood" over and against a disembodied, abstract, legal account of subjectivity. According to Noble, sentimentalism "affirms an embodied, affective personhood empowered to resist repressive legal definitions of personhood and to affirm one's own self-definition of a personhood grounded in integrity and personal convictions."[15] Noble thus emphasizes that the physicality of sentimentalism has the effect of producing a strong sense of subjective identity: something about the immediate and material nature of emotional affect is allied to a capacity for "self-definition" or freedom from constraining laws ("repressive legal definitions" of the self).[16] What is at stake in the link to the body shared by aesthetics and sentimentalism? If we return to Williams's definition of *aesthetics*, an "isolated subjective sense-activity" is central to the meaning of the term. I suggest that sense-activity matters to aesthetic theory because it registers a form of subjectivity: sense-activity is what gives us access to the category of subjectivity. Aesthetics aims at producing feeling subjects who, insofar as they feel, are able to understand their own subjectivity as free—personal, unconditioned, and creative. It is the subjective feeling of freedom and personhood that eighteenth-century aesthetic theory links to the ideal of human freedom and the (putatively) universal rights of man that are central to liberal political theory. In related terms, sentimentalism links the capacity of individuals to feel deeply (often, to suffer) to an essential, shared humanity.

How, then, do we move from felt experience in the material world to the universalizing claims of human rights and freedom? In the aesthetic theory of both Kant and Schiller, to which I now turn, the subjective sensations of aesthetics and sentimentalism are decisively linked to the politics of liberalism. In the "antinomy of reason," Kant asks how it is possible that we are both free and not free. How can humans be determined by the laws of the natural, material world (in the sensible, phenomenal realm) and yet still be essentially free and have moral agency (in the noumenal or supersensible realm)?[17] In the Third Critique, Kant proposes the idea that aesthetic judgment mediates between the sensible and supersensible realms and thus makes visible human freedom in the material world. According to Kant, the highest and most moral human end is freedom—a noninstrumental, nonconstrained relation to the world and to moral choice—yet people cannot exist in the world without being constrained by the rules that govern its material dimension. Aesthetic judgment is ultimately able to bridge this gap between the sensible and supersensible aspects of human existence because it involves an experience of the material world unconstrained by law: "The judgment is called aesthetic for the very reason that its determining ground cannot be a concept, but is rather the feeling (of the internal sense) of the concert in the play of the mental powers as a thing only capable of being felt."[18] In response to the beautiful object, for example, the subject's mental powers are set free—are able to "play"—rather than conform to any fixed concept, and this mental play is precisely the evidence of our capacity for freedom in the material world. Aesthetic judgment enables the realization of pure subjectivity in which what counts is not any quality of the beautiful object—any positive embodiment of freedom in the object—but the free play of the understanding and the imagination in the absence of a completed cognition. The aesthetic judgment is, Kant argues, both subjective and universal: it produces an experience that is universal for all subjects because it evokes subjectivity itself in its free and moral nature.

If Kant's turn to the aesthetic represents the solution to a philosophical problem (how are we determined and yet free?), this aesthetic claim must also be seen as the solution to a political problem: how can humans be free, autonomous agents and yet subject to law at the same time? In many respects, this is the question posed by the revolutions of the eighteenth century in the Atlantic world. If all people have a right to liberty (as the highest end of humankind), how should they best be governed so as to preserve rather than destroy this basic human right? Kant uses aesthetic judgment to define both human lawfulness and freedom, to explain how a moral law within might be universally accessible and thus produce the kind of citizen who would not require an oppressive ruling authority. In this sense, the tradition of aesthetic liberalism that Kant inaugurates might be seen as the counterpart to the efforts of Locke or Rousseau to imagine just forms of the social contract—forms of liberal government. Rather than imagining a structure of governance that would enable individual freedom, Kant produces an account of the liberal subject—the subject who could be capable of self-government and thus able to sustain liberal forms of rule. In the hands of Schiller, writing after Kant and—more important—writing in the wake of the French Revolution, the politics of aesthetics as a mode of liberal-subject production are explicit. Schiller argues that political revolution will fail unless a populace endowed with "moral character" is ready to sustain it: "The fabric of the natural State [of compulsion, of autocracy] is tottering, its rotting foundations giving way, and there seems to be a physical possibility of setting law upon the throne, of honouring man at last as an end in himself, and making true freedom the basis of political associations. Vain hope! The moral possibility is lacking, and a moment so prodigal of opportunity finds a generation unprepared to receive it."[19] According to Schiller, it is only the "aesthetic education" of the people that will make republican revolution sustainable. "[I]f man is ever to solve that problem of politics in practice," he writes, "he will have to approach it through the problem of the aesthetic, because it is only through Beauty that man makes his way to Freedom" (*AE*, 9). While Schiller turns decisively away from advocating political revolution on the order of that seen in France, he nonetheless aims at staging a revolution from within the subjective heart of the people—a revolution that, he imagines, will ultimately effect lasting change in existing forms of government.

How, then, might aesthetics effect a revolution? Schiller offers an answer related to Kant's, but it is significantly more concrete. Influenced by the progressive account of history by the Scottish philosopher Adam Ferguson, Schiller transforms Kant's aesthetic bridge (thrown between sensible and supersensible, material and moral) into a developmental program. In order to be lifted from an originary state of compulsion, in which only the laws of nature apply, toward a moral state, which recognizes ethical laws of reason, "man" must enter the aesthetic state where nature and compulsion are replaced by choice and freedom. In order to realize his moral essence, "[man] does not stop short at what Nature herself made of him, but has the power of retracing by means of Reason the steps she took on his behalf, of transforming the work of blind compulsion into a work of free choice, and of elevating physical necessity into moral necessity" (*AE*, 12). Here the aesthetic is described as transforming the compliance of humankind with external force—whether that force be political or natural—into a matter of choice. Nothing signifies this aspect of human volition so clearly as the aesthetic, because beauty is precisely what is not required—it is decorative, appended, the product of will and desire rather than necessity. Schiller describes the transformative power of the aesthetic in terms of "semblance" and "play": the "play-drive" (*Spieltrieb*) is a creative capacity that enables man to engage in the world in terms that are precisely not instrumental (*AE*, 61, 97). Only aesthetic understanding allows one to move away from mindless material need and compulsion; after this liberating aesthetic experience, we can begin to freely shape our world in accordance with the higher, universal laws of reason. "[T]here is no other way of making sensuous man rational," concludes Schiller, "except by first making him aesthetic" (*AE*, 161).

Like Kant, Schiller uses the aesthetic to produce an account of the liberal subject who becomes aware of his or her freedom through the act of aesthetic judgment. Like Kant, Schiller suggests that this free play of the senses enables individuals to be free and also to follow a universal moral law, thus producing freedom and lawfulness at once. Yet unlike Kant, Schiller lodges some of the power of the aesthetic in the aesthetic object itself rather than only in the subjective experience of aesthetic judgment. The aesthetic thus acquires a concrete nature for Schiller that it never has for Kant. The result of this concretization of beauty and aesthetics in the object is the possibility of a didactic program attached to the aesthetic through which subjects can not only discover their own freedom but also be taught to do so. In political terms, this means that aesthetic education can serve as the means for the production of a liberal political community. No longer relying on the Kantian presumption of the universality of an aesthetic "*sensus communis*," Schiller is able to lodge the claim of value in the beautiful object, which then serves as an Arnoldian touchstone of communal and cultural value. According to Schiller, "beauty alone can confer upon [man] a social character. Taste alone brings harmony into society, because it fosters harmony in the individual" (*AE*, 215). The aesthetic thus performs a remarkable political feat for Schiller: it both enables freedom and constructs social unity and agreement. The aesthetic instructs individuals about their own capacity for freedom while allowing the liberal polis to operate as a community of taste. In other words, it is not simply freedom that aesthetic education enables but a freedom rather miraculously aligned with social normativity and lawfulness.

The coincidence of freedom and social normativity in Schiller's aesthetic state has made for a bifurcated critical legacy. In the hands of a critic such as the neo-Marxist Herbert Marcuse, Schiller proposes a radical critique of bourgeois hegemony embodied in the labor-resistant notion of play and its relation to aesthetics; in the hands of Terry Eagleton or David Lloyd, however, Schiller's aesthetics function as a model for the internalization of disciplinary control in which brute force is not transformed into freedom via the aesthetic but into the intractable mechanisms of disciplinary culture. The compulsion that controls the subject is no longer conceived as simply a physical power (the laws of gravity or even the force of autocracy) but as a cultural and political force (the market forces of late capitalism, Gramscian hegemony), in which the aesthetic plays an accomodationist role. This polarized view of Schiller's aesthetics might be seen to inform much of the broader contemporary discussion: either the aesthetic assists in breaking free of social stricture and is located radically outside of and beyond oppressive social norms, or it covertly functions to enforce normativity by masking the operations of power, helping to lodge ideology in the hearts and minds of docile subjects.[20]

Yet as Martin Jay suggests, an alternative reading of Schiller (and of aesthetics more broadly) is possible: rather than identifying aesthetic judgment with lawfulness and morality (and hence with internalized repression and hegemony), one might discern a space of heterogeneity within Schiller's effort to conjoin freedom and lawfulness. Because Schiller does not wholly collapse the moral into the aesthetic, the aesthetic sustains the possibility of social heterogeneity. As Joseph Chytry argues, for Schiller, "The free play of faculties characteristic of aesthetic awareness ought to lead to awareness of the power of reason and the notion of a moral law, and any equation of this free play with the moral law itself reflects a serious misunderstanding of the experience."[21] In other words, Jay and Chytry indicate that the free play and formalization that characterize the aesthetic are not coextensive with the formalizing effects of hegemony but, rather, temporally distinct from one another. This temporal distance is enormously significant because it defines the mode in which the aesthetic and the law (morality) are conjoined. If the two are united reflectively, as Jay and Chytry argue, then this relation is open to political negotiation and contestation; it is thus not simply coercive and the subject is not entirely passive in his or her consent to social normativity. I cite Jay and Chytry, then, not to buttress the claim that aesthetics is indeed productive of freedom, as Schiller argues, but to suggest that the idea of heterogeneity within the aesthetic offers a means of locating a space of analysis and negotiation through which to understand the operation of aesthetics as related both to freedom and hegemonic social and political formations.

The reflective link between aesthetics and morality, for Schiller, is directly related to sentimentalism. In his treatise *On Naïve and Sentimental Poetry* (1795–96), written after *On the Aesthetic Education of Man* (1794–95), Schiller defines the ideal literary aesthetic object of the modern period as sentimental poetry. The treatise defines two forms of the aesthetic ideal: one ancient (naive poetry) and one modern (sentimental poetry). Whereas the ancients lived in harmony with nature and thus produced a naive poetry that was beautiful without a sense of self-consciousness, moderns sense their distance from nature and generate a self-reflexive poetics in which the ideal (as separate from nature rather than contained within it) is addressed in tension with the material world.[22] Sentimental poetry, then, defines for Schiller a mode of fusing the ideal with the sensuous, just as the "play-drive" in his aesthetic theory conjoins materiality and ideality. Schiller's concept of the sentimental, then, emphasizes not simply a felt response to the world but a self-conscious, formalizing response to sensation. As such, it seems markedly heterogeneous. Although it welds form and matter, it also opens a certain distance between the two in the self-reflexive moment of formalization. Far from imposing form as the natural and immediate effect of sensation, sentimental poetry underscores the considered work of connecting the materiality of nature with the ideality of form and, in so doing, makes visible the heterogeneity that obtains between the two. In naive poetry, this heterogeneity is not at stake, whereas in sentimental poetry it is definitive. Following Chytry and Jay's reading, then, we might describe Schiller's sentimental poetry as linked to an aesthetic that cannot be entirely collapsed into ideology (the violent imposition of form) insofar as it locates the possibility of freedom in the reflective space between matter and form.

Yet if sentimental poetry exemplifies the possibilities of aesthetic education for Schiller, does the sentimental writing of nineteenth-century women in the United States retain the same set of theoretical and political concerns? In other words, is the work of Osgood, Lydia

Sigourney, or Harriet Beecher Stowe related in any way to the aesthetic theory of Schiller? Both Schillerian aesthetics and American sentimentalism, I would argue, do indeed share a concern with establishing the freedom (the autonomy and constraint) of the liberal subject—a concern with the restructuring of subjectivity in relation to liberalism and capitalism. There is some evidence that Schiller's work exerted a direct influence upon nineteenth-century writers and editors in the United States. Rufus Wilmot Griswold, for instance, editor of the popular and influential anthologies *The Poets and Poetry of America* (1843) and *Female Poets of America* (1849), was clearly familiar with Weimar classicism and its lines of aesthetic argument. In the introduction to *Female Poets of America*, for instance, Griswold extols the moral value of aesthetic sensibility, citing Johann Joachim Winckelmann—a key figure in inaugurating Weimar classicism, whose generative contribution to Schiller's work involved his insistence upon the potential moral effect of the work of art on private and public sensibility.[23] References to Schiller also appear in numerous periodicals of the era, including the *International Magazine*, a journal Griswold edited from 1850 to 1852, as well as the *North American Review* and the transcendentalist journal the *Dial*, which served as primary conduits of German idealism and romanticism.[24] That Schiller was read beyond the circle of Margaret Fuller and company is evident in the 1859 poem by Frances (Fanny) Anne Butler Kemble, "Lines: On Reading with Difficulty Some of Schiller's Early Love Poems." The speaker in Kemble's poem finds much of Schiller's work foreign and unrelated to her, except for his powerful evocations of the suffering of women. Kemble thus homes in on the feminized pathos of Schiller's sentimentalism to define a universalized voice of sensibility and sympathy: "In foreign accents writ, that I did ne'er / Or speak, or hear, a woman's agony / Still utters a familiar voice to me."[25]

Yet while Margaret Fuller evidently discussed Schiller's aesthetic theory with her conversation groups in Boston, the work of Schiller that circulated in the United States was primarily his poetry and plays rather than his aesthetic treatises. Indeed, an English translation of *On the Aesthetic Education of Man* was not published in its entirety in England until 1844 or in the United States until 1861.[26] Thus, although Schiller had a U.S. readership, it would be incorrect to argue that his aesthetic theory had a widespread, direct influence on sentimental women writers in the United States. Rather, I suggest that they share a common genealogy—a common grounding—in the politics of bourgeois liberalism and the transformations of subjectivity linked to that politics, as well as a common grounding in Scottish Common Sense moral philosophy and aesthetics. We might view Schiller, then, as the articulate spokesperson for a cluster of ideas that emerged about sentimentalism and aesthetics based in part on the Scottish tradition, including the writings of Adam Ferguson, Blair, Alison, and Kames, which were widely published and taught in the United States.[27] Claims for the pedagogical quality of the aesthetic are particularly pronounced in nineteenth-century U.S. sentimental discourse, and this vein of thought is clearly indebted to the Scottish Common Sense school. Gregg Camfield has shown the influence of Scottish Common Sense philosophers on sentimental literature in the United States, particularly on Stowe's work. Camfield demonstrates that Stowe was well schooled in the philosophy of Alison and Blair, "two of the most important popularizers of Common Sense philosophies." As Camfield points out, Alison "gave America its most cogent and most popular exposition of aesthetics" and "distilled much of the thought of the Scottish Enlightenment into his *Essays on Taste*," including that of Smith, Hutcheson, and Kames.[28] In particular, Alison emphasizes that emotion or sensibility is linked to moral development; the moral sense within is influenced by taste, and taste can be taught as a means of creating a moral community. Like Schiller, Alison contends that taste combines the experience of the material world with the imaginative capacity, and morality lies precisely in this capacity.

In Alison's concern with the imaginative (or what he typically defines as the "associative") aspect of aesthetic judgment or taste, he mirrors Schiller's interest in the free play of thought that defines human autonomy and capacity for moral action. Yet Alison insists far more than Schiller on the claims of morality that are produced in this experience. According to Alison, it is through aesthetic experience that "the material universe around us becomes a scene of moral discipline."[29] The moral law that is made evident through the use of imagination thus has a far more substantive presence for Alison than for Schiller. Alison describes the pedagogical power of the aesthetic in the following terms:

[I]t is of so much consequence in the education of the young, to encourage their instinctive taste for the beauty and sublimity of nature. While it opens to the years of infancy or youth a source of pure and of permanent enjoyment, it has consequences on the character and happiness of future life, which they are unable to foresee. It is to provide them, amid all the agitations and trials of society, with one gentle and unreproaching friend, whose voice is ever in alliance with goodness and virtue, and which, when once understood, is able both to sooth misfortune, and to reclaim from folly. It is to identify them with the happiness of that nature to which they belong; to give them an interest in every species of being which surrounds them; and, amid the hours of curiosity and delight, *to awaken* those latent feelings of benevolence and of sympathy, from which all the moral or intellectual greatness of man finally arises.[30]

While the moral sense is within each individual (not within the object), aesthetic experience allows the individual to discover or "awaken" it. As this passage indicates, the morality that aesthetic judgment helps to awaken, for Alison, is more closely linked to sympathy—to the shared norms of community behavior and mutual understanding adumbrated in Adam Smith's *The Theory of Moral Sentiments*—than to a Kantian ideal of freedom and autonomy. A sentimental aesthetic, thus articulated, involves the capacity to bind a community through feeling and through affectively internalized moral codes.

If we turn to accounts of sentimental writing in the United States, we can see the ubiquity of Scottish Common Sense claims concerning the relation of the moral and the aesthetic. Caroline May's anthology, *The American Female Poets* (1848), for instance, praises Frances Osgood's poetry in terms that evoke Alison's notions of taste and aesthetics: "[G]race, wit, fancy, feeling, and a delicious adaptation of sound to sense, are equally observable. . . . But Mrs. Osgood possesses, also, loftier qualities than those which merely fascinate. There is a fine *moral awakening power*, in her noble and spirited lines . . . which evidently proves that she can be—more than fanciful, witty, and tender,—an eloquent *teacher of wisdom and truth*."[31] Using language identical to Alison's, May describes the aesthetic effect of the sentimental poem as that of "awakening" a moral sense. Or consider Griswold's praise for the writer Elizabeth Oakes Smith: "[T]hrough all her manifold writings, indeed, there runs the same beautiful vein of philosophy, viz.: that truth and goodness of themselves impart a holy light to the mind, which gives it a power far above mere intellectuality; that the highest order of human intelligence springs from the moral and not the reasoning faculties."[32] The highly wrought moral tone of sentimental writing might be here recognized as the product of aesthetic theory, rather than solely the language of Christian reform, as critical treatments of sentimental writing often claim. Beauty is taken to awake a moral sensibility and effect a didactic purpose. The didactic and disciplinary claims of sentimentalism thus emerge in conjunction with a theory of aesthetic education.

As in Osgood's poem "Woman," morality and beauty are often associated with women's domestic position in sentimental discourse. For feminist critics—even those inclined to celebrate the work of women writers in the period—it has been difficult to view the sentimental elevation of domesticity to moral calling as anything other than prescriptive and repressive for women. Yet placed within the context of Schiller's aesthetics, it seems possible to view ideas of free play and autonomy as constituting a strong line of logic threaded through sentimental celebrations of domesticity. For instance, adornment, semblance, and play are all important aspects of the domestic space within sentimental discourse. While women are intensely identified with the private space of the home in sentimental literature, this space is also figured as determined by free will, love, and desire rather than by material need or compulsion. The space of the home, imbued with feminine affect, thus helps to produce the freedom of the liberal subject through affective abundance and nonutilitarianism. Jürgen Habermas thus describes the bourgeois family as representing the freedom of the liberal individual: "To the autonomy of property owners in the market corresponded a self-presentation of human beings in the family. The latter's intimacy, apparently set free from the constraint of society, was the seal on the truth of a private autonomy exercized in competition."[33] Habermas suggests that the capitalist marketplace gives individuals freedom and autonomy (or the illusion of it), and that this freedom is culturally identified with privacy and the space of the home where individuals are seemingly able to act as they wish. In slightly different terms, Pamela Haag defines the freedom of the marketplace and that of the family as historically differentiated forms of autonomy in the United States: freedom was initially conceived primarily in economic terms in the nineteenth century but later became increasingly associated with the private space of the home. While classic liberalism described freedom in terms of laissez-faire economic policies, this freedom began to disappear with increased state regulation of the marketplace and labor relations at the close of the nineteenth century. Although Haag locates this shift from classic (economic) liberalism to modern (domestic-sexual) liberalism in the early twentieth century, the logic that associates the nuclear family with freedom and citizenship is abundantly evident in nineteenth-century sentimental texts.[34]

What occurs in the home in Osgood's poem "Woman," for instance, is described as "the poetry of life" and the production of song, rather than, say, the production of dinner and the caretaking of children. As historian Jeanne Boydston has argued, a "pastoralization" of women's household labor occurred following the market revolution in which domestic work by women was increasingly viewed outside the rubric of economics. That is, women's work in the home was not seen as a contribution to the family's financial well-being but as a moral and aesthetic endeavor.[35] This pastoralization is writ large in sentimental discourse, a central premise of which is that labor does not occur in the household. Reva Siegel, for instance, points out that a sentimental logic of deinstrumentalization (pastoralization) structures women's legal status in the nineteenth century, particularly with respect to marriage:

> [Sentimental] marriage was an affective relation that subsisted and flourished in a private domain beyond the reach of law. A wife could not enforce a contract with her husband compensating her for work performed in the family sphere because such labor was to be performed altruistically, rather than self-interestedly: for love, not pay. . . . By the turn of the century, courts seeking to justify wives' continuing legal disabilities described marriage as an emotional relationship subsisting in a private realm "beyond" the reach of law.[36]

Labor "for love, not pay" was a matter of choice rather than compulsion, and was thus portrayed less as labor than as the unfettered expression of emotion and volition. In her introduction to *The American Female Poets*, May quite literally enacts the sentimental and aesthetic pastoralization of women's labor. A passage that begins by describing women as domestic workers ends by describing women as pure and autonomous, affective (loving) agents:

> It must be borne in mind that not many ladies in this country are permitted sufficient leisure from the cares and duties of home to devote

themselves, either from choice, or as a means of living, to literary pursuits. Hence, the themes which have suggested the greater part of the following poems have been derived from the incidents and associations of every-day life. And home, with its quiet joys, its deep pure sympathies, and its secret sorrows, with which a stranger must not intermeddle, is a sphere by no means limited for woman, whose inspiration lies more in her heart than her head. Deep emotions make a good foundation for lofty and beautiful thoughts. The deeper the foundation, the more elevated may be the superstructure. Moreover, the essence of poetry is beauty; "the essence of beauty is love." And where should women lavish most unreservedly, and receive most largely, the warmest, purest, and most changeless, affection, but in the sacred retirement of home "where love is an unerring light, / And joy its own security"?[37]

The "cares and duties" in the opening sentence of this passage indicate that domestic work is a form of constraint on women. By the close of the paragraph, however, labor has been replaced by love, and women are able to expend love "unreservedly"—that is, without constraint of any kind. The domestic setting is thus transformed from a space of constraint to one of freedom, from the location of work to the location of aesthetic experience and moral truth. We might, indeed, invoke Schiller's words to describe precisely the rhetorical labor of this passage in which the author "transform[s] the work of blind compulsion into a work of free choice, and . . . elevate[s] physical necessity into moral necessity" by redefining domesticity as love rather than work (*AE*, 12).

The way in which women, in particular, are seen to occupy a pastoralized space associated with aesthetic autonomy may go some way toward accounting for the feminization of sentimentalism in nineteenth-century American letters. If sentimentalism has its origins in a European tradition of masculine fellow-feeling as Julie Ellison has argued, then it seems important to understand how and why sentimentalism has become so strongly identified with women writers and women's culture in the United States.[38] While it is increasingly possible to identify versions of masculine sentimentality in the period, even these associations are correlated to an account of feminization and domesticity. Griswold, for instance, proclaims in his account of genteel poetics that "the most essential genius in men is marked by qualities which we may call feminine."[39] If in the nineteenth-century United States liberalism defined itself increasingly in relation to doctrines of privacy—if as Haag argues, the home becomes the location of freedom rather than the marketplace—then we might see this shift as a transvaluation of the masculine "parliamentary" fellow-feeling identified by Ellison as the origin of the sentimental. From political fellow-feeling, sentimentalism becomes identified with a pastoralized aesthetic (associated with freedom and anti-utilitarianism) that appears in the writings of Schiller and is writ large in the domestic ideology of nineteenth-century sentimental women writers in the United States.

Yet if the pastoralization of the domestic sphere gave it a nonutilitarian, aesthetic value, we must also note that locating the ideal of the family space outside an economy of necessity was itself a fantasy. Habermas remarks, for instance, that the family represents itself as the space of freedom in order to make possible the perpetuation of capital and labor, to reproduce (as Marxist feminist critics have shown) the material conditions of production. I have pointed to the continuities between aesthetic notions of autonomy and sentimental discourse in part because this linkage has generally not been examined in critical accounts of sentimentalism. But any notion of pastoralization of domestic liberty is certainly subject to the same critique levied against the ideal of aesthetic autonomy—namely, that this form of "liberty" is far from free, and it is decisively linked to forms of social hegemony and coercion. In short, then, sentimental discourse would seem to pose the quandary we have seen in critical debates concerning aesthetics: sentimentalism concerns either autonomy or hegemony; either it stands radically outside the compulsory forms of market-oriented behavior or it is deeply embedded within them. As with the question of Schiller's aesthetics, then, I suggest that the term *heteronomy* might be useful in negotiating the binarized terms in which this debate is cast.[40]

In order to explain the relation of aesthetic heteronomy to sentimentalism, I turn to a second poem by Osgood, which meditates on the difficult nature of aesthetic value as linked to domesticity and womanhood. In "Lines Suggested by the Announcement That 'A Bill for the Protection of the Property of Married Women Has Passed Both Houses' of Our State Legislature," Osgood examines the connection and disjunction between aesthetic autonomy and economic value. As the title of the poem indicates, Osgood is responding to the passage of a bill that enabled married women to retain some separate property rights, including earnings for work performed outside the home. Surprisingly, however, Osgood is critical of the logic of the bill, suggesting that its passage is not a clear victory for women. She begins the poem's address to the legislators by delineating a dualism between matters of the heart or spirit and those of the material world:

> Oh, ye who in those Houses hold
> > The sceptre of command!
> Thought's sceptre, sunlit, in the soul,
> > Not golden, in the hand!
>
> Was there not one among ye all,
> > *No* heart, that Love could thrill,
> To move some slight amendment there,
> > Before you passed the bill?
>
> We make our gold and lands secure;
> > Maybe you do not know,
> That we have other property,
> > We'd *rather* not forego.[41]

Implicitly opposing the "ye" (male legislators) and the "we" (married women), Osgood aligns men with the logic of the material world and women with that of an immaterial spiritual and emotional realm. The "other property" she refers to in the third stanza is thus property that has internal rather than external value: it concerns the heart and the soul rather than the marketplace where "gold and lands" are traded.

The poem seeks to set forth the claims of women to this "other property," which is not protected by the bill that has just passed in the legislature:

> There *are* such things in woman's heart,
> > As fancies, tastes, affections;—
> Are no encroachments made on these?
> > Do *they* need no "protections"?
>
> . . . .
>
> We waste on [men] our "golden" hours,
> > Our "real estate" of Beauty,
> The bloom of Life's young passion—flowers—
> > And still they talk of "Duty."

> Alas for those, whose all of wealth
>   Is in their souls and faces,
> Whose only "rents" are rents in heart,
>   Whose only tenants—graces.
>
> How must that poor protection bill
>   Provoke their bitter laughter,
> Since they themselves are leased for life,
>   And no *pay-day* till after!

Osgood thus indicates that the property that women possess is aesthetic: the "real estate" they own is "Beauty"—a beauty related to taste, refinement, and morality, all of which make the home a place of value. Yet "Beauty" is not protected in the women's property bill and thus has no value within the legal and political terms dictated by the marketplace. Two opposed readings of the poem thus seem plausible. On one hand, Osgood seems to applaud the fact that the aesthetic (and thus moral) value of women is transcendent and remains distinct from the grasp of the market and the legislature, yet she simultaneously seems to demand some form of recognition of the invaluable nature of women's aesthetic "real estate." Is it, then, the case that women's aesthetic value is intrinsic or extrinsic to a masculine economy? Given Osgood's penchant for incisive wit, particularly with respect to matters of gender, and her skill as a writer, she appears to be more than simply confused on this issue. She appears, rather, to be bringing into sharp focus the contradictory nature of women's value as posed in aesthetic and sentimental terms.

From a feminist perspective, it seems strange and unsettling that Osgood would contest the passage of the women's property act, which was crucial to dismantling the traditional, debilitating policies of coverture for women. On the other hand, Osgood's poem also protests the bill in the name of a concept of women's value that resists integration into simple economic terms; indeed, part of women's aesthetic value lies in that very resistance—in the dualism proposed from the outset of the poem. Osgood ends the poem with a reference to the private sphere as women's domain, which holds intrinsic value for men too:

> By all the rest you fondly hope,
>   When ends this lengthened session,
> That household peace, which Woman holds
>   Thank Heaven! at *her* discretion.

> If a light of generous chivalry,
>> This wild appeal arouses,
> Present a truer, noble bill!
>> And let it pass—*all houses*!

In her reference to "all houses," Osgood ultimately conjoins the public space of the legislative house with the private space of the domestic home, indicating that the private space is located in an important political relation to the public sphere. Osgood's poem indicates a contradictory set of values: a desire to simultaneously join and dissever public and private, sentimental aesthetics and the marketplace, the feeling heart and formal legal standing.

How might one make sense of this radical oscillation in the claims of Osgood's sentimentalism? I suggest that the ground of this ambivalence is written into sentimentalism itself. By definition, sentimentalism involves both emotion and a subsequent reflection upon that emotion—a putting to use of emotion, as for instance, when it opens a subjective path toward autonomy or moral sense. As in Schiller's notion of sentimental poetry, matter and form are conjoined in the reflective, sentimental conjunction of the two. In the context of U.S. sentimental writing, June Howard points out that sentimentalism, even in its vernacular usage, is tied to a notion of excess. It involves a kind of emotion, she argues, that is recognizably cultivated, even constructed: "*[S]entiment* and its derivatives indicate a moment when emotion is *recognized* as socially constructed."[42] The excessive nature of sentimentalism might be seen to lie in the way in which emotion is placed in the service of other ends. While emotion is produced subjectively and thus generates within the individual a sense of subjective autonomy, it is nonetheless then connected to a higher moral and political end in sentimental discourse. Sentimentalism thus concerns both an affective immediacy (subjective autonomy) and a formal heteronomy—the connection of emotion to political and cultural ideals and aims. The social construction of sentimentalism Howard refers to might thus be seen as the heteronomy within the sentimental or the way in which its very materiality and subjectivity get transformed into formal and universalizing claims. Howard concludes: "Most broadly, when we call an artifact or gesture sentimental, we are pointing to its use of some established convention to evoke emotion; we mark a moment when the discursive processes that construct emotion become visible."[43] The irony of this moment of heteronomy is that it at once makes sentimentalism valuable—it gives it political and cultural meaning—and exposes it as false or mediated by culture rather than immediate, and thus as constraining rather than liberating.

In using the opposition between heteronomy and autonomy to describe the dialectic nature of sentimental discourse, I use an analytical framework Rancière has proposed with respect to aesthetics. According to Rancière, the aesthetic is itself defined by a dialectics of autonomy and heteronomy. On one hand, a philosophical tradition has linked aesthetics to modernist notions of the autonomy of the work of art. Yet on the other hand, the experience of autonomy—Schiller's free play or *Spieltrieb*, or Kant's lawfulness without law—is placed in the service of a greater political narrative concerning social cohesion, freedom, and morality. Schiller's "aesthetic State" perfectly embodies this contradiction. The autonomy realized in aesthetic judgment becomes the building block for the liberal state, and the autonomy of the aesthetic is thereby rendered purposive, heteronomous. The autonomy of the work of art may thus stand as a resistance to the mechanisms of state, market, and culture or, alternatively, may serve as the political (heteronomous) vehicle to advance the claims of those regimes upon "consenting" subjects. According to Rancière, then, the force of the aesthetic lies in the very dialectic between a resistance to constraint (autonomy) and a metapolitical claim for the reforming force of the aesthetic (heteronomy): "[T]he life of art in the aesthetic regime of art consists precisely of a shuttling between these scenarios, playing an autonomy against a heteronomy and a heteronomy against an autonomy, playing one linkage between art and non-art against another such linkage."[44] Osgood's poem, I suggest, shuttles between these two poles as well, imagining versions of women's aesthetic value as outside the market and imagining that this very value will transform the materialist nature of the market.

Rancière's analysis indicates why the aesthetic (like sentimentalism) has tended to be viewed in contemporary criticism either as a form of ideology or as its opposite—the site of emancipation from ideology. To the extent that the aesthetic is seen as valuable in the twentieth century and beyond, it is because it embodies a dream of the outside—of a location beyond social and cultural control. Sentimentalism, in which formalizing aims are so evident, recognizable, and even excessive, thus seems entirely distant from this dream of exteriority, and it is for this reason that sentimentalism is so seldom viewed as the location of aesthetic value today. Yet if following Rancière, we recognize the implausibility of the dream of the outside—even the extent to which this dream is always already embedded within the ideological space of the inside—then the heteronomous failures of the sentimental may look less like duplicity and more like the plausible means of playing through and giving scope to the inevitably interrelated spaces of inside and outside.

One of the most trenchant examinations and critiques of sentimental discourse in recent years appears in the work of Lauren Berlant, who has argued that in conjoining affect with message, sentimentalism tends to privatize suffering and to foreclose the possibility of political debate concerning the causes of suffering. Berlant has thus persuasively argued that sentimentalism is willfully apolitical and depoliticizing insofar as it recasts political issues in terms of private feeling. "[W]hen sentimentality meets politics," she contends,

> it uses personal stories to tell of structural effects, but in so doing it risks thwarting its very attempt to perform rhetorically a scene of pain that must be soothed politically. Because the ideology of true feeling cannot admit the nonuniversality of pain, its cases become all jumbled together and the ethical imperative toward social transformation is replaced by a civic-minded but passive ideal of empathy. The political as a place of acts oriented toward publicness becomes replaced by a world of private thoughts, leanings, and gestures.[45]

Berlant suggests that casting politics as a set of feelings, particularly feelings of suffering, makes these feelings resistant to debate or negotiation. Yet I would argue, in turn, that because the subjective, autonomous feelings of sentiment are never autonomous, they remain the subject of debate and the location of political meaning and value.[46] Sentimentalism fails, aesthetically, because it overreaches—because it reveals the ideological, formalizing effects of the aesthetic link between feeling and form. I mean to suggest, however, that we can locate in this excess (as, I think, Schiller did) modes of possibility rather than simply failure. Rather than pursue the dream of the outside, one might examine the possibilities of the self-reflective, formalizing moment of sentimental heteronomy. This is not precisely a rallying cry for sentimentalism or a claim that sentimentalism instantiates a liberatory politics so much as an argument that sentimentalism is allied with both the possibilities and the limitations of the aesthetic. The critical divide that currently separates aesthetics from cultural studies opposes two versions of aesthetics: one in which aesthetics operates as a form of ideology (the cultural studies model) and one in which aesthetic value operates precisely against the restrictive force of cultural normativity. Yet the community of taste (a *sensus communis*, an "aesthetic state") generated in aesthetic judgment is indissolubly linked to the concept of aesthetic autonomy and the politics of liberalism. As such, it seems important to view aesthetic judgment in its connection with community formation and thus with heteronomy, as well as to see sentimentalism as linked to versions of political agency, to the *reflective* connection of emotion to culture that enables (rather than forecloses) political negotiation. In short, it seems possible to regard both aesthetics and the devalued aesthetic terrain of sentimentalism in far more dialectical fashion, as terms related to one another rather than wholly distinct. Ultimately, then, one might locate aesthetic and political possibilities—conjunctions and disjunctions, negotiations between inside and outside—within rather than beyond the formulaic feelings of sentimental discourse.

Yale University

Notes

1   Frances Sargent Locke Osgood, "Woman," in *Nineteenth-Century American Women Poets: An Anthology*, ed. Paula Bernat Bennett (Malden, Mass.: Blackwell, 1998), 74–75.
2   Herbert Ross Brown, *The Sentimental Novel in America, 1789–1860* (New York: Pageant, 1959), 369; Ann Douglas, *The Feminization of American Culture* (New York: Farrar, Straus, and Giroux, 1977), 255, 256.
3   Suzanne Clark, *Sentimental Modernism: Women Writers and the Revolution of the Word* (Bloomington: Indiana Univ. Press, 1991), 9. See also Andreas Huyssen, *After the Great Divide: Modernism, Mass Culture, Postmodernism* (London: Macmillan, 1988).
4   See Jane Tompkins, *Sensational Designs: The Cultural Work of American Fiction, 1790–1860* (New York: Oxford Univ. Press, 1985); and Shirley Samuels, ed., *The Culture of Sentiment: Race, Gender, and Sentimentality in Nineteenth-Century America* (New York: Oxford Univ. Press, 1992). For additional recent work in the field of sentimentalism and culture, see Richard Brodhead, *Cultures of Letters: Scenes of Reading and Writing in Nineteenth-Century America* (Chicago: Univ. of Chicago Press,

1993); Gillian Brown, *Domestic Individualism* (Berkeley and Los Angeles: Univ. of California Press, 1990); Mary Chapman and Glenn Hendler, eds., *Sentimental Men: Masculinity and the Politics of Affect in American Culture* (Berkeley and Los Angeles: Univ. of California Press, 1999); Glenn Hendler, *Public Sentiments: Structures of Feeling in Nineteenth-Century American Literature* (Chapel Hill: Univ. of North Carolina Press, 2001); Mary Louise Kete, *Sentimental Collaboration: Mourning and Middle-Class Identity in Nineteenth-Century America* (Durham, N.C.: Duke Univ. Press, 2000); Lori Merish, *Sentimental Materialism: Gender, Commodity Culture, and Nineteenth-Century American Literature* (Durham, N.C.: Duke Univ. Press, 2000); Marianne Noble, *The Masochistic Pleasures of Sentimental Literature* (Princeton, N.J.: Princeton Univ. Press, 2000); and Laura Wexler, *Tender Violence: Domestic Visions in an Age of U.S. Imperialism* (Chapel Hill: Univ. of North Carolina Press, 2000).

5   Joanne Dobson, "Reclaiming Sentimental Literature," *American Literature* 69 (June 1997): 279.

6   Emory Elliott, "Introduction: Cultural Diversity and the Problem of Aesthetics," in *Aesthetics in a Multicultural Age*, ed. Emory Elliott, Louis Freitas Caton, and Jeffrey Rhyne (Oxford, Eng.: Oxford Univ. Press, 2002), 14.

7   Immanuel Kant, *The Critique of Judgement*, trans. James Creed Meredith (Oxford, Eng.: Clarendon, 1952), 71.

8   See Jacques Rancière, "The Aesthetic Revolution and Its Outcomes: Emplotments of Autonomy and Heteronomy," *New Left Review* 14 (March–April 2002): 133–51.

9   See Brodhead, *Cultures of Letters*; Wexler, *Tender Violence*; Douglas, *Feminization of American Culture*; Brown, *Domestic Individualism*; Merish, *Sentimental Materialism*; Dobson, "Reclaiming Sentimental Literature"; Noble, *Masochistic Pleasures*; and Kete, *Sentimental Collaboration*.

10   Raymond Williams, *Keywords: A Vocabulary of Culture and Society* (New York: Oxford Univ. Press, 1985), 32.

11   *Oxford English Dictionary*, 2d ed., s.v. "aesthetic."

12   Immanuel Kant, cited in *OED*, s.v. "aesthetic."

13   "Aesthetics is born as a discourse of the body," writes Terry Eagleton. "That territory is nothing less than the whole of our sensate life together—the business of affections and aversions, of how the world strikes the body on its sensory surfaces, of that which takes root in the gaze and the guts and all that arises from our most banal biological insertion into the world" (*The Ideology of the Aesthetic* [Oxford, Eng.: Basil Blackwell, 1990], 13).

14   Karen Sánchez-Eppler, *Touching Liberty: Abolition, Feminism, and the Politics of the Body* (Berkeley and Los Angeles: Univ. of California Press, 1993), 26–27.

15   Marianne Noble, "The Ecstasies of Sentimental Wounding in *Uncle Tom's Cabin*," *Yale Journal of Criticism* 10 (fall 1997): 302.

16 Both Sánchez-Eppler and Noble emphasize the extent to which the physicality of sentimentalism creates sympathetic connections among individuals. For Noble in particular, the force of this sympathy is to create a nonindividualist mode of subjectivity, which she provocatively explores in terms of masochistic dynamics. In emphasizing her claim that a free subjectivity results from feeling, I'm reading Noble somewhat against the grain of her own thesis, yet it strikes me as significant that the feeling of self generated in her account of sentimental emotion is autonomous with respect to certain forms of existing law. In other words, sentimental feeling is related to the production of autonomous subjectivity at some level, even if that subjectivity is also cast as intersubjective.

17 In *The Critique of Judgement*, Kant explains the nature of the disjunction between the sensible and the supersensible: "The realm of the concept of nature under the one legislation [Understanding], and that of the concept of freedom under the other [Reason], are completely cut off from all reciprocal influence that they might severally (each according to its own principles) exert upon the other, by the broad gulf that divides the supersensible from phenomena. The concept of freedom determines nothing in respect of the theoretical cognition of nature; and the concept of nature likewise nothing in respect of the practical laws of freedom. To that extent, then, it is not possible to throw a bridge from the one realm to the other" (36–37).

18 Ibid., 71.

19 Friedrich Schiller, *On the Aesthetic Education of Man, in a Series of Letters*, ed. and trans. Elizabeth M. Wilkinson and L. A. Willoughby (Oxford, Eng.: Oxford Univ. Press, 1967), 25. Further references are to this edition and will be cited parenthetically as *AE*.

20 According to Eagleton, for instance, the project of Schillerian aesthetics is deeply implicated in ideological forms of constraint: "[T]he aesthetic signifies . . . a kind of 'internalised repression,' inserting social power more deeply into the very bodies of those it subjugates, and so operating as a supremely effective mode of political hegemony" (*Ideology of the Aesthetic*, 28). David Lloyd, in turn, describes the formalizing aim of Schiller's aesthetics as one that eliminates heterogeneity in the name of a unified State: "The effect [of aesthetic ideology] is to pose a single type for human individuality in which the specific differences which might characterize human experience are annulled" ("Arnold, Ferguson, and Schiller: Aesthetic Culture and the Politics of Aesthetics," *Cultural Critique* 2 [winter 1985–86]: 166). Alternatively, George Levine argues: "However thoroughly absorbed into dominant ideological formations the aesthetic has been, it has always served also as a potentially disruptive force, one that opens up possibilities of value resistant to any dominant political power" ("Introduction: Reclaiming the Aesthetic," *Aesthetics and Ideology*, ed. George Levine [New Brunswick, N.J.: Rutgers

Sentimental Aesthetics **521**

Univ. Press, 1994], 15). For a lengthier discussion of the critique of aesthetics as ideology, see Martin Jay, *Force Fields: Between Intellectual History and Cultural Critique* (New York: Routledge, 1993), 72–84.

21 See Jay, *Force Fields*; and Josef Chytry, *The Aesthetic State: A Quest in Modern German Thought* (Berkeley and Los Angeles: Univ. of California Press, 1989), 90; cited in Jay, *Force Fields*, 79.

22 Friedrich Schiller, *On Naïve and Sentimental Poetry*, in *Friedrich Schiller: Poet of Freedom*, trans. and ed. William F. Wertz Jr. et al., 3 vols. (New York: New Benjamin Franklin House, 1990), 3:323–41.

23 "One endowed with an [aesthetic] apprehension . . . ," Griswold writes, "becomes purer and more elevated, in sentiment and aspiration, after viewing an embodiment of any such conception as that specimen of genius materialized, the Belvidere Apollo, 'at the aspect of which,' says Winckelman, 'I forget all the universe: I involuntarily assume the most noble attribute of my being in order to be worthy of its presence'" (preface to *The Female Poets of America* [Philadelphia: Carey and Hart, 1849], 8).

24 On Griswold's involvement with the *International Magazine* (which became *Harper's Magazine* in 1852), see Joy Bayless, *Rufus Wilmot Griswold: Poe's Literary Executor* (Nashville, Tenn.: Vanderbilt Univ. Press, 1943), 205–11. On the reception and publication of Goethe and Schiller in the United States, see Thomas L. Buckley, "The Bostonian Cult of Classicism: The Reception of Goethe and Schiller in the Literary Reviews of the *North American Review, Christian Examiner*, and the *Dial*, 1817–1865," in *The Fortunes of German Writers in America: Studies in Literary Reception*, ed. Wolfgang Elfe, James Hardin, and Gunther Holst (Columbia: Univ. of South Carolina Press, 1992), 27–40. Margaret Fuller also apparently read and discussed the aesthetic theories of Goethe and Schiller in a literary conversation group she convened in Boston in 1839; see Amanda Ritchie, "Margaret Fuller's First Conversation Series: A Discovery in the Archives," *Legacy* 18, no.2 (2001): 216–31.

25 Frances Anne Butler Kemble, "Lines: On Reading with Difficulty Some of Schiller's Early Love Poems," in *Nineteenth-Century American Women Poets: An Anthology*, ed. Paula Bernat Bennett (Malden, Mass.: Blackwell, 1998), 48–49.

26 In 1844, J. Weiss translated and published *On the Aesthetic Education of Man, in a Series of Letters* in England, and in 1861 Charles M. Hempel published a translation in Philadelphia as part of a translation of Schiller's complete works; see Wilkinson and Willoughby, "Appendix II," *On the Aesthetic Education of Man*, 338–39.

27 On the relation between Schiller and moral-sense theory, see Stanley Mitchell, "Aesthetics and Politics in the Age of the French Revolution," in *1789: Reading, Writing Revolution: Proceedings of the Essex Conference on the Sociology of Literature, July 1981*, ed. Frances Barker et al. (Col-

chester, Eng.: Univ. of Essex, 1982), 180–97. "Shaftesbury's . . . category
of 'moral sense,'" Mitchell writes, "is reproduced in Schiller's 'beautiful
soul' (*schöne Seele*), and an instinctively harmonious personality-type in
whom duty and desire do not have to conflict, as in Kantian ethics" (188).
See also R. H. Stephenson, "Weimar Classicism's Debt to the Scottish
Enlightenment," in *Goethe and the English-Speaking World*, ed. Nicholas
Boyle and John Guthrie (Rochester, N.Y.: Camden House, 2002), 61–
70; Manfred Kuehn, *Scottish Common Sense in Germany, 1768–1800: A
Contribution to the History of Critical Philosophy* (Kingston, Ont.: McGill-
Queen's Univ. Press, 1987); Wilkinson and Willoughby, introduction to
Schiller, *On the Aesthetic Education of Man*, xxviii; and Josef Chytry, *The
Aesthetic State*, 72. According to Wilkinson and Willoughby, Schiller was
reading Lord Kames's work while writing *On the Aesthetic Education of
Man* (lxxiv).

28   Gregg Camfield, "The Moral Aesthetics of Sentimentality: A Missing
Key to *Uncle Tom's Cabin*," *Nineteenth-Century Literature* 43 (December 1988): 328, 331. See also Marianne Noble, "Sentimental Epistemolo-
gies in *Uncle Tom's Cabin* and *The House of the Seven Gables*," in *Separate
Spheres No More: Gender Convergence in American Literature, 1830–1930*,
ed. Monika M. Elbert (Tuscaloosa: Univ. of Alabama Press, 2000): 261–81;
and Lori Merish, *Sentimental Materialism*.

29   Archibald Alison, "Of the Sublimity and Beauty of the Material World," in
*Essays on the Nature and Principles of Taste. With Corrections and Improve-
ments by Abraham Mills* (New York: Carvill, 1830), 414.

30   Ibid., 417–18, my emphasis.

31   Caroline May, headnote, *The American Female Poets* (Philadelphia: Lind-
say and Blakiston, 1848), 381–82, my emphasis.

32   Griswold, *Female Poets of America*, 177.

33   Jürgen Habermas, *The Structural Transformation of the Public Sphere: An
Inquiry into a Category of Bourgeois Society*, trans. Thomas Burger (Cambridge: MIT Press, 1989), 46.

34   See Pamela Haag, *Consent: Sexual Rights and the Transformation of American Liberalism* (Ithaca, N.Y.: Cornell Univ. Press, 1999).

35   See Jeanne Boydston, *Home and Work: Housework, Wages, and the Ideology of Labor in the Early Republic* (New York: Oxford Univ. Press, 1990).
See also Amy Dru Stanley, "Home Life and the Morality of the Market,"
in *The Market Revolution in America*, ed. Stephen Conway and Melvyn
Stokes (Charlottesville: Univ. Press of Virginia, 1996); and Nancy Cott,
The Bonds of Womanhood: "Woman's Sphere" in New England, 1780–1835,
2nd ed. (New Haven: Yale Univ. Press, 1997). In *From Bondage to Contract: Wage Labor, Marriage, and the Market in the Age of Slave Emancipation*, Amy Dru Stanley's discussion of wage labor is useful in demonstrating that the reality of leisure was not available to many women—particularly nonwhite and working-class women—but the ideology of domes-

tic leisure nonetheless had real effects insofar as it shaped public policy (New York: Cambridge Univ. Press, 1998).

36　Reva Siegel, "Why Equal Protection No Longer Protects: The Evolving Forms of Status-Enforcing State Action," *Stanford Law Review* 49 (May 1997): 1119. On the sentimentalization of marriage in legal discourse in the nineteenth century, see Laura Korobkin, *Criminal Conversations: Sentimentality and Nineteenth-Century Legal Stories of Adultery* (New York: Columbia Univ. Press, 1999).

37　May, introduction to *The American Female Poets*, vi.

38　See Julie Ellison, *Cato's Tears and the Making of Anglo-American Emotion* (Chicago: Univ. of Chicago Press, 1999).

39　Griswold, *Female Poets of America*, 7. See also Chapman and Hendler, eds., *Sentimental Men*.

40　The long-standing critical debate over the value and meaning of sentimental writing in the United States reflects this binary opposition. Most famously, Douglas describes sentimentalism as a capitulation to capitalism and a market economy, whereas Tompkins views sentimental writing as embodying resistance to patriarchy and women's passivity. For useful discussions of this debate, see Chapman and Hendler's introduction to *Sentimental Men*; and Laura Wexler, "Tender Violence: Literary Eavesdropping, Domestic Fiction, and Educational Reform," in *The Culture of Sentiment*, 12–32. For a recent discussion of Douglas's work on sentimentalism, see *differences* 11 (fall 1999), a special issue devoted to the work of Ann Douglas (*America the Feminine*, ed. Leonard Tennenhouse and Philip Gould).

41　Frances Sargent Locke Osgood, "Lines Suggested by the Announcement That 'A Bill for the Protection of the Property of Married Women Has Passed Both Houses' of Our State Legislature," *New York Tribune*, 17 April 1848.

42　June Howard, *Publishing the Family* (Durham, N.C.: Duke Univ. Press, 2001), 219.

43　Ibid., 245.

44　Rancière, "The Aesthetic Revolution," 150.

45　Lauren Berlant, "Poor Eliza," *American Literature* 70 (September 1998): 164.

46　Paula Bennett's work on sentimental poetry published by women in newspapers and journals has made visible the fact that the terms of debates over affect, gender, and aesthetics were taking place in the public sphere of print (*Poets in the Public Sphere: The Emancipatory Project of American Women's Poetry, 1800–1900* [Princeton, N.J.: Princeton Univ. Press, 2003]).

Wai Chee   Aesthetics at the Limits of the Nation:
Dimock   Kant, Pound, and the *Saturday Review*

How powerful is the nation as a taxonomic (rather than jurisdictional) unit? Who gets to classify, who gets to name the phenomena of the world? Do human beings naturally congregate as sovereign states, or can we imagine a different ordering of humanity, something like Bruce Ackerman's "world constitutionalism" or Jürgen Habermas's "postnational constellation"?[1] Habermas thinks that this new associative form will replace the conventional nation-state:

> [The] conventional model is less and less appropriate to the current situation. While the state's sovereignty and monopoly on violence remain formally intact, the growing interdependencies of a world society challenge the basic premise that national politics, circumscribed within a determinate national territory, is still adequate to address the actual fates of individual nation-states.[2]

Habermas made this prediction, of course, before the U.S.-led war against Iraq in 2003. As Etienne Balibar shows, that war has actually inverted Habermas's model, highlighting not a postnational constellation but state sovereignty globally deployed.[3] It is in this context—in the aftermath of a powerful nation unilaterally imposing its terms on the world—that taxonomy becomes not entirely academic. What concepts do we have that might challenge this unilateral naming? What concepts might help strengthen the claims of a "global civil society,"[4] currently trivialized and in danger of being emptied out?

In what follows, I propose a term that so far has not been examined in conjunction with this global civil society, although historically it has played an important part, namely, *the aesthetic*.[5] Terry Eagleton, not exactly a fond champion, pointed out some years ago that

American Literature, Volume 76, Number 3, September 2004. Copyright © 2004 by Duke University Press.

while the category of the aesthetic takes its cue from bourgeois hegemony, it nonetheless "provides an unusually powerful challenge and alternative to . . . dominant ideological forms," for its "contradictory" energies are such as to keep alive a "residually common world."[6] That residually common world can be reclaimed. It can be recharged, reactivated, and realigned, I argue, to serve as a rallying point against the unilateralism of nations. For the long backward extension of the aesthetic invokes a map that predates the nation-state, one that allows for multilateral ties, more complex and far-flung than those dictated by territorial jurisdictions. The aesthetic, in this way, gestures toward a paradigm of the humanities as a *species-wide* discipline, planetary in its archives, and planetary in its operating networks.

I am not the first to see the aesthetic in this light. Immanuel Kant, in *Critique of Judgment* and in his political writings, especially *Perpetual Peace*, has already done much to lay the groundwork for such a claim. Kant sees the aesthetic as a species-wide category of experience, emanating from the human perceiver rather than the perceived object. What interests him is not the ontological status of the thing we judge to be beautiful but the mental operation that enables us to make that judgment.[7] This mental operation is the pivot of humanity. According to Kant, it is the clearest evidence we have of a noncontradictory relation between the subjective and the universal. Because beauty is a quality each of us determines, it affirms our freedom as separate judges. This freedom, however, is held in check by one constraint: universal assent. Judgments about beauty must be acceptable to everyone else, a constraint that marks the projected scope as well as the limiting condition for subjective opinion. The aesthetic is both local and global in this sense, both particular in its judgment and generalizable in its ground for judgment. Through this duality, the species is able to individuate each of its members even as it affirms its integrative common ground. A manifold oneness both connects us and makes each of us singular. This is why we count as a species, a taxonomic order encompassing every human being on earth.

Of course, for Kant, this claim on behalf of the aesthetic is argued on strictly a priori, or logically necessary, grounds. Empirical data, according to him, prove nothing definite; no binding maxim can rest upon them. I reverse his strategy. Relying heavily on empirical data—in this case, the much publicized attack against one set of poems, Ezra Pound's *The Pisan Cantos* (1948), the work of an alleged aesthete and a traitor to his nation—I make a tentative claim on behalf of the aesthetic as a term activated on both ends of the political spectrum: state sovereignty on one hand, global humanity on the other. Kant's theory, tested by this empirical archive, will be fully vindicated, and ironized beyond recognition. The spectacle of an American poet recklessly embracing the aesthetic heritage of the world, and recklessly giving himself over to an anti-American cause, fulfils just what Kant predicts, but only by giving it a bad name. The aesthetic here is indeed a challenge to the national, although no one would find it reassuring. Even so, and perhaps because it is not reassuring, this vexing term continues to name a deviant zone, namable at the taxonomic limits of the nation. An alternate conception of the species emerges here, possibly (and in this case demonstrably) monstrous, but in its vision of a global humanity, going all the way with Kant.

And Kant goes far. In *Perpetual Peace*, he offers this blueprint:

> The condition which must be fulfilled before any kind of international right is possible is that a lawful state must already be in existence. . . . Now we have already seen above that a federative association of states whose sole intention is to eliminate war is the only *lawful* arrangement which can be reconciled with their *freedom*. Thus politics and morality can only be in agreement within a federal union, which is therefore necessary and even *a priori* through the principles of right. And the rightful basis of all political prudence is the founding of such a union in the most comprehensive form possible.[8]

Writing in 1795, in a Prussia under the thumb of Frederick William II, Kant had every reason to dream about a "federative association of states," a world polity not under that thumb.[9] This world polity, however, is meant not to supersede the state but to protect it.[10] For the sole charge of this entity is to eliminate war, which, for Kant, is the most vicious destroyer of nations: both in the literal sense of bringing down particular regimes and in the subtler sense of killing off civil liberties in a militarized state. Only a world polity can put an end to this dual destructiveness. Only a world polity can care for the human species as a whole, protecting individual freedom by safeguarding international peace.

And yet living in a Europe ravaged by war, Kant knew better than to see this international peacekeeper as anything other than a utopian dream. *Perpetual Peace*, while not ironic in the substance of what it proposes, is overflowing with irony when it comes to the likelihood of its ever being adopted. The treatise begins with the caption, "The Perpetual Peace," followed by this line: "A Dutch innkeeper once put this satirical inscription on his signboard, along with the picture of a graveyard."[11] Only among the dead is peace a viable option. Among the living it will always be a stillborn hope, dead on arrival.

Hannah Arendt, struck by Kant's uncharacteristic irony, has argued that *Perpetual Peace* is just a self-mocking indulgence, "reveries" that "Kant himself did not take . . . too seriously." This overtly political essay and several others like it do not amount to much, Arendt insists. They do not represent the full extent of Kant's thinking, for "there exists a political philosophy in Kant but . . . in contrast to other philosophers, he never wrote it." Where, then, is this "nonwritten political philosophy" to be found? Arendt devotes the whole of her *Lectures on Kant's Political Philosophy* to this question.[12] Her answer is perverse. The "nonwritten" can only be inferred, she says, and inferred from the most unlikely source, namely, a treatise that on the face of it has nothing whatever to do with politics: "Since Kant did not write his political philosophy, the best way to find out what he thought about this matter is to turn to his 'Critique of Aesthetic Judgment,' where, in discussing the production of art works in their relation to taste, which judges and decides about them, he confronts an analogous problem."[13]

A theory of aesthetics doubling as a theory of politics? The judging of beauty "analogous" to the keeping of peace? This counterintuitive approach has not persuaded everybody.[14] Still, the paradigm Arendt sets forth cannot be more ambitious. Any hope for a species-wide ordering of the humanities—and any hope for a species-wide ordering of the world—will have to come to terms with her argument.[15] In what follows, I test Arendt's hypothesis. Reading *Critique of Judgment* as she advises, as a meditation on two fronts, I explore it as a deeply architectured and therefore robustly nonironic version of *Perpetual Peace*. The aesthetic theory here affirms the unity of the species by way of the faculty of judgment, offered by Kant as evidence of the deep agreement among human beings, extendable to the political realm and grounding his proposal for eliminating war.

Of course, whether war can ever be eliminated is a distressing question at the moment. Do we, as members of the same species, have anything in common and, if so, can that common ground be strengthened to the point of guaranteeing peace? This is a supremely uncomfortable subject for all of us, not just Kant and Arendt. And nothing adds more to the discomfort than the example of Ezra Pound. To gesture toward species unity, in Pound's case, meant not only to be against war but also to be a fan of Mussolini, a propagandist for the Italian fascist state, and in his Rome Radio broadcasts, a traitor to his native country. Very few of us see a hopeful future in Pound's dubious example. If such empirical data mean anything at all, they point to a fault line deep in Kant's theory (and Arendt's reading of it) that runs all the way through the projected hope of species unification. That hope is probably too fragile to bear all the weight put upon it. In fact, it is probable that its ugly twin, disunity, will end up bearing that weight, as an unhappy but not altogether unhopeful condition, giving rise to its own negative dialectic. But this is getting ahead of the story.

It is useful to begin with *Critique of Judgment* and its aspirations for the species. The key vehicle of these aspirations is something called "common sense," defined in §20 as that "subjective principle which determines what pleases or displeases only by feeling and not by concepts, but yet with universal validity."[16] Here, then, is the crucial Kantian pivot, the overlap between the subjective and the universal, between the species-individuating and species-integrating poles of the aesthetic. This dynamic is further elucidated in §40, where the commonness of aesthetic judgment is given a sharper definition through its Latin name:

> But under the *sensus communis* we must include the idea of a sense *common to all*, i.e. of a faculty of judgment which, in its reflection, takes account (*a priori*) of the mode of representation of all other men in thought, in order, as it were, to compare its judgment with the collective reason of humanity. . . . I say that taste can be called *sensus communis* with more justice than sound understanding can, and that the aesthetical judgment rather than the intellectual may bear the name of a sense common to all, if we are willing to use the word "sense" of an effect of mere reflection upon the mind, for then we understand by sense the feeling of pleasure. We could even define taste as the faculty of judging of that which makes *universally communicable*, without the mediation of a concept. (*CJ*, 136, 138)

"Taste," the most private of our senses, is singled out by Kant as the most public, its contents most universally communicable, its field of action of the largest scope. It is an odd choice. Taste is not usually given this kind of global mandate. Unlike sight, a faculty deemed objective because of its representation of external objects, taste is not objectively representational. It registers only a feeling, our like or dislike of something presented to the palate, but it yields no descriptive image. Sight tells us about the measurable shape, size, and color of an apple; taste tells us no such thing. It says only that this apple is delicious or passable, a judgment entirely internal to us, with no outward extension in the world. Taste is bounded by the bounds of our subjectivity. It is the most primitive of our senses.

It is this primitive sensory faculty that occupies the central place in Kant's aspirations for the species. Not only is taste identified with aesthetic judgment, in that capacity it is given the further, all-important task of species unification. It is the aesthetic—rather than the intellectual—that is the unifying force for Kant, and the distinction between these two says much about his conception of humankind. The intellectual is a specialized category, a high-end, high-order phenomenon; it rests on a cognitive apparatus, requiring the "mediation of a concept." Intellectual activities take place on an upper stratum of our mental life. This high-end phenomenon is not *"universally communicable."* Mathematics, for instance, cannot be explained to everyone; it is the privilege of a few. The aesthetic, on the other hand, is the province of everybody. It requires no mediation at all, no high-flying concept, nothing special, since it comes from just a "gut feeling," the liking or disliking occasioned by what comes our way. That feeling expresses itself as the judgment that the encountered object is good or bad, beautiful or ugly, delicious or passable. And it does not take much to arrive at that judgment. Aesthetic feeling (according to Kant) is instinctive and instantaneous; it is preconceptual at the very least and, in some cases, perhaps even precognitive. It is the most basic feature of human life, the only part of our mental existence that is truly across-the-board, available to every member of the species.[17] And it is because it is so basic, because it occupies the lowest rung of the mind, that "the aesthetical judgment rather than the intellectual may bear the name of a sense common to all."

Aesthetic judgment is the name Kant gives to the baseline of humanity. The word *beautiful*, most common of words, is that baseline. There is no phenomenon that cannot be positively or negatively described by this term, and no human being who will not at some point resort to using it. Kant is not usually regarded as a patron saint of cultural studies, but he should be. Aesthetics and cultural studies do not have to be segregated, as if the latter were solely the province of the mindlessly low and the former solely the province of the snobbishly high.[18] Kant, on the contrary, sees the beautiful as a low-end phenomenon, experienced across the board, encompassing the full range of objects in the world and the full range of judges. "It is by beauty," Ernst Cassirer says of Kant, that humankind "passes beyond the sphere of empirical individuality . . . to a common basis—to that basis which in the *Critique of Judgment* is called *das übersinnliche Substrat der Menscheit*, the intelligible substratum of humanity."[19] That is why the word *beautiful* is so basic, why its usage gives the species its lowest common denominator. Arendt, enlarging on this point, has read *Critique of Judgment* as a theory about "an original compact of mankind as a whole, and derived from this idea is the notion of humanity, of what actually constitutes the humannness of human beings, living and dying in this world, on this earth that is a globe, which they inhabit in common, share in common, in the succession of generations."[20]

What are the chances of this idealized sense of the human actually materializing among human beings? Can the aesthetic, the *sensus communis*, the substratum of humanity, overcome the appetite of nation-states for war? Much depends on the ontological status of the term *human*, the depth of that substratum. Is the *sensus communis* a constitutive unity that binds its members at every level, unifying any individual judgment with the judgment of everyone else as a fait accompli? Or is the *sensus communis* merely regulative, not really a substratum at all, but much more tenuous, secured only through a negotiated give-and-take, with each judge appealing to a kind of species tribunal for validation? Paul Guyer, in his careful analysis of these two definitions of the *sensus communis*, one strong and one weak, argues that they represent an unresolved tension in Kant.[21] That tension has large consequences for the claim of the aesthetic and its ability to unite humankind against the nation and against war.

In §19, Kant seems to come down firmly on the side of the strong claim. "The judgment of taste," he says, "requires the agreement of everyone, and he who describes anything as beautiful claims that everyone *ought* to give his approval to the object in question and also describe it as beautiful. . . . We ask for the agreement of everyone else, because we have for it a ground that is common to all; and we could count on this agreement" (*CJ*, 74). This is clear indeed. The ground for agreement is a given antecedent, truly a substratum; we can count on it. Kant is not, of course, so misguided as to think that this ground has in any way been actualized in the world. Even a fool can see that there is no consensus about beauty just yet. But a consensual ground potentially exists. In fact, it logically has to exist, for otherwise our feeling of beauty would have been entirely arbitrary. And it is because this feeling is not entirely arbitrary, because it is justified by some pre-existing and nonidiosyncratic norm, that it can count as a judgment in the first place. A judgment, to be such, carries the binding force of an ought. It points to a generalizable rule as its genetic condition. We call something beautiful with the understanding that we are passing a normative verdict, that other human beings might concur with this norm, and that, under ideal conditions, they ought to.

Aesthetic judgment affirms the unity of the species as a logical necessity. As Eagleton says, "It is as though, prior to any determinate dialogue or debate, we are always already in agreement, *fashioned* to concur; and the aesthetic is this experience of pure contentless consensus where we find ourselves spontaneously at one without necessarily even knowing what, referentially speaking, we are agreeing over."[22] Such logical agreement seems not to mesh with the known facts of human life. Even in Kant, complications set in almost right away. The normative "ought," for instance, sometimes has a petulant air to it, as in §22:

> In all judgments by which we describe anything as beautiful, we allow no one to be of another opinion, without, however, grounding our judgment on concepts, but only on our feeling, which we therefore place at its basis, not as a private, but as a common feeling. Now this common sense cannot be grounded on experience, for it aims at justifying judgments which contain an *ought*. It does not say that everyone *will* agree with my judgment, but that he *ought*. (*CJ*, 76)

Here the *ought*, rather than being the bearer of a logical necessity—a predicable common ground—becomes instead a fiat. It is a counterfactual statement that flies in the face of what obviously disagrees with it. That disagreement can only be an aberration as far as it is concerned. Judgment here is regulative in the worst sense. Extended from an individual opinion and generalized into a universal norm, it takes any nonconcurrence as a mistake, an *ipso facto* error, to be duly corrected. The premise of unity, in other words, carries in reserve a punitive clause. It carries in reserve the right to name as deviant those who disagree with its normative common sense.

Kant is so wedded to the idea of aesthetic judgment and the *sensus communis* being one and the same that he cannot fully acknowledge this punitive scenario. Nor can he acknowledge another scenario, also punitive, in which the *sensus communis*, far from being one with the aesthetic, instead cordons it off, draws a sharp line around it, as a marked target, a negative definitional pole. The aesthetic then becomes a name for what this imagined community jointly castigates and exorcizes as an agreed-upon object of condemnation. The twentieth century has witnessed many enemies of the people branded with that label. The United States has had its share of these, and none more vexing than Ezra Pound.

The condemnation of Pound reached a climax when the *The Pisan Cantos* was awarded the first Bollingen Prize in 1949. To Robert Hillyer (then President of the Poetry Society of America and a winner of the Pulitzer Prize), this was the last straw, the ultimate affront of a "new estheticism, the literary cult to whom T. S. Eliot and Ezra Pound are gods."[23] Hillyer was not alone in being thus affronted. The formidable *Saturday Review of Literature*, which published Hillyer's articles, fully shared his outrage. In an accompanying editorial, Norman Cousins and Harrison Smith, editor and president of the *Saturday Review*, made their own case against Pound and named his offense in no uncertain terms:

> Like Mr. Hillyer, we were profoundly shocked to see the name of the United States Library of Congress, and therefore that of the United States Government, associated with the Bollingen $1,000 award to Ezra Pound. It is not enough to say that Ezra Pound is a traitor. It is not enough because it is important to know exactly what kind of traitor he is, and what he is a traitor to. Ezra Pound is not merely the traitor who deserts his country in order to impart secrets which are useful to the enemy. . . . [but] the world's No.1 sneerer at America and its traditions and its people.[24]

Pound might have been called a fascist, or an anti-Semite, but these names did not figure largely in the *Saturday Review* editorial. Instead, the name of choice that trumped all other names was "traitor." This was the proper designation for Ezra Pound, according to the *Satur-*

day Review, which used it with relish. Technically speaking, of course, Pound's "treason" against the United States was somewhat nebulous, not at all cut-and-dried.[25] He had not, after all, acted as a spy; he had not passed on valuable secrets to the enemy. He had been guilty only of "sneering" at the United States in his radio broadcasts.

Still, *traitor* was the right name, and the *Saturday Review* was on good authority in using it. This word—or at least its more technical, punishable sibling, *treason*—had originated from the legal proceedings initiated by the U.S. Attorney General. On 26 July 1943, Pound was indicted by a grand jury in the District of Columbia for violation of the Treason Statute (Section 1, Title 18, United States Code, 1940 Edition):

> That Ezra Pound, the defendant herein . . . being a citizen of the United States, and a person owing allegiance to the United States, in violation of his said duty of allegiance, knowingly, intentionally, wilfully, unlawfully, feloniously, traitorously, and treasonably did adhere to the enemies of the United States, to wit, the Kingdom of Italy, its counsellors, armies, navies, secret agents, representatives, and subjects, and the military allies of the said Kingdom of Italy, including the Government of the German Reich and the Imperial Government of Japan, with which the United States at all times since December 11, 1941, have been at war, giving to the said enemies of the United States aid and comfort within the United States and elsewhere.[26]

The phrase "United States" appears obsessively, like some sort of mantra. The grand jury needed to invoke it repeatedly, for it was this sanctified name that in turn gave a name to Pound's offense. Treason is an offense against the state; more than that, it is an offense defined *by* the state, named as a prosecutable relation to its "enemies," and in that naming, the sovereignty of the state is affirmed at the very point of its alleged breach. This is a nation-based taxonomy in its full glory; treason is its star player.

That starring role is not limited to courtroom verdicts. As the *Saturday Review* editorial makes amply clear, the word is versatile and it can do double duty, serving up literary condemnation as much as political indictment. And there is no reason why it should not be versatile in this way, interchangeably a literary and political term, for *traitor* is indeed a judgment operating on both registers if we see literature strictly in national terms, if we judge Pound solely and exclusively as American. Pound has not been a good American: not in his political loyalties, and not in his literary affiliations. With nationality as the sole yardstick, his "poetical and propaganda activities" can rightly be condemned by using one and the same term. Robert Hillyer was merely executing that logic when he entitled his first article "Treason's Strange Fruit":

> Ezra Pound is quite simply under indictment for treason because during the last war he served the enemy in direct poetical and propaganda activities against the United States. . . . In view of Pound's hatred for the democracy of his native country, it is ironic that among the conditions of the award is the stipulation that the recipient must be an American citizen. By some tenuous legality Pound may be a citizen, but he knows nothing and cares less about civic obligations. . . . He has seldom set foot in America since he was twenty-three. His country's elections, wars, aspirations, and exploits have left him untouched if not hostile. ("TSF," 16)

As an American, Ezra Pound was deficient indeed. Anyone judging him by that criterion would have reason to spurn him, to resent his legal citizenship as an empty designation, without substance. Against that taxonomic imposture, Hillyer, the *Saturday Review*, and the grand jury of the District of Columbia were united in their outrage and in their determination to set things right. The false name, *American citizen*, had to be stripped away, and the real name, *traitor*, pronounced with the combined authority of the court and a mass-circulating periodical.

Since it was a question of calling things by the right name, it was not just Pound who had to be overhauled. He was the easy target in "Treason's Strange Fruit," but Hillyer actually had in mind a larger prey. The problem with the Bollingen Prize, he said, was not only that the wrong man got the award but also that the judges decided to give it to him in the first place. Who were these judges? They were a group known as the Fellows of the Library of Congress in American Letters, and included, among others, Conrad Aiken, Robert Lowell, Katherine Anne Porter, Karl Shapiro, Allen Tate, and Robert Penn Warren, as well as two names that Hillyer listed with parenthetical asides: "Wystan Hugh Auden (a native of Great Britain who is now an American citizen)" and "T. S. Eliot (a native of the United States who has become a British citizen)" ("TSF," 9). Hillyer did not mind Auden, but Eliot incensed him. And so the article that began with the treason of Pound ended up with the treason of Eliot, heavily underlined:

> Eliot's whole life has been a flight from his native St. Louis, Missouri. He has gone far, and doubtless, if he survives Masefield, he will be the next English laureate. In America he is so enhedged with nebulous divinity that people are shocked, as by blasphemy, at anything said against him. This is occasioned not so much by his writings as by the awe for a man who managed to get contemporary America out of his system, an aspiration of many new poets and critics. . . . What is to be done? The 1949 Bollingen Award is a permanent disgrace and cannot be expunged. But preventive measures against a similar choice can be taken. The first step would seem to be for the expatriate T. S. Eliot to be dropped from the jury. ("TSF," 28)

Once again, those magic words—"American" and its opposite, "expatriate"—are made to do double and triple duty, naming in one and the same convenient gesture the crime of treason, the crime of being a bad poet, and the crime of being a bad judge. Since everything boils down to nationality, since nothing escapes its classifications, its sovereignty is thereby absolute. It will not tolerate any competing lexicon, any word that offers a different description of a poet or a judge on a prize-selection committee.

The aesthetic was unforgivable for just that reason. The idea that poetry might be written (or read) with an evaluative criterion other than its Americanness was treasonable in itself. Hillyer's dislike of the offending word began with its spelling. His object of condemnation was the "new estheticism"—and no good American would spell it any other way. Under this spelling, he obviously included those "Americans and one expatriate on the Bollingen jury," those "esthetes [who] crowned Pound as their laureate" ("TSF," 11). But as he made clear in the title of his second article, he also meant to include a much larger group, which he named "Poetry's New Priesthood." This priesthood comprised a group of readers, those "self-styled 'new critics,'" who had the nerve to look to beauty as an evaluative criterion. Hillyer found it ominous that these "new esthetes" had gone so far as to compile a taxonomy of their own, with the title "A Glossary of the New Criticism."[27] Not finding words such as *traitor* and *treason* in that glossary, Hillyer hurled at these delinquent judges a charge they were to receive again and again: "To a world eager for the clearest vision of poets they offer only the analysis of disillusioned irony, word by word" ("PNP," 8). Close reading was downright unpatriotic. What made it even worse was that the practice seemed to be quite common; college professors and even high school teachers were addicted to it:

> Their power is enormous, especially in the colleges and even the preparatory schools. A large proportion of funds for cultural purposes from the great charitable foundations is earmarked for their use. *Poetry: A Magazine of Verse* seems to be falling into the hands of the new esthetes. In their April number the editors comment on what a hard time poor Ezra Pound must have had from lack of appreciation and add that "nothing is more understandable than that he should have adopted a rather cross attitude towards America." Some day someone is going to adopt a rather cross attitude towards the editors of *Poetry*. Maybe America. ("PNP," 8)

Hillyer was right. Just two months after the publication of his *Saturday Review* articles, a Joint House and Senate Committee directed the Library of Congress to stop sponsoring the Bollingen Prize.[28] "America" did indeed decide to have nothing to do with poetry. And for good reason. Twentieth-century poets and their readers were not exactly flag-waving patriots: Louise Bogan, Robert Lowell, Wallace Stevens, Robert Penn Warren, and Allen Tate were all opposed to World War II.[29] The fact that *Poetry* magazine had actually come out with a mild apology for Pound gave Hillyer just the ammunition he needed. The war is not over yet, he insisted, for treason is in our midst: "[T]he clouds of an intellectual neo-Fascism and the new estheticism have perceptibly met and on a horizon too near for comfort" ("PNP," 38).

Here then is the charge that trumps all others: aestheticism and fascism are one. Uncannily, Hillyer is echoing a much more famous dictum from none other than Walter Benjamin: "Fascism is the introduction of aesthetics into political life."[30] It is a powerful indictment, an almost unanswerable term of reproach. And yet as Russell Berman points out, in simply equating aesthetics with fascism, Benjamin has flattened a much more complicated process, flattened, in particular, the mediating role played by the nation.[31] In the United States, that mediating role turned Benjamin's indictment on its head. Here the aesthetic, far from being staged as official spectacle, as it was in Germany and Italy,[32] is deployed instead as a common-sense term of condemnation, a shorthand for all that gives offense. It is lined up with the word *treason* and the word *fascism* to name any deviance from the patriotic norm.

That naming must be seen in the context of another word then current—*un-American*—one of the most remarkable words in the twentieth century. The designative power of the House Committee on Un-American Activities was fully behind it. This committee, appointed by Congress in 1938 and exclusively targeting Communists and fellow travelers in the decades to follow, initially had a different mission, with a different group of subversives on its agenda. The name of the committee was coined by Representative Sam Dickstein of New York, who proposed: "There should be a standing committee of this House known as the Committee on Un-American Activities, which should watch every subversive group in this country." He was thinking especially of the Nazis. According to him, there were 25,000 men and women in Nassau County alone, "going crazy, dressed in uniforms and goose-stepping their way for miles at all hours of the night." And outside Nassau County, "there are 200,000 people in this country who should have their citizenship papers canceled," for they are "men of the Bund ready to put on uniforms and to use a gun."[33]

From that beginning, the word *un-American* would go on to enjoy a rather different career.[34] At every point of its flourishing, it was an index to U.S. nationalism, an index to a taxonomy that named its positive term through a marked and denounced negation. Americanness needs a subversive foil, called by different names, but each affirming in reverse the ideal it is said to have subverted. The *Saturday Review*'s attack on the "new estheticism" must be seen in this light. The "introduction of aesthetics into political life" was very much an exercise in name-calling, branding the culprit through its guilt by association with an enemy abroad. Those who launched the attack and those being attacked were both aware of the stakes involved. As the fellows of the Library of Congress in American Letters said in a formal response to the *Saturday Review*, "This charge of irresponsible aestheticism . . . linked sometimes with charges of Fascist-mindedness," in effect imposes a "standard-brand positive Americanism as a test for literary worth."[35]

In the case of Pound, though, the links between aestheticism and fascism were not only real but proudly advertised. *The Pisan Cantos* wore its politics on its sleeves. Canto LXXIV begins by mourning the death of Mussolini:

> The enormous tragedy of the dream in the peasant's bent
>   shoulders
> Manes! Manes was tanned and stuffed,
> Thus Ben and la Clara a Milano
>   by the heels at Milano[36]

Benito Mussolini and his mistress, Clara Petacci, were overtaken by the Italian Partisans on 27 April 1945 and shot, their bodies brought back to Milan and hanged by the heels. To Pound, the hope for human-kind in general and for the Italian peasants in particular died that day. Mussolini, after all, had embarked on ambitious agricultural reforms, including reclaiming 150,000 acres of the Pontine Marshes in 1931 and distributing them to 75,000 peasants; he had made the promise that each of those peasants would have a house of his own in 80 years.[37] Pound, obsessed with economic reform since his ten-year stint at the British socialist magazine the *New Age*, was particularly drawn to this aspect of fascism, its promised redistribution of wealth.[38] He thought Mussolini's estimate too modest: "I don't the least think he expects to take 80 years at it, but he is not given to overstatement. . . . It is possible the Capo del Governo wants to go slow enough so as not to see, in his old age, an Italy full of fat peasants gone rotten. . . . All this is poesy and has no place in a critical epistle."[39]

Politics was indeed aesthetics for Pound, called by the name *poesy*. And it was in tribute to that poesy that he would write, with poetic license, his most controversial piece: *Jefferson and/or Mussolini*. As its title indicates, this treatise is dedicated to the proposition that the American President and the Duce have much in common. In Pound's own words, "The heritage of Jefferson, Quincy Adams, old John Adams, Jackson, Van Buren is HERE, NOW in the Italian peninsula at the beginning of the fascist second decennio, not in Massachusetts or Delaware."[40] It is an outrageous claim, a theory of American (and Italian) history with which hardly anyone would agree.[41] As Pound himself said, this manuscript had the distinction of being refused by "40 publishers."[42] What sort of judgment inspired him to write some-thing so out of step with everyone else? As evinced by the reference to Mussolini's "poesy," that judgment seems to have been largely aes-thetic in nature. "His god is beauty," D. H. Lawrence once said of

Pound.[43] That god gave him a historiography as well as a poetics. It is much more beautiful, much more striking, to think of the shape of human history as an arc rather than a straight line, the legacy from Jefferson and Adams swerving to the side, curving to Europe, winding up in the hands of an Italian. In Canto LXXIV, Pound himself has made poesy out of a similar claim, chronicling an arc of cultural transmission also swerving to the side:

> But a snotty barbarian ignorant of T'ang history need not
>   deceive one,
> nor Charlie Sung's money on loan from anonimo[44]

The Chinese (like the Greeks) are fond of calling foreigners barbarians. Pound adopts that word, the prejudiced word of an ancient civilization. And it is he, Pound, who can afford to be prejudiced in that Chinese way, for it is he, the non-native, who has T'ang history in his safekeeping, while the supposed native, Charlie Sung, clearly has in his safekeeping something very different.

Jefferson and Mussolini, Mussolini and Pound: there is a symmetry between these two sets of relationships.[45] The arc of cultural transmission that makes the Italian the recipient of an American legacy also makes the American the recipient of a Chinese legacy. It is a beautiful symmetry. But "beauty" of this sort, intoxicating to Pound, is nonsensical to most people. Aesthetic judgment is most often, and most powerfully, a lone judgment. Its force is never generalizable, for that force is measured by its peculiar grip on one person, a grip that bears the imprint of one subjectivity, as it does no one else's. It is at this point, where an across-the-board taste turns into something much more luminous (and much more obsessive) for one particular person, that aesthetic judgment can be said to be a salient mental event, an event that marks that person. That mark can never serve as a blueprint for human unity, for its very intensity inflects it, rigs it as subjective, the terrain on which disagreement thrives. The aesthetic thus points to a deep division among human beings; it is a prelude to war rather than a deterrent to it. "Art cannot concretize Utopia, not even negatively," Adorno has argued. "Without a perspective on peace art would be untrue, just as untrue as it is when it anticipates a state of reconciliation. The beautiful in art is the illusion of peace in empirical reality."[46]

That "illusion of peace" would hit Pound with full force. Writing his

Cantos as a grand epic of humankind, a rejection of war, he ended up by himself, in a cage, a traitor and a prisoner in the American Disciplinary Training Center at Pisa. He concedes as much:

> sunt lumina
> that the drama is wholly subjective
> stone knowing the form which the carver imparts it
> the stone knows the form[47]

The poesy of fascism is subjective drama. The "form" of symmetry between Jefferson and Mussolini, and between Mussolini and Pound, is known only to Pound himself. It is emphatically not shared by the Grand Jury of the District of Columbia and the readers of the *Saturday Review*. But if it is true that the aesthetic is no more than subjective, no more than the individualized ground for disagreement, that "no more" nonetheless carries a nontrivial force when that disagreement happens to be pitted against a patriotic norm so naturalized as to become common sense. Disagreement with that norm is suicidal then; it is terrifying to witness.

In his sixth radio broadcast, the first recorded after the Japanese attack on Pearl Harbor, Pound opened with this offhand remark: "On Arbour Day, Pearl Arbour Day, at 12 o'clock I retired from the capital of the Old Roman Empire to Rapallo to seek wisdom from the ancients."[48] The ancients in question were Confucius and Mencius, whose Chinese ideograms, "of extreme beauty," he was trying to translate.[49] The national catastrophe of Pearl Harbor meant nothing to Pound. He did not mourn the casualties; he did not pour his patriotic furor on Japan; he did not call the Japanese barbarians. On the contrary, he noted only this:

> Anybody who has read the plays entitled Kumasaka and Kagekiyo, would have AVOIDED the sort of bilge printed in Time and the American press, and the sort of fetid imbecility I heard a few nights ago from the British Broadcasting Company . . . . the Awoi no Uye, Kumasaka, Nishikigi, or Funa-Benkei. These are Japanese classical plays, and would convince any man with more sense than a pea hen, of the degree of Japanese civilization.[50]

Pearl Harbor or not, Japan would always remain for Pound a luminous name. His admiration for that country, like his admiration for Mussolini, was aesthetic: he had translated those Japanese classical plays himself, from Ernest Fenollosa's notes, and the task had seemed not a task but simply "the pleasure of arranging beauty into words."[51] That beauty must have meant nothing to his compatriots. In any case, beauty is beside the point in the wake of Pearl Harbor.

Is beauty beside the point or not? And what does it mean to speak of the beauty of ancient plays when unsightly corpses are crying out for vengeance? Then as now, Pound's will always be a minority voice, laughable in its naive and stubborn attachment, blind to the patriotic fury of a wounded nation. Kant is right about this at least: the aesthetic is not intellectual; it is the most primitive of our faculties. It is not astute, not savvy, not wise—which is why, in spite of Pearl Harbor, Pound still saw nothing wrong with this radio broadcast:

> The United States had been for months ILLEGALLY at war, through what I considered to be the criminal acts of a President whose mental condition was NOT, as far as I could see, all that could be or should be desired of a man in so responsible a position.[52]

Statements like this explain why the word *aesthetic* will always be a virtual synonym for the word *un-American*.

Yale University

Notes

1   Bruce Ackerman, "The Rise of World Constitutionalism," *Virginia Law Review* 83 (May 1997): 771–97; and Jürgen Habermas, *Postnational Constellation*, trans. Max Pensky (Cambridge: MIT Press, 2001). While Habermas is primarily interested in the postnational constellation as democratic politics, other theorists approach it as a globalized imagination; see, for example, Arjun Appadurai, *Modernity at Large: Cultural Dimensions of Globalization* (Minneapolis: Univ. of Minnesota Press, 1996).
2   Habermas, *Postnational Constellation*, 69–70.
3   Etienne Balibar, "What Is a War?" public lecture, School of Criticism and Theory, Cornell University, 23 June 2003. For Balibar's analysis of nationalism and the nation-state, see Etienne Balibar and Immanuel Wallerstein, *Race, Nation, Class: Ambiguous Identities* (London: Verso, 1991), 37–68, 86–106.
4   Mary Kaldor, *Global Civil Society: An Answer to War* (Cambridge, Eng.: Polity Press, 2003).
5   The past five years have witnessed a resurgent interest in the aesthetic. However, there has been no attempt to link it to the idea of a global civil

society; see, for instance, *Revenge of the Aesthetic: The Place of Literature in Theory Today*, ed. Michael P. Clark (Berkeley and Los Angeles: Univ. of California Press, 2000); Gerard Genette, *The Aesthetic Relation*, trans. G. M. Goshgarian (Ithaca, N.Y.: Cornell Univ. Press, 1999); Elaine Scarry, *On Beauty and Being Just* (Princeton, N.J.: Princeton Univ. Press, 1999); James Soderholm, ed., *Beauty and the Critic: Aesthetics in the Age of Cultural Studies* (Tuscaloosa: Univ. of Alabama Press, 1997). See also the slightly earlier volume *Aesthetics and Ideology*, ed. George Levine (New Brunswick, N.J.: Rutgers Univ. Press, 1994).

6   Terry Eagleton, *The Ideology of the Aesthetic* (Cambridge, Mass.: Basil Blackwell, 1990), 3, 2.

7   As a subject-centered theory, *Critique of Judgment* will always be of marginal interest to those who see aesthetics as object-centered. For a lucid critique of Kant from the latter standpoint, see Genette, *The Aesthetic Relation*, 61–72.

8   Immanuel Kant, *Perpetual Peace*, in *Kant's Political Writings*, ed. Hans Reiss, trans. H. B. Nisbet (Cambridge, Eng.: Cambridge Univ. Press, 1970), 129.

9   As Hans Reiss points out, Frederick the Great was much offended by Kant's *Religion within the Limits of Reason Alone* (1793), and he issued a Royal Command forbidding Kant from writing any more on religion; see introduction to *Kant's Political Writings*, 2.

10   For a discussion of Kant's federalist conception of world government, see Carl Friedrich, *Inevitable Peace* (Cambridge: Harvard Univ. Press, 1948).

11   Kant, *Perpetual Peace*, in *Kant's Political Writings*, 93.

12   Hannah Arendt, untitled lectures, in *Lectures on Kant's Political Philosophy*, ed. Ronald Beiner (Chicago: Univ. of Chicago Press, 1982), 7, 31, 19, 61. Arendt delivered the Kant lectures at the New School for Social Research during the fall semester of 1970. She presented an earlier version of them at the University of Chicago in 1964. She was scheduled to lecture again on Kant at the New School in 1976, but her death came in December 1975. These lectures were in preparation for *Judging*, which was to have been the third and concluding volume of *The Life of the Mind*.

13   Ibid., 61.

14   For a lucid and respectful dissent from Arendt, see Patrick Riley, "Hannah Arendt on Kant, Truth, and Politics," in *Essays on Kant's Political Philosophy*, ed. Howard Williams (Cardiff: Univ. of Wales Press, 1992), 305–23.

15   Arendt is not the only one to see *Critique of Judgment* as a theory about a global humanity. In a brief but suggestive volume, Dieter Henrich has also argued that the Third Critique grounds a theory of international human rights. Unlike Adrendt, Henrich makes his argument by linking *Critique of Judgment* not to *Perpetual Peace* but to *Critique of Pure Reason*; see *Aesthetic Judgment and the Moral Image of the World* (Stanford, Calif.: Stanford Univ. Press, 1992). See also Mark F. Franke, *Global Limits:*

Immanuel Kant, International Relations, and Critique of World Politics (Albany: State Univ. of New York Press, 2001).

16 Immanuel Kant, *Critique of Judgment*, trans. J. H. Bernard (New York: Hafne/Macmillan, 1951), 75. Further references are to this edition and will be cited parenthetically as *CJ*.

17 Pierre Bourdieu is mistaken, I think, when in his brief discussion of *Critique of Judgment* he says that Kant's aesthetics are based on "disgust at the facile" and the refusal of the "simple, primitive form of pleasure" (*Distinction: A Social Critique of the Judgment of Taste*, trans. Richard Nice [Cambridge: Harvard Univ. Press, 1984], 87–88).

18 Rita Felski has also urged us to think of aesthetics as a category running across the full spectrum of the humanities (in "Aesthetics and Cultural Studies," a presentation at the Americanist Colloquium, Yale University, March 2003).

19 Ernst Cassirer, "Critical Idealism as a Philosophy of Culture," in *Symbol, Myth, and Culture: Essays and Lectures of Ernst Cassirer, 1935–1945*, ed. Donald Phillip Verene (New Haven: Yale Univ. Press, 1979), 88.

20 Arendt, untitled lecture, in *Lectures*, 76.

21 See Paul Guyer, *Kant and the Claims of Taste* (Cambridge: Harvard Univ. Press, 1979), 297–307.

22 Eagleton, *Ideology of the Aesthetic*, 96.

23 Robert Hillyer, "Treason's Strange Fruit: The Case of Ezra Pound and the Bollingen Award," *Saturday Review of Literature*, 11 June 1949, 10. Further references will be cited parenthetically as "TSF."

24 Norman Cousins and Harrison Smith, "Ezra Pound and the Bollingen Award," *Saturday Review of Literature*, 11 June 1949, 20.

25 Eventually Pound was deemed "mentally unfit" for trial and remanded to St. Elizabeths Hospital, where he was kept for twelve years (1946–58). For a full archive, see Julien Cornell, *The Trial of Ezra Pound: A Documented Account of the Treason Case by the Defendant's Lawyer* (New York: John Day, 1966).

26 *Indictment by the Grand Jurors in the District Court of the United States for the District of Columbia, 26 July 1943*; quoted in Charles Norman, *The Case of Ezra Pound* (New York: Funk and Wagnalls, 1968), 62–63. This is the first of the two indictments against Pound. For a detailed account of both indictments, see 62–82.

27 Robert Hillyer, "Poetry's New Priesthood," *Saturday Review*, 18 June 1949, 7; further references will be cited parenthetically as "PNP." "A Glossary of the New Criticism" was published in *Poetry: A Magazine of Verse*, November 1948–January 1949, 7–9, 38.

28 The directive was announced by Senator Theodore Francis Green of Rhode Island and reported in the *Washington Times-Herald* on 20 August 1949; see preface to *The Case against the "Saturday Review of Literature"*

(Chicago: Modern Poetry Association, 1949), v. Since 1949, the Bollingen Prize has been sponsored instead by Yale University.

29 See Marjorie Perloff, "Fascism, Anti-Semitism, Isolationism: Contextualizing the case of EP," *Paideuma* 16 (winter 1987): 7–21. As Perloff shows, the intellectuals affiliated with the *Partisan Review* were almost uniformly against the war.

30 Walter Benjamin, epilogue to "The Work of Art in the Age of Mechanical Reproduction," in *Illuminations*, trans. Harry Zohn (New York: Schocken Books, 1969), 241.

31 Russell Berman, "The Aestheticization of Politics: Walter Benjamin on Fascism and the Avant-Garde," *Stanford Italian Review* 8, nos. 1–2 (1990): 35–52, especially 49.

32 See, for instance, George L. Mosse, *The Fascist Revolution* (New York: Howard Fertig, 1999), 45–54, 183–98; Mary Ann Frese Witt, *The Search for Modern Tragedy: Aesthetic Fascism in Italy and France* (Ithaca, N.Y.: Cornell Univ. Press, 2001); and Simonetta Falasca-Zamponi, *Fascist Spectacle: The Aesthetics of Power in Mussolini's Italy* (Berkeley and Los Angeles: Univ. of California Press, 1993).

33 Resolution brought to the House floor, April 1937; *Congressional Record*, 21 December 1937; quoted in Walter Goodman, *The Committee: The Extraordinary Career of the House Committee on Un-American Activities* (New York: Farrar, Straus, and Giroux, 1968), 16, 18.

34 The Committee on Un-American Activities actually made an appearance in the *Saturday Review* at the same time as the Bollingen controversy. John S. Wood, chair of the committee, had sent a letter to school superintendents to obtain a list of textbooks for inspection. The *Saturday Review* was firmly opposed to this action; see "Speaking of Tests," *Saturday Review of Literature*, 9 July 1949, 22.

35 Library of Congress Information Office, Press Release No. 590, "Statement of the Committee of the Fellows of the Library of Congress in American Letters in Reply to Published Criticisms of the Bollingen Prize in Poetry," 10.

36 Canto LXXIV, in *The Cantos of Ezra Pound* (New York: New Directions, 1996), 445.

37 See Richard B. Lyttle, *Il Duce: The Rise and Fall of Benito Mussolini* (New York: Atheneum, 1987), 97–98. For Mussolini's roots in Italian socialism (specifically, the syndicalism of Georges Sorel), see A. James Gregor, *Young Mussolini and the Intellectual Origins of Fascism* (Berkeley and Los Angeles: Univ. of California Press, 1979). Gregor draws on the monumental archival work of Renzo De Felice, the foremost Italian historian of fascism, whose eight-volume biography of Mussolini has unfortunately not been translated into English. For a short introduction to De Felice's work, see *Fascism: An Informal Introduction to Its Theory and Practice;*

An Interview with Michael A. Ledeen (New Brunswick, N.J.: Transaction Books, 1976).

38 Pound wrote for A. R. Orage's the *New Age* from November 1911 to January 1921. For a detailed account of Pound's tie to British socialism and its legacy in his admiration for Mussolini, see Wendy Stallard Flory, *The American Ezra Pound* (New Haven: Yale Univ. Press, 1989), 42–130; Leon Surette, "Ezra Pound and British Radicalism," *English Studies in Canada* 9, no. 4 (1983): 435–51; and Tim Redman, *Ezra Pound and Italian Fascism* (New York: Cambridge Univ. Press, 1991), 17–50.

39 Ezra Pound, *Jefferson and/or Mussolini* (New York: Liveright, 1935), ix.

40 Ibid., 12.

41 I should point out, however, that Mussolini did have excellent press in the United States all through the 1920s; see John P. Diggins, *Mussolini and Fascism: The View from America* (Princeton, N.J.: Princeton Univ. Press, 1972), 3–73.

42 See Pound's prefatory statement in *Jefferson and/or Mussolini*: "The body of this Ms. was written and left my hands in February 1933. 40 publishers have refused it. No typescript of mine has been read by so many people or brought me a more interesting correspondence" (iv).

43 D. H. Lawrence to Louisa Burrows, 20 November 1909. "He is a well-known American poet—a good one," Lawrence writes. "He is 24, like me, but his god is beauty, mine, life" (*Lawrence in Love: Letters from D. H. Lawrence to Louie Burrows*, ed. James T. Boulton [Nottingham, Eng.: Univ. of Nottingham Press, 1968], 46).

44 Pound, Canto LXXIV, *The Cantos*, 446.

45 Philip Kuberski has also noted the importance of Mussolini as a poetic precursor for Pound; see *A Calculus of Ezra Pound* (Gainsville: Univ. of Florida Press, 1992), 16–18. For an account of the affinity between Pound and Mussolini based on a theory of translation as well as a theory of economics, see Paul Morrison, *The Poetics of Fascism* (New York: Oxford Univ. Press, 1996), 16–59.

46 Theodor Adorno, *Aesthetic Theory*, trans. C. Lenhardt, ed. Gretel Adorno and Rolf Tiedemann (London: Routledge and Kegan Paul, 1984), 48, 366.

47 Pound, Canto LXXIV, *The Cantos*, 450.

48 Radio Broadcast #6, "On Resuming," 29 January 1942, in *Ezra Pound Speaking: Radio Speeches of World War II*, ed. Leonard W. Doob (Westport, Conn.: Greenwood, 1978), 23.

49 Ibid. As Burton Raffel points out, Pound is probably the greatest poet-translator in American literary history, translating from a dozen languages: Italian, French, Spanish, Provencal, Latin, and Greek (the languages he knew best); German and Old English (which he knew reasonably well); Chinese (of which he had a smattering); and Japanese, Egyptian, and Hindi (which he knew not at all); see *Ezra Pound: The Prime Minister of Poetry* (Hamden, Conn.: Archon Books, 1984), 61–62.

50 Pound, Radio Broadcast #6, in *Ezra Pound Speaking*, 26.
51 Ezra Pound and Ernest Fenollosa, introductory note to *The Classic Noh Theatre of Japan* (1917; reprint, New York: New Directions, 1959). In 1913, following Fenollosa's sudden death in 1908, Fenollosa's widow gave all her husband's manuscripts to Pound: "eight notebooks in all," according to Hugh Kenner, "plus the volumes of notes on *Noh* drama, plus the books in which he was drafting his lectures on Chinese poetics, plus a sheaf of loose sheets" (*The Pound Era* [Berkeley and Los Angeles: Univ. of California Press, 1971], 198).
52 Pound, Radio Broadcast #6, *Ezra Pound Speaking*, 23.

Thomas H.
Kane

Mourning the Promised Land: Martin Luther
King Jr.'s Automortography and the National
Civil Rights Museum

When Martin Luther King Jr. delivered his final
speech on the night of 3 April 1968 in Memphis, the weather was
nearly biblical in its foreboding: the shutters of the Mason Temple
flapped open in the winds, the city was blanketed in the darkness of
power outages, and civil defense sirens wailed their warning. "[A]t
some points" during the speech, notes Jesse Epps, "where there would
have been applause, there was a real severe flash of lightening and a
real loud clap of thunder that sort of hushed the crowd."[1] Through its
proximity to King's death, "I've Been to the Mountaintop" haunts representations of the man. Eerie, unnerving, and prophetic all at once,
the speech, in which King contemplates his own death, elicits a melancholic response. In its uncanny afterlife, or what I call automortography, King's last speech can be instrumental in reading the legacy
of the Civil Rights movement, especially as it is represented in the
National Civil Rights Museum built on the site of the Lorraine Motel
where King died. Together, the speech and the museum's space provide a lens through which to view the relation between the melancholic, the aesthetic, and politics.

My essay will first consider how King's automortography can lead
us to become melancholically oriented—mobilized—to see his project
as unfinished, to see "history [as] open for continual re-negotiation."[2]
Shifting next to a description of my visits to the National Civil Rights
Museum during the summer of 2001, I will consider how the temporal and spatial aesthetics of the museum are similarly animated by a
melancholic aesthetic. Both the speech and the space, through their
aesthetics and their relation to King's death, are objects of continual

American Literature, Volume 76, Number 3, September 2004. Copyright © 2004 by
Duke University Press.

automortographic witness. The museum's participatory exhibits cue the structures of feeling that linger in the American cultural imaginary, placing the visitor precisely at the point where the aesthetic and the political intersect. But in the end, do the exhibits present, like King's speech, an unfinished history, or do they encourage a closing of minds, locking King and the Civil Rights movement in the past?

Automortography, or the attempted representation of one's own death, describes the subject becoming an object (in the form of the corpse) and entails attempts by survivors to reanimate that subject through the object of the automortographic act. Like the aesthetic, which is "caught between subjectivity and objectivity," automortography enables the subject to fantasize about a posthumous objectification and the survivors to return, through melancholic sentiment and repetition, to that moment of fantasy.[3] Because it is performative, the automortographic act is akin to the aesthetic: its construction enables an emotional projection (by self and other) and ruminations on mortality and the intersection of identity and community.

Automortography may be autobiography's kin, but it is more concerned with the *mort* of death than the *bio* of life. Instead of relying on the logic of the mature self reflecting (on) the progress of the immature self, automortography shows the self anticipating an impending death and scripting the response of the posthumous audience. The split in the self is not retrospective but forward-looking, occurring in what Donald Pease has described as the "future anterior tense" where one can imagine what will have been.[4] In automortography, "what will have been" is one's own death; the dying self, uncannily projected past the grave, imagines its absence. The repetition at the heart of these acts of dying enables the survivors' melancholic attachment to automortography, opening up the space of the self with collective potential. In King's case, his automortographic final speech is replayed annually on National Public Radio and has been incorporated into exhibits at the National Civil Rights Museum. This speech has the ring of prophecy, and has enlisted thousands in King's unfinished project.

Automortography opens an avenue for discussing the larger phenomenon of mortography—those texts, widely distributed and consumed, that in their spectacular representation of death mark the "wound culture" in the United States that Mark Seltzer sees in the highly mediated consumption of violence.[5] Mortographic texts cross genres and forms, in many cases serving as some of our shared texts: the evening news; television shows about crimes, hospitals, and supernatural violence; celebrity biographies; slasher films; popular music, particularly so-called goth music and gangsta rap; written texts, including true-crime accounts, many mystery novels, and tales of loss framed as self-help books; and the host of attempts to grapple with large-scale tragedy, such as the Holocaust or September 11. Sharon Holland believes that mortographies, "as they focus on the cacophony of the bereaved, and not the dead, move us away from the space of death, constantly reminding us of our own grief; this paradigm allows death to remain a spectacle."[6] Mortography trades on the spectacle of death, reproducing a sentimental economy of citizenship by denying the space of death and muting the dead.

In contrast, automortography occurs within and frequently against such a culture and thus suggests a potential counterhegemony to mass sentimentality. Through the unique location of the *auto* in automortography, the uncanny self produces an affect of wonder in its audience, inviting questions about the construction of the subject, history, and power. Such self-reflection, by avoiding "self-confirming" mortography, provides grounds for a more active form of citizenship.[7] The dead speak for themselves in an arresting manner, showing the automortographic self as an aesthetic projection that remains unfinished even in death, thus compelling the audience to see itself as instrumental in the construction of that self—which is not essential or singular but performative and potentially collective.

While death might suggest finitude or closure, the *auto* in automortography is an opening, an invitation. Just as the dying wish to disturb their own finitude through the production of automortography, the audience or the survivors seek to revivify those subjects through automortographic witness. Not marked by an affirmation, automortography nonetheless holds political and social possibility. As Heather Love argues about queer politics, "political change can happen not only through disavowing loss but also through cleaving to it."[8] The melancholic economy at the heart of automortography can defy propriety and facilitate a specific sense of witnessing that transgresses a subject-object split. Kelly Oliver uses the term *witnessing* to signify both bearing witness to one's experience and being an eye witness, simultaneously articulating a subjective and objective position.

In automortography, these two notions of witnessing meet in the uncanny *auto*: in either composing or receiving an automortographic act, I come to realize that "without a witness I cannot exist."[9] But this witnessing is not confined to the sense of sight, as these acts of automortography stand as artifacts of affective witnessing. Through melancholic feeling, clusters of witnesses, who are sensitive to bearing witness as well as witnessing, form counterpublics.[10] In automortography, we—certain self-selected and selecting people—bear witness not just to the death of another but also to the witness of the dying.

Automortography is a melancholic genre re-presenting unfinished selves to unfinished publics. David Eng and David Kazanjian have described melancholia as "both a formal relation and a constellation of affect," which together "offer . . . a capaciousness of meaning for losses encompassing the individual and the collective, the spiritual and the material, the psychic and the social, the aesthetic and the political."[11] Because it traces and transgresses the subject-object split, automortography is uniquely situated to intervene in discussions of melancholic affect. Instead of skirting the complexity of phenomenology under the banner of anti-essentialism, automortography grapples with the specific, distinct manner in which a feeling of melancholy is transferred and circulated from the dying self to the posthumous audience. In King's case, the phenomenology of his voice—its tenor, pitch, timbre, and pace (the way he lingers, for example, on the word "seen" in the sentence "I've seeeeen the promised land")—are aspects of his aesthetic that stir the posthumous audience.[12] John Forgas's recent work on the "multi-process theory" of affect can be illuminating here because it shies away from the essentialism of psychobiology but still attempts to grapple with the phenomenology of interiority; it acknowledges that affects and their "effects are neither simple nor uniform." Instead, feelings are "highly context sensitive."[13] For my purposes, melancholia is not, in Silvan Tomkins's terms, a "negative affect," because the loss that initiates the melancholia is accompanied by the residual presence of that loss. Automortography is the anticipated posthumous presence that foments the sadly pleasurable and pleasurably sad constellation of affects that motivates automortographic witness.[14]

This logic of self-representation in the face of death has special resonance in African American cultural production where self-assertions have been vexed historically and where tropes of death and mortality abound. Recent important theoretical work on African American mourning and death does not concentrate on issues of self-representation.[15] And while there are compelling studies of an African American autobiographical tradition, they skirt issues of mortality, for the most part.[16] Even since 1960, however, we have several important examples of African American automortography, including works by W. E. B. DuBois, Malcolm X, Audre Lorde, Arthur Ashe, Tupac Shakur, and June Jordan. To different degrees, these writers attempt to follow DuBois's wish to create "not so much my autobiography as the autobiography of a concept of race," even as they are motivated by impending violence or death.[17] The results of such a substitution of self for race ring both heroic and apocalyptic, as the individual death can signify the death of racism or the death of the race. Interrogating the intersection of social death and phenomenological death, each African American automortographer confronts the question, How does self-creation in an African American context include the staging of a posthumous self?

Mountain Climbing

In support of striking sanitation workers demanding a living wage, King returned to Memphis on 3 April 1968, where only a week earlier he had led a demonstration that degenerated into violence when a more radical group, the Invaders, began looting and confronting police. King and members of the Southern Christian Leadership Conference had been ushered to safety. King saw the sanitation strike as a testing ground for his Poor People's Campaign that was to conclude with another march on Washington in the summer. In his speech on the night of 3 April, after having ascended the pulpit high above the congregation and in his richly sonorous voice thanked Ralph Abernathy for his extensive introduction—a reflection on their friendship—King moved from the broadly historical to the elevation of the local, to the autobiographical, and finally to the sublime image of the "promised land." Relying throughout on chiasmus, he brings the mythic into relation with the familiar at the same time that he elevates the personal and the local to global, historical significance. This double movement implicates the audience in the grand narratives of history and myth. King elevates the sanitation workers' dispute to the level of some of history's greatest battles, including those of the ancient

Israelites and the Greeks, and greatest moments, such as the Reformation and the emancipation of U.S. slaves. At the same time, he anchors his high-flying rhetoric with gestures to the mundane, describing particular details that allow his audience to share his vision. For instance, when he mentions the Good Samaritan, he includes details about the rough terrain and the narrow, physically dangerous road, which he had visited himself. He also gives his listeners practical political objectives, advocating an economic nationalism and a boycott of Sealtest and Coca-Cola, among other companies. Grounded in a kind of literary-realist aesthetic, these references to the ordinary provide a material contrast to the transcendent, allowing his grandest claims to resonate. Moreover, King's banal act of sneezing during the speech takes on historic resonance when he recalls a prior attempt on his life.

In New York in 1958, a "demented" woman at a book-signing for King's first book had planted a letter opener in his chest very near his heart.[18] Recounting this event in the Mountaintop speech, King recalls that while recovering in a Harlem hospital, he received letters from dignitaries and politicians, including the president and vice-president of the United States. But he claims that he doesn't remember those letters. The letter he remembers came from a ninth-grade white girl. King quotes her: "I read in the paper of your misfortune, and of your suffering. And I read that if you sneezed, you would have died. And I'm simply writing to say that I'm so happy that you didn't sneeze" ("M," 221). King then takes this detail and spins it out by repeatedly deploying the refrain, "If I had sneezed."

King's oratory relies on anaphora, the repetition of a phrase or trope that endows a piece with momentum or even a sense of ascendance. Anaphora may be similar to the "fort/da" game in Freud's famous essay on melancholia, as the rhetoric offers a pleasurable repetition, but it is distinct in its provision of a cognitive map for the listener or reader, setting out the boundaries of that imagined space at the same time that it serves as a kind of inculcation, an invitation to participate.[19] King's sneeze, and its rhetorical repetition, fosters a vital connection with his audience, creating a crucial automortographic opening through which his survivors can view him and reconstruct him after his death, lifting them into history. While King's refrain "If I had sneezed" goes a long way to humanize him and unite him with his audience, it also allows him to reflect on the great strides made in the Civil Rights Movement:

I want to say that I am happy that I didn't sneeze. Because if I had sneezed, I wouldn't have been around here in 1960, when students all over the South started sitting-in at lunch counters. And I knew that as they were sitting in, they were really standing up for the best in the American dream. And taking the whole nation back to those great wells of democracy which were dug deep by the Founding Fathers in the Declaration of Independence and the Constitution. If I had sneezed, I wouldn't have been around in 1962, when Negroes in Albany, Georgia, decided to straighten their backs up. And whenever men and women straighten their backs up, they are going somewhere, because a man can't ride your back unless it is bent. If I had sneezed, I wouldn't have been here in 1963, when the black people of Birmingham, Alabama, aroused the conscience of this nation, and brought into being the Civil Rights Bill. If I had sneezed, I wouldn't have had a chance later that year, in August, to try to tell America about a dream that I had had. If I had sneezed, I wouldn't have been down in Selma, Alabama, to see the great movement there. If I had sneezed, I wouldn't have been in Memphis to see a community rally around those brothers and sisters who are suffering. I'm so happy that I didn't sneeze. ("M," 221)

In this final instance of anaphora, King animates an aesthetic of melancholy with the repetition of the words "If I had sneezed," reminding his audience of his mortality, and pleasurably (in a rhetorical sense) circling back to it. Standing in for his death, the simple and banal action of a sneeze allows him to measure the accomplishments of the movement and tie them to his own bodily functions—perhaps risking a closure of the movement in his death. But King is very careful, particularly in choosing a point of view, not to collapse his body into the movement; instead, these are events that would have happened without him. Rhetorically, he stages himself as a witness to these events more than a catalyst. But in retrospect, only a day later when he did sneeze, metaphorically speaking, this history seems more fixed and more closely dependent on King's body, his life. The anaphora adds the sense of losing what might have been: the *next* Birmingham, Selma, Memphis. It is important that King placed this highly automortographic anecdote as his penultimate point. If he had started with this gesture, there would have been nowhere else to go, rhetorically. Instead, we've been climbing higher with him—the anaphora of "if I had sneezed" offering a precarious foothold on King's sublime mountaintop.

With clear religious overtones of cleansing, even purification, King's rhetorical performance seems, in retrospect, to approach ritual. But rituals are also performances. As Richard Schechner notes, "Rituals, and the behavior arts associated with them, are overdetermined, full of redundancy, repetition, and exaggeration." Yet the "ritual process opens up a time/space of antistructural playfulness" that is the power of the uncanny.[20] This "antistructural playfulness" is the site of possibility in King's last act, and in automortography generally, coming within the structure of the text but gaining power by the extratextual rupture of King's death. As Michael Osborn observes, "[M]uch of the language of this speech . . . is the language of ritual. But the occasion was certainly not epideictic, not at least in any traditional sense of that term." We see King anticipating his own absence and almost delivering the formal funerary or stately address associated with epideictic rhetoric, "belonging to an occasion after some critical event has occurred."[21] What is uncanny, prescient, and persistently affecting is the speech's strange temporality. For most of us, the speech comes after King's death; we approach it as epideictic. We read the automortographic cues as ritualistic—overdetermined, yet suggesting and inviting an "antistructural playfulness."

The Sublime Climb

Anaphora having carried his audience to the heights, King delivers his closing lines relying on chiasmus. These lines not only offer a reflective mode within his "realist" aesthetic but also make the heady claim for King as a latter-day Moses. After running through all the movement's accomplishments, King shifts into the present, describing the pilot's voice-over on his flight from Atlanta that morning. There had been bomb threats against King, but he relays this information through the voice of the pilot, ventriloquizing to relate the dire news about his own vulnerability. While use of the pilot allows King to objectify himself (the subject becoming an object), what's significant is that he includes the threats in his speech at all. It's a move that risks disconnecting him from his audience even while it elicits sympathy or pity, and it's a move that a day later will script the surviving audience's witness.

In the final lines of "I've Been to the Mountaintop," King links the bomb threats in Atlanta with the potential for violence in Memphis—the city that only a week earlier failed to live up to his nonviolent ideal. In the process, he deploys two important images, the mountaintop and the promised land, that continue to resonate long after his death and that place his automortography in relation to the aesthetics of the sublime.

> And then I got into Memphis. And some began to say that threats, or talk about the threats . . . were out. What would happen to me from some of our sick white brothers.
>
> Well, I don't know what will happen now. We've got some difficult days ahead. But it doesn't matter with me now. Because I've been to the mountaintop. And I don't mind. Like anybody, I would like to live a long life. Longevity has its place. But I'm not concerned about that now. I just want to do God's will. And He's allowed me to go up to the mountain. And I've looked over. And I've seen the promised land. I may not get there with you. But I want you to know tonight, that we, as a people will get to the promised land. And I'm happy, tonight. I'm not worried about anything. I'm not fearing any man. Mine eyes have seen the glory of the coming of the Lord. ("M," 222)

King describes his ascendance at the same time that his vocal performance takes flight; his oratory is alternately contemplative and defiant until cresting in his last words. His final line is unfinished, a melancholic allusion for his audience and survivors to resolve. In an ecstatic clutch, King relies on the sublime to deliver his final lines, having climbed to his verbal peak to shout them over the heads of his listeners. "The camera loves King—" writes Michael Eric Dyson, describing the film footage of King's speech in Memphis only a week earlier, "loves the way the skin between his eyes furrows, loves the way he half-consciously licks his lips, loves the way his eyes twinkle and pierce as he recruits nearly every facial muscle to punctuate his sublimely intense preaching."[22] A week later, one can see King using similar facial and rhetorical force as the mortal mountaintop winds blow tears from his eyes; a day later, his tears will signify his mourning for himself.

While Dyson uses the phrase "sublimely intense" in a colloquial fashion, the origins of the sublime are worth our reflection, particularly as the sublime unites King's use of mountain imagery with tropes of mortality and a particular version of the aesthetic. Since the romantics, mountains have been associated with the supernatural or the cosmic because of their awe-inspiring dimensions. King uses the mountain trope as a stage for his performance, and a day later it approaches the cosmic. In a description that reverberates strangely with Dyson's words, John Ruskin claims that "mountains are, to the rest of the body of the earth, what violent muscular action is to the body of man. The muscles and tendons of its anatomy are, in the mountain, brought out with fierce and convulsive energy, full of expression, passion and strength."[23] Placing this passage next to Dyson's description of King's facial mannerisms makes King's performance, his bodily gestures, seem mountainous. King becomes the mountain—the thing his people will have to get over to get to the promised land. It is King's "fierce and convulsive energy" that is read as a death-throb a day later.

In their discussion of romanticism and the sublime, Claudia Bell and John Lyall describe mountaintops as "sites of particular revelation but also precarious places where one's psychic composure might tumble when faced by the vertiginous grandeur of the view."[24] Along with many other automortographic last acts, King's mountaintop has just such an effect. The mountaintop is a culturally "precarious place" and a "site of particular revelation." With its strange relation to his death, King's mountaintop creates a kind of psychic vertigo, hanging in the balance between life and death, movement and stasis.

While the sublime is often associated with landscapes (particularly mountains), its philosophical origin is temporal, exposing the seam between the mortal and the immortal, the finite and the infinite. The sensation of the immortal or divine that Edmund Burke and, later, Immanuel Kant found in landscapes was, for Kant, an ambivalent blend of pleasure and terror: "The feeling of the Sublime is, therefore, at once a feeling of displeasure, arising from the inadequacy of imagination in the aesthetic estimation of magnitude to attain to its estimation by reason, and a simultaneously awakened pleasure, arising from this very judgement of the inadequacy of the greatest faculty of sense."[25] For Kant, the combination of feelings emerges out of the limits of human reason and the simultaneous recognition that there is something that exceeds human reason. Sublimity is a kind of wonder, a mix of pleasure and pain, at once affirming and reducing the viewer. In his discussion of the avant-garde, Jean-François Lyotard shows just how the sublime contains a temporal dimension because it is "kindled by the threat of nothing further happening." The audience, "[s]truck with astonishment, is thus dumb, immobilized, as good as dead."[26] The sublime stymies its audience. We might ask, then, to what extent a national platform of dissent based on race and class has been stymied by King's death. To what extent has the sublimity of his mountaintop resulted in immobilization? If the melancholy that the speech elicits is pathological (based on a compulsive repetition), then one might see it as fulfilling the "threat of nothing further happening." For some, no doubt, this is the case. But automortography, with its performative play between object (corpse) and subject, allows a strategy that glimpses the sublime without being fully or pathologically stymied. The sublime is witnessed but not confronted.

Like the mountaintop, King's image of the promised land is laden with historical and cultural import. It recalls the earliest Puritan visions of the "new land" as an Edenic fulfillment of divine prophecy.[27] This promised land is a part of the shared cultural imaginary that operates in the spiritual and secular United States. Roger Aden stresses this shared sense of a promised land but applies it to behavior found in contemporary fan cultures: "By 'promised lands,' I mean the symbolic visions shared by a culture that provides a destination, unique to the culture." Aden argues that in taking "symbolic pilgrimages," fans engage in "purposeful play" in the construction of and participation in their promised lands.[28] Similarly, King's powerful words encourage the pilgrims who continue to engage in "purposeful play" at the site of the Lorraine Motel, now part of the National Civil Rights Museum.

Mobilizing Melancholy

In narrating my own trips to the National Civil Rights Museum in 2001, I will explore the spatial cues a visitor encounters to consider how the museum stages and uses the material and imagined legacy of King's death and automortography. While the resignation in the final lines of "I've Been to the Mountaintop" might speak to historical closure, the uncanny relation of the words to King's death presents an opening, compelling us, his audience, to look over the edge: of the movement, of mortality. Similarly, although building a museum on the site where King was killed might suggest the end of the Civil Rights movement, a visitor's experience of moving through the museum's space provides a kind of opening, allowing another avenue into residual structures of feeling and further illuminating the point where the aesthetic and the political intersect. The affective cues in the space are also those that make automortography a powerful, if melancholic, genre. Like King's mountaintop with its precarious footing, the space of the museum produces psychic vertigo. Like the vertigo of King's speech—which encourages speculation and wonder that counteract a sense of loss— the vertigo in the museum's space results from the visitor's participation in its staged exhibits, and from the distinct temporality of museums, where time is reified yet visitors are encouraged to fantasize about engaging in the history represented. In other words, both the speech and the space invite participation and reflection because of their uncanny aesthetic and their proximity to King's death.

Politics and aesthetics—and the politics of aesthetics—meet in the construction of museums. In the case of history museums, where visitors' temporal distance from events can often be apparently bridged through "living history" exhibits, affect proves instrumental in revivifying past moments. History museums exploit a simultaneity that Judith Butler sees at the heart of loss: the acknowledgment that "the past is irrecoverable and the past is not past."[29] The simultaneous irrecoverability and presence that loss generates animates both automortography and history museums. In the case of the National Civil Rights Museum, this animation is achieved through a kind of temporal plasticity—in the dual sense of malleability and artificiality. The museum not only bends time but also relies on inauthentic items resembling the actual ones (a coffee cup, a used ashtray) to revive the moment of King's visit and death. Plasticity also marks my position as a critic. Because my account is drawn from visits to the museum in 2001, my narrative is melded to my subjectivity and to that moment, even as it acknowledges the changes that have taken place. Most significantly, on 28 September 2002, the museum opened the eleven-million-dollar expansion into the rooming house where the assassin took aim; it is a space devoted to entertaining conspiracy theories and contemplating the legacy of the movement. This new exhibit stands as proof of the temporal and psychic opening that is central to automortography; the space of the museum and the history represented in it are changeable.[30]

In its space and its mission, the museum exhibits a tension between the desire to forge an active sense of the work for civil rights and the fact that the chosen site seems to speak to the death of the movement in the death of King. This tension is present even in the politics of the space, which deploys many "new museum" aesthetics, such as displays equipped with video and sound, and interactive exhibits populated with mannequins that aid in placing us back in the moment. At the same time, the choice of site and the strict teleology of the displays suggest closure. In museological terms, the museum's sensory-rich exhibits "fracture and augment the meanings" of the history represented, even as the visitor is directed through the narrow historical movement of the space that is always proceeding (upward) toward the space of King's assassination.[31] After a reading of the comprehensive aesthetics of the museum, I will examine this tension as it is manifested in the preservation of the two motel rooms where King stayed for the kinds of unintended melancholia that this space elicits.

The museum's origins are also marked by tension. The site of the Lorraine Motel was purchased in the late 1980s in the hope that a museum might gentrify the neighborhood and attract capital to the area between the tourist destination of Beale Street and the motel (several blocks to the south). But there was also a political hope for the site. At the time of the museum's opening in 1991, its founder, D'Army Bailey, claimed that the site would be "a propaganda vehicle to create more soldiers and generals to carry on our fight for equality, by teaching them and showing them what we came through."[32] To place the museum at the location where King was shot and killed might be seen as working against such an explicitly political mission, but it is King's death that serves—as the museum's brochure tells us—as the "emotional focus and historical climax" of the tour. In looking under the hood of this "propaganda vehicle," we can see how "history, and history museums, are inescapably political, and always have been."[33] In determining the museum's mission and the ideological implications of its display, we will have a clearer reading of the vexed and contested legacy of the Civil Rights movement.

Relying on the latest museological notions and technologies, the National Civil Rights Museum claims to be a bullhorn for the oppressed, for those denied civil rights. This is commendable, but in speaking *for*, whom might it silence? In an otherwise celebratory look at contemporary museum practices, Hooper-Greenhill wonders if the "total experience (in living history or interactive exhibits), the total immersion (in gallery workshops and events), can have the function, in the apparently democratised environment of the museum marketplace, of soothing, of silencing, of quieting questions, of closing minds."[34] One wonders if the apparently democratic aesthetic of participatory exhibits in the National Civil Rights Museum enforces an opening to an unfinished history, which is its stated mission, or a "closing of minds." Having left the museum after only a few years, Bailey lamented the stalling of his "propaganda vehicle" and has recently decried the museum's latest expansion into the rooming house.[35] In serving as a guide through the museum, I will attempt to trace this tension and show how the "total experience" of the preserved rooms contains a kind of unscripted, vertiginous affect marked by the strange split between the irrecoverability and presence of King.

The museum space is animated by aesthetic and temporal splits. Indeed, the opening film (and nearly all the subsequent video displays) is projected onto two screens, side by side; one half of the film ends with the words "I HAVE" moving in from the left frame while "A DREAM" moves in from the right. Splitting the dreamer from the dream, literally, the split screens are a metaphor for the ideological as well as phenomenological operations of the museum, signifying the tension between some of the new-museum aesthetics and the necessity to affirm the site and its history; the museum has to legitimize its place in civil rights history, but that legitimization risks suggesting an end to the movement in the death of King.

According to the *New York Times*, "Of all this country's monuments and shrines, few hold the visceral power of the National Civil Rights Museum in Memphis."[36] It derives this "visceral power" from its interactive aesthetic, which is designed to produce a melancholic affect in its visitors. The interactive exhibits juxtapose mannequins representing the movement's participants with documentary footage and sounds from the events in which they participated. The museum is thus able to stage what Alan Wallach considers a successful exhibition: "not a book on the wall, a narrative with objects as illustrations, but a carefully orchestrated deployment of objects, images, and texts that give viewers opportunities to look, to reflect, and to work out meanings."[37] What remains in question is how much the museum fosters the opportunity "to reflect, and to work out meanings." For the moment, the museum's success emerges from its ability to enable visitors to interact with history through its multimediated displays.

The use of bodily representations in the displays also seems to reflect the ideological splits of, and in, the museum. In most cases, the plaster figures featured in many of the displays are the foot soldiers of the movement, ordinary people who stepped out of anonymity momentarily in order to make a politically and historically significant act before returning to their lives outside the frame of official history. The participants' ordinariness is meant to connect with the visitor, to enlist an identification that will transcend the temporal rift. Strangely but significantly, all the figures—the bus driver, Rosa Parks, the figures at the lunch counter, the National Guardsmen and marchers, striking garbage workers—are colored gray and are made of the same material. It's as if race has been diminished or erased in the space of the museum. Traveling back in time, where we can place ourselves, our bodies, in these spaces of historical significance, we hover next to these people. This history is being staged for those who weren't there, weren't born yet. As with the black-and-white photographs that line the walls, the grayness of the figures might imply a stasis of history, induce nostalgia, and enforce a temporal distance that the interaction would seek to overcome.[38] At the same time, the color of the mannequins suggests that the Civil Rights movement was about rights and not race, that the discrimination was arbitrary. This suggestion can be affectively powerful, though inaccurate, reminding visitors that they too could have been victims, that they too could have been among these silent heroes. (The oppressors are not silent; they frequently speak in the videos, spewing racist threats.)

The aesthetic of selective silence serves to deepen identification with the victims, enabling the educational mission of the museum. But do these interactions mask a form of control? Do they "soften the contradictions and disguise the inequalities"?[39] Participating in the museum's multisensory displays, we climb onto a bus and inhabit the space of violation and struggle in the bus boycott.[40] At the same time, we hear the vicious voice of the bus driver grow angry and hostile in chastising us. We are allowed, through touch, sight, and sound, to feel the kind of resistance that Rosa Parks and others had to muster. Meanwhile, Parks sits there stoically—incredibly powerful in her silence (or is she dead, the historical residue?). While the effigy of Parks is not given any voice, we read on the placard above her head that she did, in fact, respond to the rebukes. The museum is playing with Parks's agency and making her into a victim again (of the white supremacist power she originally confronted) because her silence has greater effect for the visitor even if it is historically inaccurate. We get a visceral or affective sense of the struggle for civil rights through this display, so that we do more than just identify with the actors or victims. *We are meant to become them.*

The National Civil Rights Museum, like other "postmuseums," attempts to violate the traditionally impenetrable "fourth wall" of display by having its visitors embody the spaces of history.[41] The museum's designer, Gerard Eisterhold, a former curator at the Smithsonian's National Museum of Natural History, says that he was trying to create "a You Are There feeling."[42] We hang about a lunch counter, ruminate on a burned out freedom-rider Greyhound, and march across a replica of the bridge in Selma. We reenact these moments in a ritual fashion and become what Carol Duncan describes as the museum's "dramatis personae."[43] But in erasing race in these interactive exhibits by having all the mannequins the same pale gray, and at the same time foregrounding race on the black and white text and the images that line the walls, the museum seems to stress racism as a historical artifact rather than present reality. In rendering racism dead in its living-history portions that eliminate racial difference, the museum trades on the visitor's desire not for the death of racism but for the death of King. Yet it is toward the end of the tour, when we reach the "space of death," that we begin to break from the script, as the museum's ostensible ritual is disturbed.[44] These rooms "of death" are the magnetic force both in the museum's history (its construction) and its construction of history (the telos it represents to the visitor).

Having marched over the Selma Bridge and ascended a hall marked by calls to "black power," we reach the spring of 1968. The hallway opens onto the tops of all the displays in the museum. Although it's obstructed, we can look back over the history of the movement, emulating King's final sermon as he reviews the history of the struggle and ties Memphis to it. Below us, the space is filled with filthy-looking garbage trucks, heaps of plastic, odorless garbage, and two sets of gray figures. The first set is strikers holding placards that read: "I AM A MAN"; the second set is a cluster of militia holding out bayonets toward the strikers. As opposed to King's final sermon that works so consciously to elevate the poor of Memphis, we are above the strikers, endowed with the advantage of historical hindsight as we literally look back over this conflict. This might be the museum's attempt to place its visitors alongside King on the mountaintop of history, to prepare us literally and psychically for our arrival, finally, at King's rooms in the Lorraine Motel.

A display case filled with artifacts from the strike and dual video screens mark the entrance to these rooms. The museum uses a sound clip of "I've Been to the Mountaintop," but it is accompanied by color slides of King instead of the newsreel—a black-and-white aesthetic with color for the first time. The slides show King in a range of emotions: pensive, expectant, smiling, angry, ecstatic, sad and perhaps distant, and finally reflective. The slides' range and their sequence are important, allowing the viewer to apprehend the contradictory messages of the images' death-like stillness and life-like emotion. They don't correspond to King's words: he smiles while he tells of the bomb threats to his plane in Atlanta that morning, and his speech ends in the throes of passion while the image is somber. But that split isn't as important as the life-affirming tenor of his voice coupled with the color imagery. How many times have we seen King in color? History has preserved him in black and white. Despite the stasis, the color of these images humanizes King at the same time that the display case and the rest of the museum historicizes him. The kinds of repetition found in his speech, in anaphora, and in the telescoping of memory and history open up the listener or viewer in ways that are similar to the rhetoric of the space of Rooms 306 and 308. King enacts in his speech, and we enact in its repeated playing—in the museum and beyond—the kind of repetitions that resonate in the preservation of these rooms. Placing the speech as the gateway, the museum at once reanimates King and implies that these rooms are his "promised land."

The Vertiginous Mountaintop

On one hand, the museum's display of the two motel rooms enacts "a mourning and militancy that returns melancholia's internalized anger to the sphere of the social and to social activism."[45] The rooms foster reaction that can be activist, and the museum publicly recognizes the activism of certain Civil Rights leaders since the death of King in the exhibit that opened in 2002, "Exploring the Legacy." On the other hand, the space of the motel rooms is also a shrine that simultaneously asks for inward reflection and a detached rumination. Both activism and reflection are happening simultaneously, and the tension between each reaction is emblematic of the irrecoverability and presence that together mark automortography. As a result, my final narrative represents the melancholic tension present in the aesthetic preservation of King's rooms; my discussion will reflect the fort/da of the space and of time, even as it clings to my visits in the summer of 2001.[46]

When we pass through the narrow passage into the space of the preserved motel rooms, we can see or feel the new-museum aesthetics break down even as the script becomes more strict and ritualized. Yet our presence and the plasticity of the display open up "antistructural playfulness." The rooms are preserved behind a clear plastic shield as if time stopped in 1968. Although their preservation as a kind of untouchable shrine might underscore narratives of historical closure, the effect of passing through this space complicates that closure. By displaying the rooms behind plexiglass, the museum suggests that they are a holy place and denies the tactile that is so much a part of the other interactive exhibits. In falling back on the visual, we return to what Alan Wallach calls the "belief in transcendence."[47] Sealed behind plexiglass, these rooms are meant to be elevated by the distance, set off from anything else we might have seen. The message is clear: this is a place of reverence, not play. Like the messages of what Hooper-Greenhill defines as a modernist museum, these are "spaces of controlled behavior, guarded and surveyed by warders who would eject those who behaved in an unruly fashion."[48] We are supposed to be isolated in reverence. In this space we can feel the pressure to conform to some behavior. The museum turns to the visual because it is attempting to distance the visitor from the death that is represented metonymically in these mundane motel objects. This underscores the gap between "social death" and phenomenological death.[49] The museum's message seems to be that social death is a role and can be played by anyone—as we have played it in the earlier portions of the tour—but biological death and the phenomenology of the corpse is untouchable. The plastic lens creates distance and enforces the reverence the display seeks.

We hear Mahalia Jackson singing a slow gospel dirge. Mingled with her voice is the sound of King's final speech each time a visitor pushes the button and repeats the clip. *"It really doesn't matter what happens now. I left Atlanta. . . ."* It drifts in, the same segment, an unconscious haunting. *"And then I got into Memphis. . . ."* Otherwise, there are quiet conversations among visitors about the geography, where we are, which window James Earl Ray used to fire the shot, which room was King's. In the first room, room 308, the shades are drawn on the outside world and the room is lit with powerful halogen lamps from above, placing it under our scopophilic gaze. Although King is the most famous embodiment of the Civil Rights movement, he never receives representation in a mannequin; in other words, he is bodily absent.[50] At mid-thigh level is a black, Lucite placard that runs the length of the room. On it are glowing bits of text—split between history and memory—gold for objective comments or King's speech and white for anecdotes and subjective reflections of eye witnesses. What we see is an immaculate motel room from 1968: rust-colored linens, an old television. The substantive text serves to enforce a spatial pause; it gives us a reason to linger. What is a rather uninteresting and perhaps even banal room can't be passed over that quickly because the words literally slow down one's pace. King's speech and its relation to his death is so compelling—elicits such melancholic desire—that one gets drawn into the text even while the room doesn't do very much. Sufficiently reverent, having reflectively read the comments, the pilgrims would seem to be fully prepared to face the fated spot. But in finishing the placard, we encounter a kind of spatial vertigo. We look up and we're facing the fire door to the outside and a large window that overlooks the parking lot. Affixed to the wall is a black-and-white photograph of what we see through the window—the backs of buildings, including the rooming house from which Ray fired his shot.[51] Repeatedly, visitors try to locate the proper window, turning to each other with questions.

Slightly disoriented by having seen the outside world for the first time since entering the museum, we turn and face room 306 and our spatial vertigo clashes with a temporal vertigo. While the placard in the museum erroneously asserts that the room is "just as King and his lieutenants left it on April 4," it is actually modeled on a photograph taken in 1966 when King had stayed there (the museum includes the image on the placard).[52] This creates temporal vertigo as we move from the moment the picture was taken in 1966 to the day King died in 1968 to today. Bathed in a halo of light, the room has been preserved in moderate disarray, as if someone has stepped out to get a bucket of ice or something. As Eisterhold has explained, this decision is the museum's effort "to indicate some evidence of habitation" ("GG," 56). In the foreground, a pitcher stands ready to refill a water glass; a full cup of black coffee squats on the bureau. There are a few ashtrays, jammed with extinguished butts. Between the beds, there is a tray table with dirty dishes peaking out from under a tossed cloth napkin, and the remnants of "King's last supper (catfish)" ("GG," 56). One of the beds is rumpled and unmade. King is absent, but the display suggests he might come back to make the bed and finish his coffee.

Instead of movement or the possibility of action, there is a mild frozen feeling, as if history stopped at that moment in this place. Although we've now returned to the exact spot, our returning has not restarted history. History bumps into itself here, risking the full disconnection of the visitors from each other and from history. As Wallace says of history museums, "The disconnection of past from present and the separation of culture from politics was itself a political act. History was to be confined to providing of entertainment, nostalgia, or interesting insights into vanished ways of life. It was not to be freed to become a powerful agent for understanding—and changing—the present."[53] This civil rights museum risks becoming a purely nostalgic, politically conservative act in its conservation of this space.[54] Viewers can, and perhaps often do, come away feeling that the fight for rights is ultimately untouchable, sealed in the crypt of this room.

But the museum's ideology is more complex than a simplistic reduction to closure. The new exhibit, "Exploring the Legacy," has extended the tour with a room that acknowledges the risks of disconnection. The space of King's motel rooms, with its transparent plexiglass, may be more of a cultural aporia than a sealed crypt of history. In fact, in using such generic, raceless objects that will be familiar to every visitor—the ashtray, the pitcher, the coffee—the museum anticipates and attempts to facilitate an identification. Stephen Greenblatt asserts that "museums can and on occasion do make it easier to imaginatively recreate the work in its moment of openness."[55] The National Civil Rights Museum seems to be attempting to facilitate just such an imaginative act in its interactive exhibits and perhaps in the preservation of the motel rooms. While Greenblatt is speaking of art objects, I think the recreation of the rooms encourages a kind of temporal openness, where the visitor can imagine the contingency of history and fantasize about his or her participation in altering events. King's unfinished coffee attests to an unfinished project.

At the same time, this openness is a ruse, to a certain extent. We know that twenty years intervened between King's death and the formation of the museum so that this couldn't possibly be *his* cup. We more or less consciously buy into the cup's metonymic function so as to elevate our own pleasure. The cup is intended to be charged with near-religious significance. (The more one is willing to see religiosity in these simulacra, the greater the importance of this space and one's pleasure.) Greenblatt describes artifacts found in the State Jewish Museum in Prague as "wounded objects" ripe with historical and cultural "resonance" because of their proximity to death; in the case of the National Civil Rights Museum, these cups and trays and beds are staged as wounded objects—they are the simulacra of wounded objects.[56] The psychic space between the intent of the museum in staging these wounded objects and our inability to completely conform to the script fosters a valuable aporia or openness. For example, on one of my visits, an older woman declared in disbelief:

"That's not really his catfish, is it?"
"No, it would have rotted by now," her younger companion responded.
"Uhmm," the first said, absorbing the catfish's artificiality.
"It's just the *representation* of that catfish," the companion said.

Having absorbed the aim of the new museums, the younger visitor can see past the questions of authenticity to appreciate the scene for its intent; she can follow the museum's script. But this conversation reveals the tension in the script between closure and opening. The artificiality or plasticity is a kind of death, and yet it is necessary to preserve the catfish—the only item, in fact, which signifies King and speaks to region if not race. In other words, preservation—in the fish, in the rooms—relies on inauthenticity in order to defy time (or death), and this causes the older woman's vertigo as she absorbs the artificiality of the catfish. The aesthetics of this display evoke confusion that testifies to the uncanny politics of the space.

We have been shuttled between the plastic falsity of the objects on display and the temporal plasticity of our own fantasy. In standing in the space between rooms 306 and 308, we find ourselves in the space King occupied, engaging in a kind of wonder, like that described by Philip Fisher as the "aesthetics of rare experiences" and like that in King's automortography.[57] We have to figure it out, like a puzzle; the

cognitive map has been ruptured, forcing visitors to actively reconstruct it. This wonder, facilitated by the uncanny plasticity of the
space, aids in creating a melancholic public.

Public Feeling

Historically, museums are aesthetic instruments of the bourgeois public sphere, but the "new museums" seek to interrogate the museum's
values and their modes of transmission—that is, their aesthetic.
The National Civil Rights Museum has absorbed this critical, self-
reflective curatorial politics, even while reproducing bourgeois sensibilities. Still, its visitors form versions of a public. For some, this
is a mortographic public, drawn to the site of King's death and fascinated by the spectacle of James Earl Ray's point of view on display in
"Exploring the Legacy." But there is another public traveling within
the same space that is critical of the museum's script and skeptical of its politics. This counterpublic finds its most strident advocate
just beyond the museum's property. Jacqueline Smith's presence both
exposes the mystified power of the museum itself and melancholically
adheres to King, pointing visitors to their role in an unfinished political
project.

Smith militantly mourns the aestheticization of King's death in the
creation of the museum. The former manager of the Lorraine Motel,
Smith was evicted when it closed its doors in 1988 to prepare for the
coming of the museum. From a couch placed outside on the corner,
she has, for sixteen years, launched campaigns against a succession of
museum initiatives, which she regards as a violation of King's legacy.
She began by protesting the construction of the museum itself, advocating that the space should be used for something more in keeping with King's message, such as a resource center for job training,
a homeless shelter, or a free college. She has designed boycotts of
Denny's and AutoZone because, in order to ameliorate the poor public images they acquired as a result of their racist hiring practices,
they have donated money to the museum's expansion project. Smith
has created an alternative public space on her Web site, where she
documents her ongoing protest, places testimonies of support for her
project, and invites participation in keeping with King's intention. She
has been forcibly moved by the police and arrested for civil disobedience a number of times—recently, for attempting to block the con-

struction of the museum's expansion. Smith creates banners decry-
ing the creation of a museum devoted to death, because she sees the
refurbishment of the rooming house as enlisted in the creation and
affirmation of Ray supporters and a monumental waste of millions of
dollars.

I am left wondering about the possibility of an audience for Smith's
reading of King's legacy. Smith stands as a shining example of the
existence of a kind of melancholy—and its potential limits. Her commitment is admirable, but it is wholly dependent on the museum.
When the museum purchased automobiles that would replicate those
parked in the lot on 4 April 1968, Smith sought out and retrieved the
actual automobile that had been parked there—and displayed it as a
critique of the inauthenticity of the museum. She refuses to acknowledge the plasticity of the site, of time, and of intent. In fact, her dissent ultimately confirms the power of civil rights that the museum
seeks to explore, even as the museum erases her eviction (evidence
of its power) in its own representation of history. With her commitment, she risks becoming the living history display of the museum she
seeks to dismantle. She risks being the human diorama that proves the
museum's point about the significance of King and this site, once her
home. Sleeping outside on the couch on the corner, she is the literal
un-Heimlich in this place. Smith may be the Antigone figure, as theorized by Butler: a figure at the limit of the subject-object that points
to a future anterior moment. She stands for the "limit" that is "the
trace of an alternate legality that haunts the conscious, public sphere
as its scandalous future."[58] Smith's automortographic efforts enable
the witnessing of this alternate legality serving as a kind of limit for
the museum visitor, regulating how far we will let our melancholy take
us. Her Antigone-like presence cleaves to King's intent, "haunting the
conscious, public sphere." But will we exhibit Smith's commitment,
or is that beyond our limit? Her work, though admirable, may let the
rest of us off the hook. We could never be (or be expected to be in
some future anterior moment) that committed, could we?

But like the uncanny relations of King's speech to his death and the
space of these rooms to the construction of history, Smith's uncanny
relation to the museum has the potential to lead passive consumers
to wonder. Her presence and her witness, like King's rhetoric and the
weird preservation of those rooms, may invite the audience's participation in a form of witnessing that marks the uncanny genre of auto-

mortography. Rather than letting us off the hook, Smith hooks us or interpellates us; her presence is an Althusserian policing of an alternate public.[59] We are called out and must turn and confront her dissent. Her commitment jars us into witnessing the force of the museum and its bourgeois politics and suggests an "alternate legality," one closer to the moral law that King tried to articulate with his Poor People's Campaign in 1968.

Automortography exposes hegemonic mortography and can inspire counterhegemonic practices and publics. In the case of King, one can see automortographic aesthetics in recent books: Charles Johnson's novel *Dreamer*, Toni Cade Bambara's *Those Bones Are Not My Child* (1999), and Michael Eric Dyson's critical biography *I May Not Get There with You* (2000) — as well as in artistic and musical expressions, including Solomon Burke's "Mountain Top," and museum curation in the Smithsonian's traveling exhibit, In the Spirit of Martin.[60] Each in its own manner, like Smith herself, cleaves to the loss of King and participates in an act of "self" creation that molds and maintains a public that refuses the King who is reduced to a dreamy sound bite each January.[61] Analogous to the modes of close reading in automortography that trace the subject-object split, each of these acts enables a psychic participation in the "spirit" of King, through participatory aesthetics, and demands a reconsideration of his politics.

King's automortographic speech offers a way of witnessing and using history that might countervail a sense of loss and that might enable a nonpathological (that is, plastic), political melancholia. In "I've Been to the Mountaintop," King tries to script its posthumous reception so as to participate in his own mourning and, simultaneously, to see the movement past his death, attempting to ensure that his death will not be read as an overdetermined ritual. Instead, history is an opening and his speech an invitation to see ourselves as historical actors and agents. His uncanny aesthetic denies both narrative and historical closure and solipsistic grief, instead encouraging a participatory wonder and a witnessing of both the irrecoverability and presence of loss. Automortographic witnesses cleave to King's aesthetic, working and feeling toward that future moment when King's promise will have been fulfilled.

Andover, Massachusetts

Notes

I would like to thank Bill Albertini, Elizabeth Bridgham, Jennifer Cane, Jim Kim, Eric Lott, Brenna Munro, and Alice Rutkowski for valuable responses to earlier versions of this essay. I am also grateful to the participants at the panel "Museums and Memory" at the 2001 American Studies Association meeting in Washington, D.C.

1   Jesse Epps, quoted in Joan Turner Beifuss, *At the River I Stand: Memphis, the 1968 Strike, and Martin Luther King* (Brooklyn: Carlson, 1989), 278.

2   David L. Eng, "The Value of Silence," *Theater Journal* 54 (March 2002): 88.

3   Marcella Tarozzi Goldsmith, *The Future of Art: An Aesthetics of the New and the Sublime* (Albany: State Univ. of New York Press, 1999), 76.

4   Donald Pease, "Doing Justice to C.L.R. James' *Mariners, Renegades, and Castaways*," *boundary 2* 27 (summer 2000): 16.

5   See Mark Seltzer, *Serial Killers: Death and Life in America's Wound Cultures* (New York: Routledge, 1998).

6   Sharon Patricia Holland, "Bill T. Jones, Tupac Shakur, and the (Queer) Art of Death," *Callaloo* 23 (winter 2000): 389.

7   Lauren Berlant, "Uncle Sam Needs a Wife," *Materializing Democracy: Toward a Revitalized Cultural Democracy*, ed. Russ Castronovo and Dana D. Nelson (Durham, N.C.: Duke Univ. Press, 2002), 147. While mortography may be "postpolitical" in Berlant's terms, automortography may ultimately fulfill what Berlant sees as the valuable aspects of such forms of emotional attachment: it "might ground resistance to political powerlessness; it might be a counterhegemonic drive . . . ; it might confirm what we already know, that publicity marks danger while private but collective spectatorship protects" ("Uncle Sam," 164). Automortography grows out of and engages with debates over citizenship and sentimentality found in Berlant's work; see also Russ Castronovo, "Political Necrophilia," *boundary 2* 27 (summer 2000): 113–48.

8   Heather Love, "'Spoiled Identity': Stephen Gordon's Loneliness and the Difficulties of Queer History," *GLQ: A Journal of Lesbian and Gay Studies* 7, no. 4 (2001): 515.

9   Kelly Oliver, *Witnessing: Beyond Recognition* (Minneapolis: Univ. of Minnesota Press, 2001), 88.

10 Automortography can be situated in relation to Michael Warner's recent discussion of publics, where the mortographic spectacle is instrumental in the formation of "the mass public subject." Automortography, then, would enable the articulation and construction of "counter publics" that operate in the name of the deceased, that is, King's followers (*Publics and Counterpublics* [New York: Zone Books, 2002], 159, 65–124).

11 David L. Eng and David Kazanjian, "Introduction: Mourning Remains," *Loss: The Politics of Mourning*, ed. Eng and Kazanjian (Berkeley and Los Angeles: Univ. of California Press, 2003), 3.

12 My use of the term *aesthetic* is close to the pre-Kantian coinage of the term by Alexander Baumgarten (1714–1762), who sees aesthetics as instrumental in the description of sensual perception and not confined to artistic representation; see Alexander Baumgarten, *Theoretische Aesthetik: Die grundlegenden Abschnitte aus der "Aesthetica"* (Hamburg: Meiner, 1983). Thus, in my essay, aesthetics is not about art or artifice as much as the impact, manipulation, and affective work of style. For a discussion of Baumgarten in relation to other German thinkers on aesthetics, see Kai Hammermeister, *The German Aesthetic Tradition* (New York: Cambridge Univ. Press, 2002).

13 John Forgas, "Affect and the 'Social Mind': Affective Influences on Strategic Interpersonal Behaviors," *The Social Mind*, ed. John Forgas, Kipling Williams, and Ladd Wheeler (New York: Cambridge Univ. Press, 2001), 67. For further discussion of what Forgas calls the affective infusion model, see Forgas, "Mood and Judgment: The Affect Infusion Model (AIM)," *Psychological Bulletin* 117, no. 1 (1995): 39–66.

14 See Silvan Tompkins, "What Are Affects?" in *Shame and Its Sisters: A Silvan Tomkins Reader*, ed. Eve Kosofsky Sedgwick and Adam Frank (Durham, N.C.: Duke Univ. Press, 1995), 56. For a discussion of the need to attend to the phenomenology of affect rather than simply defer to a politically progressive but intellectually facile anti-essentialism, see Eve Kosofsky Sedgwick, *Touching Feeling: Affect, Pedagogy, Performativity* (Durham, N.C.: Duke Univ. Press, 2003).

15 See, for example, Deborah McDowell, "Recovery Missions: Imaging the Body Ideals," in *Recovering the Black Female Body: Self-Representations by African American Women*, ed. Michael Bennett and Vanessa D. Dickerson (New Brunswick, N.J.: Rutgers Univ. Press, 2001), 296–317; Deborah McDowell, "Reading Family Matters," in *Haunted Bodies: Gender and Southern Texts*, ed. Anne Goodwyn Jones and Susan V. Donaldson (Charlottesville, Va.: Univ. of Virginia Press, 1997), 389–415; Holland, "Bill T. Jones, Tupac Shakur"; Sharon Patricia Holland, *Raising the Dead: Readings of Death and (Black) Subjectivity* (Durham, N.C.: Duke Univ. Press, 2000); and Karla F. C. Holloway, *Passed On: African American Mourning Stories, A Memorial* (Durham, N.C.: Duke Univ. Press, 2002).

16 See, for example, Maurice O. Wallace, *Constructing the Black Masculine: Identity and Ideality in African American Men's Literature and Culture, 1775–1995* (Durham, N.C.: Duke Univ. Press, 2002); Kenneth Mostern, *Autobiography and Black Identity Politics: Racialization in Twentieth-Century America* (New York: Cambridge Univ. Press, 1999); and Crispin Sartwell, *Act Like You Know: African American Autobiography and White Identity* (Chicago: Univ. of Chicago Press, 1998).

17 W. E. B. DuBois, *Dusk of Dawn*, in *W. E. B. DuBois: Writings* (New York: Library of America, 1986), 551.

18 Martin Luther King Jr., "I've Been to the Mountaintop," in *A Call to Con-*

science: The Speeches of Martin Luther King, Jr., ed. Clayborne Carson and Kris Shepard (New York: Warner Books, 2001), 220. Further references to this speech are to this edition and will be cited parenthetically as "M."

19   See Sigmund Freud, "Beyond the Pleasure Principle," in volume 18 of *The Standard Edition of the Complete Psychological Works of Sigmund Freud*, trans. James Strachey (London: Hogarth, 1955), 3–64.

20   Richard Schechner, *The Future of Ritual: Writings on Culture and Performance* (New York: Routledge, 1993), 230, 233.

21   Michael Osborn, "The Last Mountaintop of Martin Luther King, Jr.," in *Martin Luther King, Jr. and the Sermonic Power of Public Discourse*, ed. Carolyn Calloway-Thomas and John Lucaites (Tuscaloosa: Univ. of Alabama Press, 1993), 156.

22   Michael Eric Dyson, *I May Not Get There with You: The True Martin Luther King* (New York: Free Press, 2001), 78.

23   John Ruskin, vol. 2 of *Modern Painters* (New York: Wiley and Sons, 1878), 27; quoted in Claudia Bell and John Lyall, *The Accelerated Sublime: Landscape, Tourism, and Identity* (Westport, Conn.: Praeger, 2001), 5.

24   Bell and Lyall, *The Accelerated Sublime*, 5.

25   Immanuel Kant, *The Critique of Judgment* (New York: Oxford Univ. Press, 1964); quoted in Slavoj Žižek, *The Sublime Object of Ideology* (New York: Verso, 1989), 203. I use Žižek's translation because it fits my context more smoothly than others.

26   Jean-François Lyotard, "The Sublime and the Avant-Garde," in *Continental Aesthetics Reader*, ed. Clive Cazeaux (New York: Routledge, 2000), 459. Michel Deguy provides another example of the relation of the sublime and death: "The mortal condition and the moment of perishing are always at stake when the *sublime* appears. The sublime is the concentration, the start of the startling that weighs in speech against death" ("The Discourse of Exultation," in *Of the Sublime: Presence in Question*, trans. Jeffrey Librett [Albany: State Univ. of New York Press, 1993], 5–24).

27   Conrad Eugene Ostwalt asserts that "the garden of America was sacred space in two different ways. It represented a sacred and paradisiacal natural world; however, it also symbolized a sacred social world where people could aspire to live without sin and in total harmony with one another" (*After Eden: The Secularization of American Space in the Fiction of Willa Cather and Theodore Dreiser* [Lewisberg, Pa.: Bucknell Univ. Press; Associated University Presses, 1990], 25). In deploying the term *promised land*, King not only borrows the costume of Moses, he also deploys familiar Puritan tropology, forcing the republic to confront its failure to fulfill the "sacred social world" where people could live "in total harmony."

28   Roger Aden, *Popular Stories and Promised Lands: Fan Cultures and Symbolic Pilgrimages* (Tuscaloosa: Univ. of Alabama Press, 1999), 4, 9.

29   Judith Butler, "Afterword: After Loss, What Then?" in *Loss*, ed. Eng and Kazanjian, 467.

30 The museum's exhibits have changed in its nearly thirteen-year history. For instance, for some period of time and causing some public debate, a laser that traced the trajectory of the killer's shot was mounted so as to be seen through the window.

31 Eilean Hooper-Greenhill, *Museums and the Shaping of Knowledge* (New York: Routledge, 1992), 205.

32 D'Army Bailey, quoted in Lynn Norment, "Memphis Motel Becomes a Shrine," *Ebony*, April 1992, 54.

33 Mike Wallace, "Museums and Controversy," *"Mickey Mouse History" and Other Essays on American Memory* (Philadelphia: Temple Univ. Press, 1996), 122.

34 Hooper-Greenhill, *Museums and the Shaping of Knowledge*, 214.

35 See Jacqueline Smith, "What's New," www.fulfillthedream.net (accessed 15 April 2004).

36 Kevin Sack, "Museums of a Movement," *New York Times*, 28 June 1998, 12.

37 Alan Wallach, "Revisionism Has Transformed Art History but Not Museums," *Exhibiting Contradiction: Essays on the Art Museum in the United States* (Amherst: Univ. of Massachusetts Press, 1998), 121.

38 *Gray* is also a term used by African Americans to describe white people.

39 Hooper-Greenhill, *Museums and the Shaping of Knowledge*, 214.

40 The vehicle gains its authenticity, we learn, because it was used in the movie *A Long Walk Home*.

41 Eilean Hooper-Greenhill, *Museums and the Interpretation of Visual Culture* (New York: Routledge, 2000). For Hooper-Greenhill, a "postmuseum" takes "many architectural forms [because its emphasis is on] . . . a process or an experience" rather than a building (152–53).

42 Gerard Eisterhold, quoted in Walter Shapiro, "The Glory and the Glitz: The New National Civil Rights Museum in Memphis Is a Classic Jumble of Laudable Intentions and Bad Taste," *Time*, 5 August 1991, 56. Further references to this source will be cited parenthetically as "GG."

43 Carol Duncan, *Civilizing Rituals: Inside Public Art Museums* (New York: Routledge, 1995), 13. Duncan argues that "the totality of the museum [is] a stage setting that prompts visitors to enact a performance of some kind. . . . From this perspective, art museums appear as environments structured around specific ritual scenarios" (1–2).

44 "Space of death" is an allusion to Michael Taussig, "Culture of Terror— Space of Death: Roger Casement's Putumayo Report and the Explanation of Torture," in *Colonialism and Culture*, ed. Nicholas Dirks (Ann Arbor: Univ. of Michigan Press, 1992), 135–74.

45 Eng, "The Value of Silence," 89.

46 My "reading" does not narrate the changes in the museum since the summer of 2001. As of 28 September 2002, visitors continue past the motel rooms through an underground tunnel to the newly refurbished room-

ing house where they view the new exhibit "Exploring the Legacy" that addresses the period after King's death.

47 Wallach, "Revisionism," 126.

48 Hooper-Greenhill, *Museums and the Interpretation of Visual Culture*, 126.

49 See Orlando Patterson, *Slavery and Social Death* (Cambridge: Harvard Univ. Press, 1983).

50 The museum has chosen not to create a gray plaster model of King: "'There was some discussion of populating Room 306 with figures,' Eisterhold recalls but acknowledges that this seemed close to blasphemy" (Osborn, "The Last Mountaintop," 56). It would be blasphemous to embody the dead—or at least offensive to bourgeois sensibilities.

51 The photograph, in the black-and-white aesthetic of a historical artifact, has been taken since the museum was built, with the large brick wall that marks the museum's property in the foreground.

52 See Kevin Sack, "Museums of a Movement: Institutions in Memphis, Birmingham, Atlanta Commemorate the Struggle for Civil Rights," *Pittsburgh Post-Gazette*, 26 July 1998, F-6.

53 Mike Wallace, "Visiting the Past: History Museums in the United States," *"Mickey Mouse History" and Other Essays*, 24.

54 This museum is distinct from those in Selma and Birmingham and from the King Center in Atlanta because of the centrality of death in its siting.

55 Stephen Greenblatt, "Resonance and Wonder," in *Exhibiting Cultures*, ed. Ivan Karp and Steven Lavine (Washington, D.C.: Smithsonian Institution Press, 1991), 43.

56 Ibid., 43. While Greenblatt's term predates Wendy Brown's "wounded attachments," Brown's phrase certainly describes part of the operation of this space and this museum; it facilitates a wounded attachment to King (see Wendy Brown, *States of Injury: Power and Freedom in Late Modernity* [Princeton, N.J.: Princeton Univ. Press, 1995]).

57 See Philip Fisher, *Wonder, the Rainbow, and the Aesthetics of Rare Experience* (Cambridge: Harvard Univ. Press, 1999).

58 Judith Butler, *Antigone's Claim: Kinship between Life and Death* (New York: Columbia Univ. Press, 2000), 40.

59 For Louis Althusser's discussion of interpellation, see *"Lenin and Philosophy," and Other Essays*, trans. Ben Brewster (New York: Monthly Review Press, 1972).

60 For a catalog of the Smithsonian exhibit, see *In the Spirit of Martin*, created and developed by Gary Miles Chassman (Atlanta: Tinwood, 2001).

61 The reduction of King's life to a short segment of the speech "I Have a Dream" reminds me of a passage from Walter Benjamin's "Theses on the Philosophy of History": "Only that historian will have the gift of fanning the spark of hope in the past who is firmly convinced that *even the dead* will not be safe from the enemy if he wins" (*Illuminations* [New York: Schocken, 1968], 255).

Christopher Nealon   Camp Messianism, or, the Hopes of
                         Poetry in Late-Late Capitalism

Recent innovative North American poetry is a good place for thinking about the status of a new aesthetics, since it's been busy writing one. I'm thinking of American and Canadian poets, most in their thirties and forties now, who are writing in light of the poetic and critical projects of Language poetry, though they are by no means simply following them out. These poets, referred to as "post-Language" writers in the small-press world in which they've emerged, raise interesting questions about new habits of literary criticism, since their poems read both as theory and poetry. Although these poets have not yet produced a body of writing like the criticism and theory of the Language poets, their poetry reads like the yield, if not the fore-grounding, of significant theoretical effort.

More specifically, many of the post-Language writers seem to have taken a kind of Frankfurt school turn in their poems, by which I mean not so much that they are crankily denouncing a culture industry—though they may—or critically miming "authoritarian" types of lan-guage—though they do—but that they have become invested in a historical story about what Theodor Adorno called "damaged life," or what Susan Stewart might call the "fate" of the material world, its pasts and possible futures.[1] Unlike Adorno or Walter Benjamin, though, many of the post-Language poets have struck a kind of camp posture toward the "damage" of late capitalism, in a way that borrows from but reinterprets both the messianism of Adorno and Benjamin and the subcultural (especially queer) trajectory of camp.

The best sketch I can offer of the Frankfurtian part of this his-torical story about a "damaged" material life is to say that it's not

American Literature, Volume 76, Number 3, September 2004. Copyright © 2004 by Duke University Press.

just a story of the culture industry whose workings Adorno and Max Horkheimer detailed at midcentury, nor even of the "late capitalism" Fredric Jameson first diagnosed in 1984;[2] it's the story of something like really, *really* late capitalism; capitalism in a fully globalized and triumphal form, the destructive speed and flexibility of whose financial instruments alone make Nixon's lofting the dollar off the gold standard in 1971 look thoughtful and conservative. Depending on how one understands the massive glut of capital unleashed on the world markets since the collapse of the Soviet Union, capitalism has either taken on a new, omnipotently viral character (traveling across national boundaries, for instance, with the power to imperil entire economies for no other reason than to keep a tiny group of wealthy investors' portfolios mobile and artificially inflated); or it is in the last, seizing phases of a horrible addiction to its own mobility. In any case, the privatizing, shock-treatment destruction of the post-Soviet economy in the early nineties, the collapse and bailout of the peso in 1995, the Asian currency crisis of 1997, and the bottoming out of the United States' supposedly posthistorical new economy in 2000—all these indicate a volatility to capital on an order of magnitude beyond even the ricochets of the early twentieth century.[3] If Adorno and Horkheimer made much of how the Enlightenment's dream of the equality of all people had become the nightmare of the interchangeability of all people, that interchangeability could now be said to have become entirely liquid, even quicksilver.

We might say that the camp aspect of post-Language writing, meanwhile, is the rueful astonishment that, against all odds, this liquidation is still not complete: post–Cold War global economic volatility has not resulted in wholesale disaster for the United States or Europe. Instead, late-late capitalism gives texture to our everyday lives more murmuringly: most of us are at least intermittently aware of being solicited day and night by a kind of manic mass culture that seeks, ever more aggressively, to stuff our attention to the gills. When Andrew Ross remarks, then, that camp "is the re-creation of surplus value from forgotten forms of labor," he touches on a polemical affection for waste, which animates not just camp in its queer subcultural matrix but also in its migrations beyond subcultural boundaries—to mass culture (which tries to capture the dynamics of camp consumption in television, for instance, in programs like Mystery Science Theater 3000, or in VH-1's "Pop-up videos," or in fake-anachronistic sitcoms like "That '70's Show") and to the literary culture of small-press poetry.[4]

Mass-cultural camp invites us all to be clever; post-Language poetic camp, I hope to show, invites us to take up a polemical affection for what's obsolete, misguided, or trivial, and to risk the embarrassment of trying it out.

So how do post-Language poets do this? How do they perform a relationship to the experience of a materiality that is both desubstantialized and supersaturating, subject to both lightning-swift consolidations and dispersals and to humiliating, vegetally slow decay? A first text for consideration:

> What gets *me* is
> > the robots are doing
> *my* job, but I don't get
> > the *money*,
> some extrapolated node
> > of expansion-contraction gets
> my money, which *I* need
> for *time travel*.[5]

What gets *me* is how compactly this terrific little poem toys with, or speaks through, an affect that has transformed North American poetry in the last decade. At first, this poem by Kevin Davies seems to be just the swift dodge of a tedious sort of lecturing, political poetry. Yes, the speaker is complaining about the theft of his wages, but he does it science-fictionally, and by way of a dated science fiction, at that: there is no Matrix here, just "robots" and "*time travel.*" But the campiness of the obsolete sci-fi conceit has something to play off against, namely, the description of the system that steals the speaker's wages, the "extrapolated node / of expansion-contraction"—itself amusing in its succinctness but not quite the same as the clanking of the worker-robots. If the poem is a dodge, then, it's not quite dodging politics with humor: the truth of the poem lies elsewhere, in its rueful awareness of the obsolescence of its conceit. This awareness is not simply reflexive—not simply a modernist recognition of obsolescence—because the poem also performs the knowledge that even its obsolescence is obsolete. This performance—I think of it as a kind of stance—is designed to make the poem's last, emphatic phrase—"*time travel*"—escape, for a moment, its camp value and reveal an extravagant demand: that the speaker get his money *and* his history back, that he be freed to burrow back behind the process that made even the expropriating robots obsolete—or, perhaps, to lurch forward to a time when obsolescence will reveal itself to have been an unfinished piece of a story about the rescue of human vulnerability from the merciless abstraction of "expansion" and "contraction."[6]

Read this way, Davies's poem is not far from the canonical modern articulation of a redemptive historiography—that is, from Benjamin's remarks in "Theses on the Philosophy of History":

> A chronicler who recites events without distinguishing between major and minor ones acts in accordance with the following truth: nothing that has ever happened should be regarded as lost to history. To be sure, only a redeemed mankind receives the fullness of its past—which is to say, only for a redeemed mankind has its past become citable in all its moments. Each moment it has lived becomes a *citation à l'ordre du jour*—and that day is Judgment Day.[7]

This scenario echoes not only the short poem by Davies but also a whole variety of post-Language writing, like this poem in Lisa Robertson's *Debbie: An Epic* (1997):

maybe
even
this
dress
shall
some
day be
a joy
to
repair[8]

And here, Davies again, from *Comp.*'s "Karnal Bunt":

Every junked
vehicle a
proposition
waiting for
the right rustic
welder
after the war that
never happened
here.
(*C*, 61)

And Rod Smith, from *The Good House* (2001):

Each reasonable house
& each waking motion
are votive, based on
the wiley insurgence
of awaiting worlds— [9]

Each of these poems (they are actually all stanzas or sections from longer poems) finds in its material at hand—a dress, "junked" cars, the "reasonable house" and "waking motion"—a mute expectation of "repair" or recuperation.

The character of this expectation is slightly different in each case. In the context of *Debbie*, it becomes clear that Robertson is implicitly imagining herself in the scene of repair; Davies understands the instances of his "junked vehicle" logically, as "propositions," but he complicates past logic the temporality of their being welded since their future is contingent on what "never happened / here"; and Smith places not only his "house" but also a human figure, with "waking motion," in the way of expectation. The language in each poem is also differently political—only whisperingly so in Robertson (though, again, elsewhere she will show her cards), but frankly combative in Davies, with his hard-to-locate "war," and slyly, ambiently resistant in Smith's "wiley insurgence / of awaiting worlds."

I realize that in offering a preliminary account of these poems my focus on modernist and midcentury points of comparison—camp modes of attachment and critique, and Frankfurtian tactics of rereading history—raises the question, What about postmodernity? It is true, of course, that the two "schools" of poetry to whom the post-Language poets are most indebted—the Language poetry of the 1980s and the New York school of the 1960s and 1970s—are both understood in American literary history as signally "postmodern." Are the post-Language poets postmodern?

This is a hard question. It is true that poets like Davies, Robertson, and Smith make use of the signal strategies of literary postmodernism as we've come to recognize it, especially its engagement with mass culture and a decoupling of signs from their referents. And it's true that these poets have also grown up with the peculiarly postmodern admixture of identity-based liberation movements and poststructural critiques of identity. But their poems seem to be written out of some set of conditions we are still struggling to name, conditions not quite matching the major accounts of the postmodern (hence, with my apologies, "late-late capitalism"). At the very least, these younger poets are motivated by a different sense of historical situation—specifically, a different sense of the unfolding of a totalizing political and economic system—than was felt by either the New York school or the Language poets.

Although vastly different, of course, both Language and New York writing developed in successive stages of the expansion of mass culture, and both drew energy from critiques of authenticity bound up in mass culture's unfolding. At midcentury, in poems like Frank O'Hara's "Having a Coke with You" and John Ashbery's "Daffy Duck in Hollywood," New York school poets made friends with popular and mass culture, deliberately braving the possibility of obsolescence or eventual inscrutability. Such risk-taking was meant to dislodge the idea of poetry from the formalist antimodernisms of "official verse culture," which presumed that poems were autonomous linguistic artifacts whose aim was to rise above their immediate surroundings and stake a claim to cultural permanence.[10]

Language school poets later developed a critique concerned not with the poet's cultural isolation as much as with the authenticity of lyric utterance—and, ultimately, of language itself—as a transparently truthful medium. Language poets, like the poets of the New York school, were interested in the relationship between mass culture and poetry, but rather than mining mass culture as a referential and affective resource, they tended to focus on its capacity to obscure social truths, especially the truth of the commodification of language. Deliberately fracturing syntax and troubling reference, Language poets developed a relationship between the poetic and the political not so much by striking the implicitly political posture of insouciance toward an official culture as by tearing away at its lies. If the relevant political backdrop for the New York school poets was the Cold War, for the Language poets, it was Vietnam.[11]

What kind of poetics the post-Language poets articulate, meanwhile, is a question understood so far primarily in terms of their relationship to Language writing rather than to the New York school, perhaps because the Language poets developed a large body of critical writing (and because they are the more immediate precursors). While I can't devote much space here to a comparison between Language and post-Language writing, I think it is important at least to mention some of the major arguments in the Language poets' critical writing in order to highlight what seems different now about the post-Language poets, especially in their understanding of linguistic materiality.

Language poets' contribution to the development of a postmodern poetics can be understood as an argument on behalf of three interrelated arguments about participatory readership, language and the commodity form, and the decentering of the postmodern political subject. These contributions have been widely discussed and analyzed; in brief, I think it's fair to say that the notion of active readership lies at the center of the Language poets' collective self-understanding.[12] Active readership points to a belief that difficult, unconventional texts, rather than being closed to readers, are actually more open than traditional literary texts because they don't smother or direct readers with too many genre cues, overdetermined tropes, clichés, or heavily rehearsed rhetorical movements—forms of what Language poets like Lyn Hejinian and Bruce Andrews refer to as "closure."[13] This "rejection of closure," as Hejinian calls it, implies a scene of reader-writer collaboration meant to rescue language not only from cliché but also from commodification, from becoming a unidirectional, informatic, PowerPoint-y medium for social control. The argument for referentially disjunct, nonclosural texts as the appropriate scene for a collaborative decommodification of language has been made most forcefully by the Language poet and critic Ron Silliman; this argument is linked, in the poetry and critical writing of Bruce Andrews, to a theory of collaboration between reader and writer that produces a mobile, protean, political subject along the lines of the "schizo" envisioned in Gilles Deleuze and Félix Guattari's *Anti-Oedipus*.[14] As Andrews puts it:

> [Language poetics] doesn't call for a reading that rejects or
>   negates the referential, or even the baldly representational
>   forces of language,
> but one that resists letting those forces be confined and
>   recuperated & territorialized.
> It would join in the adventure of keeping them active at the micro
>   level, as singular & literal events—
> constantly varying, skidding, interpenetrating, mutually
>   transforming, out in the open, on the surface

.   .   .   .

> Works are responses, and the praxis of the reader reconstructs
> this responsiveness
>
> . . . .
>
> Here we're not looking for mastery, but passionate or even
> dizzying embrace—of an *implicated* social body.[15]

These concerns with active readership, the decommodification of language, and the production of a new, political subject, fully enfolded
(*"implicated"*) in a mobile social body, are formally present in many
Language poems. One canonical example is Hejinian's *My Life*, which
in its first edition contained thirty-seven sections of thirty-seven sentences each, one section-sentence for each year of Hejinian's life (the
second edition, written eight years after the first, adds eight sentences
to the thirty-seven original sections, and eight new sections: guess
why). These playfully arbitrary formal conceits allow Hejinian to foreground the variety of means she deploys to establish connectivity
among her sentences:

> Back and backward, why, wide and wider. Such that art is
> inseparable from the search for reality. The continent is greater
> than the content. A river nets the peninsula
>
> . . . .
>
> The Spanish make a little question frame. In the case, propped on
> a stand so as to beckon, was the hairy finger of St. Cecilia,
> covered with rings
>
> . . . .
>
> An extremely pleasant and often comic satisfaction comes from
> conjunction, the fit, say, of comprehension in a reader's mind to
> content in a writer's work. But not bitter.[16]

Hejinian moves from one sentence to the next according to different
principles in different instances, and it is this connective variety that
gives the poem life. Sometimes the sentences move with a gesture
toward logic. The second sentence in this section, for instance, begins,
"Such that." Or the sentences might represent two phrasings of the
"same" idea: "The continent is greater than the content" is followed
by "A river nets the peninsula," which allows Hejinian to begin to iso-
late the difference particular figures make when called into the service
of the same concept—in this case, the concept of content surrounding,
rather than being encased by, form.

It is this last concept, really an argument, that seems typical of the attitude toward linguistic materiality expressed in Language writing. While it is true enough to say that Language writers are concerned with linguistic materiality (since they are poets, it is nearly tautological to notice this), what's distinctive is their relation to the aspectual character of this materiality. Language writing argues for understanding the medium of language as a kind of perpetually mobile surround, which Hejinian typically calls "context":[17] placement, situation, conjunction, animating constraint—the "net" and the "frame"—all serve to establish a scene that invites the reader to experience the toggle between material and referential aspects of language as curious, as "a little question frame" that "nets" content but lets it go. Poems like Hejinian's articulate linguistic materiality in terms much like those of a monist Deleuzian plenitude, where differences are not metaphysical or categorical but *"implicated"*; they are folds. The relationship between form and content in Language poetry takes on the character of a materio-linguistic snapshot, where what is form one minute might be content the next. It is a poetics of fluidity, and if we listen for it, I think we can hear in it the echo of the post–1968 hope for a new, more fluid politics.

This set of beliefs and practices around the materiality of language is significantly different from the testamentary, expectation-laden materiality in the work of the post-Language poets who most interest me. The historical reasons for this difference are of course complex, and they are still being debated. Hejinian has recently suggested, controversially, that the new generation of poets has not been politicized as the Language poets were by the singular, defining experience of the war in Vietnam.[18] While this doesn't amount to the now-familiar Baby Boomer charge that Generation X is "apathetic" or "de-politicized" (which Silliman has suggested), it does raise the question of how different political moments breed different structures of political and poetic feeling. This is of course a complicated question; we might take a first attempt at answering it by way of the very largest abstractions to hand and try to understand the political affects of the two generations and the formal strategies that animate their work as expressing emphatically different moments in the unfolding of a late-capitalist totality:

> As for the current situation, . . . [we can see] how the very mood and methodology of the analyses varied across the great internal polarity of voluntarism and fatalism (or determinism) according to

the changes in the objective situation, and its great cyclical rhythms that alternate from situations of great promise and change . . . to those of a locked social geology so massive that no visions of modification seem possible. . . .[19]

Fredric Jameson wrote this passage at the beginning of the 1990s, as part of an explanation of why he felt Adorno's work might, after what he felt were the poststructuralist highs of the 1970s and 1980s, be freshly relevant for political thinking. In 1990, at least, Jameson believed that Adorno, because of his willingness to work in isolation from an identifiable political movement, was a good model for the way critical thinking and political solitude might have to go together in a new postmodern dispensation that had done away with the types of cultural and historical memory that mass movements need. More than ten years later, Jameson seems to have been both right—there is undeniably a revival, in the English-language academy, of interest in Adorno—and wrong: late capitalism, perhaps in the emergent form of empire, is being written about as though it were all the more legible— and therefore more vulnerable to opposition—to a new generation of "anti-globalization" activists.[20]

The post-Language poets to whom I now want to turn, however, exhibit neither a postrevolutionary political apathy nor a specific set of anti-globalist affiliations. They are not "movement" poets. But they do write with an acute knowledge of the susceptibility of their materials to historical change. What I would like to suggest in the rest of this essay is that the recent affective and strategic shift in American poetry can be described as a shift in attitudes toward the character of late-capitalist totality. We might say that where the Language poets discovered a reserve of uncapitalized materiality in the lively, "aspectual" character of language—so that the open-endedness of texts might outpace their superscription by languages of power—the post-Language poets, battered by another generation's-worth of the encroachments of capital, are not so ready to rely on those aspectual reserves. They can discern them in language, of course, and in material objects, but it's not their focus; instead, as I'll try to show, they expend their considerable talents on making articulate the ways in which, as they look around, they see *waiting*.

Perhaps the best place to begin is with a poem from Joshua Clover's manuscript *The Totality for Kids*. Since 1996, when he published his first book, *Madonna Anno Domini*, Clover has been trying to develop a new poetry of the city, with Paris as his model—a kind of post-Benjaminian, post-Situationist city, whose moods and contours are revealed by way of a perpetual and unstable movement between concretion and abstraction. Like Ashbery's poems, Clover's foreground the pathos of conceptualization—how recursive it is, how helpless, even in its glories; but unlike Ashbery, Clover develops a quietly messianic sense that the city, and the aesthetic experience it fosters, awaits redemption. In this view, he follows Benjamin, for whom even ephemera—especially ephemera—could whisper to listening ears the story of how a mute material existence, completely overwritten by capital, might still one day become a tool for breaking it apart. As Clover puts it in the last poem in *The Totality for Kids*, "What's American about American Poetry?":

> They basically grow it out of sand.
> This is a big help because it was getting pretty enigmatic.
> Welcome to the desert of the real,
> I am an ephemeral and not too discontented citizen.
> I do not think the revolution is finished.[21]

The Baudrillardian "desert of the real," now more familiar to us from *The Matrix*, is—after all—a biblical desert of unredeemed wandering. Baudrillard's famous essay "The Precession of Simulacra" opens with a simulacral "quotation" from Ecclesiastes and begins as a meditation on the death of God. But Clover has none of Baudrillard's enraged despair with the Left. Although "the revolution" that Clover counterposes to "the desert of the real" is happening in a suspended grammar, detached from an object, that suspension may occur just because "the revolution" has a temporality hard for him to see. Even the poem's fainting last line—"I drift, mainly I drift"—recalls the situationist *dérive*, the deliberately unregulatable "drift" that is meant to restore life to a too-regular city.

"Ceriserie," Clover's first poem in *The Totality for Kids*, meditates hungrily on where such life might hide:

> Music: the unless of a certain series.
> Mathematics: Everyone rolling dice and flinging Fibonacci, going
>   to the opera, counting everything.
> Fire: The number between four and five.
> Gold leaf: Wedding dress of the verb *to have*, it reminds you of of.

There is a tiny messianic message, let me start by saying, even in the "unless of a certain series": that music can withhold exact certainty from the "certain series," or that there can be no truth unless there is music—not the rushed cacophony of everyone "going to the opera, counting everything," but the music of "fire," of what's *between* the numbers, unaccountable. "Fire" is the poem's first foray into another materiality, the *serie-serie* of the "Ceriserie," the series-series that both rests humbly in the interstices of the tossed dice of items in series and also promises to overthrow them by lighting up as pun and performance: "Fire" is the tissue binding "four" and "five"—the tissue that, un-knotted and bright red, turns items into relationships, and numbers into words.

Not so "Gold leaf," which a few lines before the ones I've quoted is associated with Enguerrand Quarton, the fifteenth-century painter who applied it so heavily. Unlike "Fire," the "Gold leaf" represents, like the "robots" in Davies's poem, a sweet, bemusing anachronism, an artistic attempt revealed in retrospect as literal-minded; as a nice try; as trumped by subsequent history; as an object, that is, of camp affection. Clover puts it this way later in the poem: "Enguerrand Quarton: In your dream gold leaf was the sun, salve on the visible world." Quarton's "salve," with which he suffused paintings like the *Coronation of the Virgin* (1454), is meant to supervene and redeem mere painterly reference, "the kingdom of the visible"; to give "the verb *to have*" a "wedding dress"; to transform the genitive into the betrothed. But Quarton, endearingly, is a bit of a mess—"swathed," earlier in the poem, "in gold paint" and "whispering come with me under the shadow of this gold leaf." He cannot see, that is, the tightening noose of a modernity that will foreclose on any historical alchemy promising to make of possession a relation, a wedding, and that will turn "Gold leaf," instead, into the chill "red rock" of *The Waste Land*.

Robertson doesn't necessarily see this as a problem. In *Debbie*, she writes:

> I do not limit myself: I imitate
> many fancy things such as the dull red
> cloth of literature, its mumbled griefs. (*D*, 609–61)

Although she shares with Clover a commitment to the recuperation of forms of material waste, Robertson has a different sense of what the candidates for recuperation might be, and by what means the recuperation might take place. Indeed, though she says she does not "limit" herself, she is interested in ornament, and its uselessness, and she is everywhere an erotic poet, collaging from both modernity and classical tradition new configurations of old figures for pleasure. Her project, in books like *The Weather* and *XEclogue* as well as in *Debbie*, has been to articulate something like a cyborg pastoral. Writing as one of "Virgil's Bastard Daughters," she highlights at every turn the arbitrary and ideological nature of what she calls "filiation," imagining in "Argument" that history is simply a "library," which might lend momentary legitimacy to a whole variety of recuperative claims: "To narrate origin as lapidary, as irrevocable, is only to have chosen with a styled authority from the ranked aisles of thought." Or elsewhere in the poem: "filius/flunks."

Though Robertson puckishly calls *Debbie* "An Epic," it is really something like a prismatic pastoral, composed of "episodes," "parts," and unpaginated interludes, all gorgeously and adventuresomely typeset in varying text sizes and shades of gray, so that not even the physical matter of the text eludes what Robertson calls "decoration." There is no plot, although there is an astonishing array of poses and also a wide variety of background characters. Though only Debbie speaks in the poem, it is filled with "nurses," "majorettes," "scholars," and "shepherdesses" who loll and stroll and set themselves in the thickly textual landscapes Robertson paints. In a signal passage from an early section called "Party Scene," the speaker asks:

> Do you remember the day we wanted
> to describe everything? We saw a
> euphoria of trees. This was the middle
> ground. Some women lounged on the clipped
> grass, shadows and intelligence moving
> lightly over their skin, compelled by
> the trenchant discussion of sovereignty.
> Others, in the background, rolled their pale
> Trousers to wade in the intimate sea:
> Their crisp gasps matched the waves. Freed scholars
> Strolled slowly in pairs along gravel
> Paths, reading from books the rhetoric
> Of perfidy. Succinct flowers thrust gauche
> Grammars into the air. In the upper
> Left corner improbable clouds grouped

> And regrouped the syntax of polit
> Esse: The feminist sky split open. (*D*, 25–41)

Few poets these days brave this kind of utopian description. Robertson manages it, I think, because of how she foregrounds the "improbable"—not just the "improbable clouds," moving as if in conversation, and not just the "gauche" grammaticality of flowers, as if their principles of growth were at last a language, but also the willful match between the crispnesses of waves and the gasps of the waders who step into them. It is, in short, a willful utopia, which overwrites the "party scene" with an aspect of fulfillment that, it is hinted, cannot be found there. The "euphoria of trees" in the "middle ground," which gets listed first, seems indeed to ground the fanciful projections that follow and preserve, even in the pastoral, a narrative of the liberation required to get there—the "sovereignty" won for women and "freed scholars" by "perfidy," by foregoing claims to legitimacy in favor of claims to ungrounded "intelligence,"which moves lightly, like weather, and opens up history: "The feminist sky split open."

It is perhaps a failure of my own imagination to want to probe such utopian passages for traces of conflict. But Robertson, too, seems to feel that the argument from "decoration"—that it is simply, gloriously, extra; that it is a supplement, and requires no ethical or political justification, no proper "origin"—can't by itself address the problem of the entanglement of decoration in an unredeemed world. In a section of *Debbie* called "As If the World's a Punctured Chit," she writes:

> The bridge and the river are
> not landscape—nor is this forest with its
> archival plenitude and entanglement.
> The clerical earth just exudes itself.
> —and the carved ruckus of milky bark
> spells a long diary of placation
> repeating ad infinitum We want
> to love. We want to love.
> Or the heart's cheap
> Dipthong snaps. Black ink trickles through my arms
> And it has written landscapes. The trees still
> pose embittered questions. Do
> bright thrones yield civil shade? Some day I shall
> laugh at even this obedience, wake

in the middling shade of the library
wander freely, calling out a name I hope (*D*, 316–31)

This is a world not only overcome by a tyranny of exchange-value—
made a "chit"—but used, "punctured," done with. It is still a richly
textual scene—the forests' knotted plenty is "archival," and the trees
are transcriptions of a "clerical earth" that is still, even deflated, writing itself—but the archive doesn't yield "euphoria" here so much as a
lonely, sad demand: "We want to love," repeated in each mute material
thrust of life up from earth, and bleeding out of every love-tattoo cut
into "milky bark." Even "the heart" breaks down into *he-art*, just what
the thundering "feminist sky" should have rinsed clear.

The lines after the "heart's cheap / Dipthong" seem crucial. Here
and elsewhere in *Debbie*, Robertson equates ink with blood, writing
with the body, and the poem with the landscape; but the embodied,
erotic writing she vaunts is written, we can see, not only as a monologue: "The trees still / pose embittered questions." What they want
to know, it turns out, is something about what the women in the earlier
pastoral were discussing, that is, something about sovereignty: "Do /
bright thrones yield civil shade?" It's a way of asking, you might say,
whether mercy is a quality of Enlightenment: unanswerable question.
And it obliges Robertson to turn, once more, to a dialectical "Some
day" that will not only shed but also recuperate the pain of mute embittered questioning: "Some day I shall / laugh at even this obedience."
It is more persuasive, in its way, than the full-blown pastoral of "Party
Scene," since it foregrounds not the fancy of pure correspondences
(between gasps and waves, clouds and syntax) but a not-quite posthistorical humanity where mediation, where language, has survived: one
"wakes" from the nightmare of history into the tree-like "shade" of a
library, no less, where there is world and time now for a future-anterior
repair, and for the enjoyment of yearning: "calling out a name."

Rod Smith approaches the problem of a damaged materiality not so
much by setting the scene for the pronunciation of a name as by meditating on the allegorical character of objects. And he finds, in his astonishing book *The Good House*, a moving inadequacy in their materiality:

The good house feels bad about
The territory
                    —the house seems
to be a verb though it dislikes

the term 'housing'—the house
seems to be a bad dog & a
live wire—the house is bored
until people come over—the house
is anxious to please guests—
it is stupid & so thinks cordon
means love—it is wise & so
chooses—

This "house" is, yes, anthropomorphized, and allegorized, given attributes and placed in relationships, but part of the achievement of *The Good House* is that the "house" is never left lying in a single rhetorical register or allowed to become only allegory, only anthropomorphic figure. It moves instead among modes of abstraction and concretion so ceaselessly that, reading the book, we are finally obliged to understand it as a kind of perpetually collapsing second-order allegory that performs and figures the vicissitudes of materiality—its dissatisfaction with itself *as material*—before our eyes, and for our ears.

This sounds essentially de Manian, I know—and Smith's writing is extraordinary in obliging readers to confront the movement between the figural and the performative that de Man argued was the very character of the materiality of language.[22] But for Smith, the character of materiality, even at its most mute, its most formal, is historical—that is, it acts out and compasses its inadequacy as material. As Smith puts it: "There are 8 houses in the heart, / there should be 9." Even the figural, these lines suggest, is not free from what it ought to be but isn't. There is no reason the "8 houses in the heart" shouldn't—or couldn't, for a more satisfied poet—complete the strophe; but the figure of the "8 houses in the heart" cannot be unhitched, for Smith, from what should be there. It is a historical and material condition of "the house" to fail to be self-sufficient:

the good house—it is heavy
the good house—it exercises
hope in the inhuman, is transformed
by it—
    becomes blatant in its strength
    & is destroyed, the good
    house must be rebuilt
    carefully. The good house

          is in conflict
ordinary houses complete
the smart bombs and are
buoyant—victorious,
brainwaves of shunt commotion,
bestial then or not house

The "inhuman" and the "bestial," here, are meant as a critique of "blatant strength" as the "buoyant" self-congratulation that forgets, in the midst of linguistic play, the *ought* at the heart of materiality— that it could be otherwise, that it could be, as Adorno might say, more humane: "there should be 9."

For Davies, meanwhile, the material world is overwhelming, and not in a nice way. As he puts it in "Karnal Bunt":

There's nothing superficial about the way all that stuff burrows
    into any available crack
in the sidewalk, growing back, covering, by logical extension if
    not in fact, *everything*. (*C*, 61)

"All that stuff," in Davies's poems, is the frightening array of material that has become commodified in late capitalism—not just the recognizably thing-like widgets on sale at the hardware store but also the "node[s] / of expansion-contraction" whose materiality lies as much in their enmeshing network of objects as in the objects themselves. In the lines above, that network congeals momentarily, as it does in the untitled robot poem, around italicized speech, around the "*everything*" that is meant at once as the moment of collating divergent objects in the "expansion-contraction" but also as the moment where the attempt to collate fails, and falls back on emphasis.

Elsewhere in "Karnal Bunt," those italics are replaced with the comedy of pretending to have a lived attachment to incommensurably abstract, and complexly nested, nominalizations:

I love to be an international unit in the measure of the loading of
    the fissures in the communal membrane into silos on a prairie
    in a basement by a government of souls in trouble at a party for
    a long time (*C*, 54)

This nesting of abstract objects, and the pointed political irony of pretending that we can "love" them, are part of an argument in Davies about the character of materiality in late capitalism. Like Smith, Davies sees the stuff of the world as wrong in its very quiddity. Where Marx, in the famous lines from "Theses on Feuerbach," italicizes the word "change"—"The philosophers have only *interpreted* the world, in various ways; the point, however, is to *change* it"—Davies writes, in one of the first poems in *Comp.*: "The point, however, is to change *it*" (*C*, 19). As with Smith, materiality for Davies is not something worked on by historical conditions but actually produced by them: to change the world will have to be to change *it*, the stuff of the world, no aspect of which is simply "pure" material, unhistorical; or, as Davies puts it a few lines later in the same poem: "Class violence at the level of the seedling." Polemical, yes; but not, in *Comp.*, ungrounded. The book's central poem, "Karnal Bunt," names a fungal disease affecting wheat—wheat that the United States, affected by Karnal bunt in the late 1990s, managed to convince its trade partners not to scrutinize too closely.[23]

What I like so much about Davies's poems is the unembarrassed glee with which he asks to be read polemically; indeed, at least one version of his argument about the saturation of the world with appalling materializations of ever-tighter webs of capitalist relation is that we should not, at this point, even be arguing about whether or not such a web exists. And, again, the polemic is italic: "*You* know, the fact that we're ruled by the money that owns the people who have the money that rules itself—. . . ." (*C*, 53).

I hope I've managed to show that the "votive" or propositional modes of expectation to which these poems gravitate implicitly distinguish them from the "dark art" of the modernism we know best, in the academy, and from the blankness and euphoria Jameson suggests belong to the art of the postmodern. It is impossible to say, reading poems like these, whether we have therefore gone backward or forward—whether, for instance, these poems return us to the type of expectation Siegfried Kracauer attributed, in the Weimar period, to "those who wait" while history horribly, unpredictably, seems to rouse itself into the form of a capital "H."[24] Certainly the comparison is tempting, though our conditions are different. What most chastens me on the edge of historical comparison, however, is the presence in these poems of types of materiality so gossamer, so nearly abstract—so nearly nonexistent—that they feel as if they could come to us only from the fragile singularity of the history of the present.

And the types of expectation by which Clover and Robertson, Smith and Davies animate such material feel similarly fragile, partly because they seem to reside neither in the form nor the content of the poems but somehow in their stance, in what Adorno would have called their "comportment." "Great works wait," he writes, and their waiting is one way to think about the relation of their form to their content, of their politics to their aesthetics: it is unfulfilled.[25] This is especially true of a poetry that recognizes that even its awareness of the obsolescence of its materials, as a literary strategy, is obsolete. It is in this sense that the poems I've been reading in this essay feel more like models than just instances—models of an aesthetics, at once enacted and theorized, groping for the future in the suffering of its materials.

I'd like to say a bit, in closing, about what I imagine are some of the questions left hanging by my discussion of these poems. First, I have foregrounded my own enthusiasm for them rather than subjecting them to critique; and second, I have focused, in reading them, on something like their content rather than their form. I have highlighted their preoccupations, that is, more than their techniques. What are the dangers for contemporary reading practice of a sympathetic, content-focused aesthetics? What might be its promise?

I think the most obvious risks run by the critical practice I've been testing here are a failure of critical distance and a literal-mindedness about content—so that a descriptive, advocating criticism is endangered by the possibility of becoming nothing more than an accompaniment to its object: packaging. Fair enough. Sympathy, and advocacy on the basis of content, runs counter to some of the most powerful and positive developments in late-twentieth-century literary studies—such as theory's claim to have extricated itself from pseudoneutral assessments of value, or the attempts in feminism, queer theory, and U.S. ethnic and postcolonial studies to reveal pseudo-innocent content as a component of historical form.

These projects make up the center of my own training, and I hold them dear. But I think we're at an impasse in literary studies, on the way to which we have sacrificed the critical potential of appreciation and advocacy in favor of what has become a rote "problematization" of texts, and a sadly narrow practice of appreciation that is only able to find subversiveness to admire. But what if the texts we admire, even the politically engaged ones, turn out to be not subversive? What if their political efficacy has been evacuated or is pending? Ascribing performative success to these objects—to pick one of our favorite strategies of the last decade—and equating that capacity for performance with agency doesn't seem to do justice to the theoretical power of the idea of performativity, which I take to lie not in our applauding the aesthetic object's performance but in our being unable to pin down when the performance is finished. Crucial to the sympathetic reading practice I want to advocate is an understanding that critical acts are not discrete. To dismiss appreciative or content-driven readings of texts on the grounds that they are insufficiently politicized, insufficiently counterhegemonic, is to mistake the work of countering hegemony (if that's what we're doing) as individual work. When I read a text that interests me, especially for its political-affective comportment, my impulse, my *critical* impulse, is: pass it on. Highlight it as best you can, read against the grain, or with it where you can, and make sure others take a look. This is as true for texts that I find repulsive as for those I admire: I don't imagine myself, as a critic, judging *by myself*.

This sense of critical reading as a self-insufficient act has historiographical implications for the dynamic of form and content. In particular, I think it is a living link both to camp and Left-messianic traditions of interpretation, for if both traditions insist that waste and trivia are potentially recuperable, they also imply that we might not be the final judges of what, in the object, was form, and what content. For instance, in reading some post-Language poems here, I have foregone looking at their (very interesting) line breaks and habits of syntax—not because these don't strike me as important but because those features of the poems are not what is most vividly emergent in them when they are grouped together. On the other hand, though I have been trying to foreground what I've called the preoccupations of these poems, those preoccupations don't quite amount to content either. I have been trying to articulate a stance or relation to a cultural problem that the poems are grappling with, which is the problem of how to have a live relationship to a material world whose temporal-spatial character is unreadable: an obsolescence on top of an obsolescence. The polemical affections of these poems for a "good house," or a "feminist sky," or for the lavish misguided-ness of an Enguerrand Quarton, are, yes, a kind of content; but they are also a relation to content—in other words, a kind of form.

It is the polemical character of this poetic stance that interests me most right now, since it is something we might imitate in our emerging critical practices. And what seems freshly polemical about some of my favorite post-Language writing—what I think we might treat as a model—is its sense that polemic is the element of the negative in affection, or in judgment. A critical or artistic attachment is polemical, dangerous even, not because of which protagonist it has chosen but because it models what it's like not to know the whole story of its object. The dream of a redeemed matter, that is, doesn't entail a positive vision of what that redemption will look like so much as a resistance to the idea that it will look like any one thing we know.

This seems to me the provoking thing about post-Language poetry's polemical affection, or its camp messianism: it is a new and interesting way of writing from within the presumption of totality. This is a large part of why I like these poems so much. And if we were to pick up on these cues and risk writing to our peers about what we admire or revile (without neutralizing our opinions in advance by assuring our colleagues that yes, we too wish for the overthrow of hegemonic systems), I don't think we'd be giving ourselves over to a depoliticized humanism, or to mere impressionistic whimsy, so much as fostering a refreshed, and refreshing, negativity. Kevin Davies:

> These cheesy little hypertexts
> are going to get better.
> I don't know
> how *much* better, but *we'll see*. (*C*, 67)

University of California, Berkeley

Notes

1   See Theodor Adorno, *Minima Moralia: Reflections from Damaged Life*, trans. E. F. N. Jephcott (New York: Verso, 1996); Susan Stewart, *Poetry and the Fate of the Senses* (Chicago: Univ. of Chicago Press, 2001).

2   See Theodor Adorno and Max Horkheimer, *The Dialectic of Enlightenment*, ed. Gunzelin Schmid Noerr, trans. Edmund Jephcott (Stanford, Calif.: Stanford Univ. Press, 2002); Fredric Jameson, *Postmodernism, or the Cultural Logic of Late Capitalism* (Durham, N.C.: Duke Univ. Press, 1991).

3   In the vast lay literature on the post–World War II financial system and its vulnerabilities, see David C. Korten, *When Corporations Rule the World* (Bloomfield, Conn.: Kumarian Press, 1995); Nicholas Guyatt, *Another*

American Century? The United States and the World after 2000 (New York: St. Martin's, 2001); Randy Martin, *The Financialization of Daily Life* (Philadelphia: Temple Univ. Press, 2002); and Harry Shutt, *The Trouble with Capitalism: An Enquiry into the Causes of Global Economic Failure* (London: Zed Books, 1998).

4   Andrew Ross, "Uses of Camp," in *Camp: Queer Aesthetics and the Performing Subject; A Reader*, ed. Fabio Cleto (Ann Arbor: Univ. of Michigan Press, 1999), 320. First published in the *Yale Journal of Criticism* (fall 1988): 1–24.

5   Kevin Davies, untitled frontispiece, *Comp.* (Washington, D.C.: Edge Books, 2000). Further references to *Comp.* will be cited parenthetically in the text as *C*.

6   In a very helpful essay called "Globalit, Inc.; Or, the Cultural Logic of Global Literary Studies," Ian Baucom makes use of the figures of expansion and contraction to characterize the current mode of capitalism (*PMLA* [January 2001]: 158–72). He deploys these terms to invest the rhetoric of globalization with a cautionary note: the "expansion" of capital, he insists, means also its "contraction," that is, its concentration in fewer hands. Baucom offers this cautionary coinage in order to work against what he sees as a potentially romanticizing tendency to model literary studies on a new global situation that is, in fact, an uneven global marketplace. I take Baucom's caution seriously; it is one reason I will rely here on the Frankfurtian diction of a *totality*, whatever its problems, rather than on the word *globalization*.

7   Walter Benjamin, "Theses on the Philosophy of History," in *Illuminations: Essays and Reflections*, ed. Hannah Arendt, trans. Harry Zohn (New York: Schocken Books, 1969), 254.

8   Lisa Robertson, *Debbie: An Epic* (London: Reality Street Editions, 1997). *Debbie* has no page numbers; further references will be cited parenthetically in the text as *D*, using line numbers.

9   Rod Smith, *The Good House* (New York: Spectacular Books, 2001), n.p.

10   For a discussion of the character of "official verse culture" (which is Charles Bernstein's phrase, coined long after the 1950s in reference to poetry of the 1980s), see James E. B. Breslin, *From Modern to Contemporary: American Poetry, 1945–1965* (Chicago: Univ. of Chicago Press, 1983).

11   For one consideration of the political background of Language poetry, especially in terms of its relation to the new social movements, see Eleana Kim, "Language Poetry: Dissident Practices and the Makings of a Movement," in Gary Sullivan's online journal *readme* (spring–summer 2001), *home.jps.net/~nada/language2.htm*. Both Kim and Barrett Watten identify the emergence of Language poetry as a politicized avant-garde with the practice of criticism (see Watten, "The Turn to Language and the 1960s," *Critical Inquiry* [autumn 2002]: 139–84). For Kim, this means that

the Language poets, in preserving a small-press "outsider" status into the 1980s, actually ended up setting the stage for their (relative) canonization in university-based literary culture. For Watten, the "turn to language" is articulated in a critical response to the failures of "radical" poets like Denise Levertov to grasp the "insufficiency of language to history" (182). For the Language poets of Watten's generation, this critique led to an exploration of the obduracy, even the opacity, of the relationship between politics and the linguistic sign.

12　The active-reader theory has received a good deal of attention from both post-Language poets and literary critics; see, for example, Alan Gilbert, "re: Reading the Active Reader Theory," *Tripwire* 6 (fall 2002): 118–24; and Charles Altieri, "Some Problems about Agency in the Theories of Radical Poetics," in *Postmodernisms Now: Essays on Contemporaneity in the Arts* (University Park: Penn State Univ. Press, 1998), 166–94.

13　For a key articulation of this theory, see Lyn Hejinian, "The Rejection of Closure," in *The Language of Inquiry* (Berkeley and Los Angeles: Univ. of California Press, 2000), 40–58.

14　Ron Silliman makes his case for understanding reader-writer collaboration as a decommodification of language in the essays collected as *The New Sentence* (New York: Roof Books, 1995).

15　These lines are from "The Poetics of L=A=N=G=U=A=G=E," an essay by Bruce Andrews; see ubuWeb, www.ubu.com/papers/andrews.html (15 April 2004).

16　Lyn Hejinian, *My Life*, 2nd ed. (Los Angeles: Sun and Moon Press, 1987), 84–85.

17　See Lyn Hejinian, *The Language of Inquiry* (Berkeley and Los Angeles: Univ. of California Press, 2000).

18　For excerpts from Hejinian's and Silliman's remarks on this topic, and for responses to them by younger writers, see "Forum: The Blank Generation?" *Newsletter of the St. Mark's Poetry Project* (February–March 2003), 9–14.

19　Fredric Jameson, *Late Marxism: Adorno, or, The Persistence of the Dialectic* (New York: Verso, 1990), 251.

20　For a recent example of this rhetoric of the emergent legibility of empire—American empire, here—see Arundhati Roy, "Mesopotamia. Babylon. The Tigris and Euphrates," *UK Guardian*, 2 April 2003, guardian.co.uk/g2/story/0,3604,927712,00.html. Roy describes the Bush administration's international posture as "tactless imprudence."

21　Joshua Clover, "What's American about American Poetry?" *The Totality for Kids*, unpaginated manuscript.

22　See, for instance, Paul de Man, "Phenomenality and Materiality in Kant," in *Aesthetic Ideology*, ed. Andrej Warminski (Minneapolis: Univ. of Minnesota Press, 1996), 70–90. There is a subtle and exceptionally elegant notion of the historicity of the materiality of writing in de Man, of course, a notion of history as the "occurrence" of the transfer, in writing, between its "cognitive" and "performative" aspects—a notion of history as "the emergence of a language of power out of a language of cognition" ("Kant and Schiller," in *Aesthetic Ideology*, 133). I cannot, here, compare the cognitivisms of, say, Adorno and de Man—another and more daunting project—but I can say, à propos of the two ways of understanding historicity and cognition, that where de Man rejects the idea of a dialectic in the materiality of language, Adorno sees the dialectic as the very form of that materiality—and sees the materiality of thought, furthermore, not as "occurrence," but as what he calls "the need in thinking," which is motivated not by the inadequacy of language to materiality but by its inadequacy to history—by the fact that our material productivity has not yet made of earth a paradise; see Adorno, *Negative Dialectics*, trans. E. B. Ashton (New York: Continuum, 1983), 408; and *Aesthetic Theory*, 33.

23 For a brief history of Karnal bunt, see "Karnal Bunt of Wheat," by R. L. Foster and B. J. Goates, www.uidaho.edu/ag/plantdisease/kbwheat.htm (15 April 2004).

24 See Siegfried Kracauer, "Those Who Wait," in *The Mass Ornament: Weimar Essays*, trans. Thomas Levin (Cambridge: Harvard Univ. Press, 1995), 137.

25 Adorno, *Aesthetic Theory*, 40.

Book Reviews

Gender and Morality in Anglo-American Culture, 1650–1800. By Ruth H. Bloch. Berkeley and Los Angeles: Univ. of California Press. 2003. x, 225 pp. Cloth, $55.00; paper, $21.95.

Democracy, Revolution, and Monarchism in Early American Literature. By Paul Downes. New York: Cambridge Univ. Press. 2002. xii, 239 pp. $55.00.

The recent flurry of transatlantic scholarship would seem to have resituated early American studies in a trans- or postnational context. Yet in the eye of the storm, two recent books defy this new critical trend. Firmly focused on cultural developments in the post-Revolutionary United States, Ruth Bloch and Paul Downes both argue for the importance of previously overlooked factors for subject formation and early nationalism in the new republic. Seeking to (re)introduce the concepts of gender and monarchism into the equation, Bloch and Downes rely on readings of literary and legal texts as well as other eighteenth-century cultural practices. Though different in methodology and theoretical underpinnings, these studies engage many of the same issues and pose similar interventions in the field.

Gender and Morality in Anglo-American Culture is a collection of Bloch's articles written from 1978 to 1994, arranged as chapters, with the addition of two previously unpublished pieces. Despite this unusual format, all the chapters cohere beautifully around the premise of "the overwhelming symbolic significance of gender and family as sites of both individual identity formation and collective socialization" (1). Bloch is more interested in broad religious and economic developments than in national histories; therefore, she discusses the origins of nineteenth-century, white, middle-class views of gender by looking back to colonial developments and, even further, to changes in the position of women brought about by the Reformation. Though Bloch's sweeping view of gender and gender roles from the sixteenth to the nineteenth century is perhaps overly general, it effectively introduces and informs her argument about the early United States.

Methodologically, Bloch objects to the hegemony of Marxist and materialist theories in women's studies, advocating instead a "culturalist" approach in which gender is seen as a symbolic quality that is "at least as much about interconnectedness as [it is] about power" (40). Bloch's first chapter offers an incisive critique of prevailing trends in feminist theory, including psycho-analysis and poststructuralism. Her own counter—or culturalist—approach is perhaps better explained by the ensuing readings than the foundational belief that "gender is embedded in wider systems of meaning" (40). Some of Bloch's chapters ("American Feminine Ideals in Transition: The Rise of the Moral Mother, 1785–1815" and "Republican Virtue: The Gendered Meanings of Virtue in Revolutionary America") are already classics of the critical canon. Others, in particular chapters 4 and 8, that concentrate on the public-private dichotomy are equally insightful.

In chapter 4, Bloch considers the ways in which colonial courtship laws influenced and prescribed an increasingly private process. Seventeenth-century American laws punished fornication, elopement, and courtship without prior consent of the father or the master much more severely than did English laws, thus reinforcing patriarchy and asserting parental control over the emotional attachments of children (81). The practice of suing for breach of promise or for seduction also became particularly popular in early America. Bloch's readings of eighteenth-century trial manuscripts reveal the ascendancy of sentimentalist ideology in the judges' verdicts and their open expression of sympathy for the female victim, especially in the case of one Clarissa Harlowe Boynton (no joke). Bloch convincingly argues that such cases show "the influence upon the law of wider cultural changes in the understanding of gender" (101), thereby demonstrating the effectiveness of her culturalist approach. All Bloch's chapters are worthwhile and, together, they form an excellent collection that is greater than the sum of its parts.

In *Democracy, Revolution, and Monarchism in Early American Literature*, which won the 2003 MLA prize for a first book, Paul Downes argues that monarchism was not only an oppositional defining force but also a persistent characteristic of revolutionary ideology and early American democratic discourse. He sets out to prove that "displaced or translated elements of monarchic political culture can be found at work in key revolutionary ideas and constructs" (5) by reading the works of Crèvecoeur, Brockden Brown, and Irving. Though Downes shares part of his textual corpus with Bloch (most notably Benjamin Franklin's autobiography), their studies differ in methodology and focus. Downes repeatedly cites the political theories of Ernesto Laclau and seems to accept the hermeneutics of deconstruction. He does not fully articulate his interpretative paradigm, however, and at times the citations of Derrida seem obfuscating or simply out of context. Downes's introductory explanations of revolutionary time and grammar and the link between sovereignty and substitution are nevertheless very well formulated.

The first (and best) chapter in the book considers the ritualized executions of effigies of George III in 1776. Downes suggests that because the American revolutionaries were unable to physically kill their King, they killed him metaphorically, in repeated staged performances of regicide. The meaning of this spectacle depends on a shared acknowledgement of the symbolic power vested in a material representation of the king's body. The revolutionaries tried to subvert "the king's privileged relationship to the order of the metaphor" (42) in order to create a new economy of power between the political subject and the material signifier. In a reading heavily influenced by Michael Warner's work, Downes claims that the brand-new Americans went on to construct their political subjectivity not on the hieroglyph but on the alphabetic sign. This chapter offers many excellent interpretations of race, patriarchy, and materiality in the context of the mock executions, and Downes succeeds in tying together a wide variety of texts to prove the residual influence of monarchism on American democratic subjectivity.

However, not all of Downes's chapters are equally convincing. His cursory consideration of Irving, for example, does nothing to strengthen his argument, which can be difficult to follow because of his fragmentary and foreshortened style. Also, the choice of texts seems to reveal a particular penchant for the dead white men, which goes unexplained. Fortunately, his afterword on Cooper's *The Spy* incorporates the previous interpretations into the bigger, monarchical picture. Like Bloch's book, Downes's study presents a valuable new reading of American Revolutionary culture, and it stands as an example of the important work that remains to be done within the confines of American studies and the geographical boundaries of the United States.

Joanne van der Woude, University of Virginia

The Artistry of Anger: Black and White Women's Literature in America, 1820–1860. By Linda M. Grasso. Chapel Hill: Univ. of North Carolina Press. 2002. xi, 249 pp. Cloth, $49.95; paper, $18.95.

The Language of War: Literature and Culture in the U.S. from the Civil War through World War II. By James Dawes. Cambridge: Harvard Univ. Press. 2002. viii, 308 pp. $39.95.

Despite this nation's revolutionary beginnings, literary criticism has generally failed to recognize the centrality of violence and dissent to U.S. culture. Violence occasionally consumes Hawthorne's dream worlds, rage crystallizes in the figure of Ahab or is transferred onto rebellious slaves, and the United States has had to address its destruction of indigenous populations and the violence and aftermath of the Civil War. Nonetheless, such violent literary and historical interludes seldom disrupt the tight, well-ordered composition of U.S. nationalism. But in a terror-obsessed present where violence has moved to center stage, Linda Grasso's *The Artistry of Anger* and James Dawes's *The Language of War* are particularly relevant to emergent theorizations of dissent and violence in the United States.

Grasso argues that anger, when acknowledged as part of the U.S. tradition, is typically coded as masculine, and women are charged with neutralizing it to ensure political order. Complicating this gendered division of social life, Grasso argues that the submerged anger of the U.S. Revolution surfaces in the writing of women who challenged their exclusion from democratic representation. Because it was coded as "treasonous" (61), women's anger is almost never the explicit theme of the texts Grasso analyzes (including Lydia Maria Child's *Hobomok*, Maria Stewart's *Productions*, Fanny Fern's *Ruth Hall*, and Harriet Wilson's *Our Nig*); rather, this anger is a powerful undercurrent in novels that thematize "illness, acts of sacrifice, supplicating tones, captivity motifs, death, hunger, and emaciated bodies" (7).

White women writers, Grasso argues, often expressed anger through displacement. Thus, the Native American character Hobomok is a conduit for a Puritan woman's—and a nineteenth-century reformer's—resistance to patriarchal culture. As this example suggests, Grasso believes that white women writers' expressions of anger frequently depend on a not-so-subtle racism and classism. Middle-class, white womanhood, with its creed of "moral emotionalism," is kept intact when women writers displace less than pious emotions onto nonwhite or lower-class characters who are chastened by women characters claiming the disciplinary power of white masculinity. African American women writers, however, resist such disciplinary efforts. Maria Stewart, for example, articulates her anger by appropriating the power of an Old Testament God who criticizes gender and racial discrimination, and Harriet Wilson's *Our Nig* refuses the ideology of moral exceptionalism that was imperfectly available to black women. Moreover, "unlike many of her white peers, Wilson does not mask her desire to secure retribution" (184).

Grasso imagines that marginalized writers occupy a space of freedom from which the constraints of the dominant culture can be resisted more easily. However, a sustained analysis of marginality as something other than the inverse of white womanhood might provide a fuller account of African American resistance to white U.S. culture. It's also worth noting that Grasso, like many Americanists, assumes that the preoccupation of marginalized writers is inevitably U.S. nationalism or its possible reformation, even though most of the texts she discusses are not national allegories.

James Dawes's study of war literatures from the Civil War to the Geneva Conventions is structured by the debate between broadly poststructuralist and neo-universalist accounts of language: is language coextensive with violence (as poststructuralism's "disciplinary model" would suggest), or is it opposed to violence (as the neo-universalist, Habermasian "emancipatory model" argues)? Given that each of these questions can be aptly answered "sometimes," it might seem that they are unproductively broad. However, Dawes uses these speculations to develop strikingly original analyses of U.S. culture. Much of the energy of *The Language of War* comes from his engagement with understudied texts (including Ulysses S. Grant's *Memoirs*, William Sherman's *Memoirs*, Louisa May Alcott's *Hospital Sketches*, Walt Whitman's *Drum Taps*, William Faulkner's *A Fable*, and documents from various Geneva Conventions), though he also offers substantial readings of several canonical texts, most notably Stephen Crane's *The Red Badge of Courage*, Ernest Hemmingway's *A Farewell to Arms*, and Joseph Heller's *Catch 22*. Dawes's theoretical approach is most influenced by Heidegger, Arendt, and Scarry, though he also cogently summarizes the work of Kant, Clausewitz, Bataille, Ricoeur, the Frankfurt school, de Beauvoir, Goffman, Foucault, Habermas, and Nagel. While sometimes obfuscating his argument, Dawes's lyrical style and theoretical divagations leave readers in a meditative mood.

Dawes juxtaposes texts and genres to great effect. His first chapter, for instance, interrogates the relation of objectivity, subjectivity, and sympathy via readings of memoirs, poetry, sketches, philosophy, and a novella. In chapter 2, Heidegger's philosophical account of tools is provocatively read against World War I novels. And in his brilliant fifth chapter, Dawes joins organizational theory with novels by Heller and Faulkner to investigate how language, discipline, and agency function in late-twentieth-century social structures.

Dawes's implicit project is to reconcile poststructural and neo-universal accounts of language: because tools, including language, can be weapons, one cannot argue (as neo-universalists do) that language is an ethical force that works against violence. But because tools, especially language, are also constructive and help to reorient or stop violence, one also cannot argue (as poststructuralists do) that language inevitably leaves a violent residue on the material world. Unfortunately, this reconciliation proceeds through a rather weak version of theory that values poststructuralism for its capacity to suspend judgment. Dawes argues that theory might be understood as a "plea for humility, as an injunction to . . . question our terms and even to leave them perpetually open to the possibility of resignification" (216). Although this is a fine plan, the poststructuralist position should not be reduced to advocacy of humility and reexamination. In short, Dawes's effort to reconcile neo-universalism and poststructuralism fails to grant that the central assumptions and methodologies of each position are largely incompatible.

Dawes's interrogation of violence, like Grasso's, challenges assumptions that U.S. culture resists violence and converts dissent into consent. Both books make clear that terrorism, violence, and radical dissent can neither be dismissed as antagonistic to nationalism nor admitted as aberrations that suture it.

Monique Allewaert, Duke University

Caribbean Autobiography: Cultural Identity and Self-Representation. By Sandra
Pouchet Paquet. Madison: Univ. of Wisconsin Press. 2002. xii, 345 pp. Cloth,
$60.00; paper, $24.95.

Scarring the Black Body: Race and Representation in African American Literature.
By Carol E. Henderson. Columbia: Univ. of Missouri Press. 2002. xiii, 184 pp.
$32.50.

Voices of the Fugitives: Runaway Slave Stories and Their Fictions of Self-Creation.
By Sterling Lecater Bland Jr. Westport, Conn.: Greenwood. 2002. xviii, 184 pp.
Cloth, $73.95; paper, $23.95.

These studies address the self-representation of people of color and the tensions that emerge between the self and cultural forces that surround it, including not only the immediate ethnic community but also expectations and assumptions of larger national and even international communities. Each author interrogates how writers negotiate a public self in the midst of these often competing influences.

In a most ambitious undertaking, Sandra Pouchet Paquet examines the multiplicity of self-expression in *Caribbean Autobiography*. Complicating the notion of autobiography as an account of personal and public elements of an individual life, Paquet introduces Caribbean culture as a multifaceted factor in itself. Paquet mirrors the Caribbean's multiplicity, due to its colonial and multiethnic past, by interpreting no less than sixteen texts that range from nineteenth-century women's narratives to twentieth-century autobiographies. Paquet expands our notions of autobiography by examining other literary forms, such as travel and conversion narratives, within traditional prose autobiography and by considering a poem as well as fragmented personal narratives. What these different genres and authors share, Paquet insists, is a tendency to create intricate identities that utilize the multidimensional backdrop of Caribbean culture.

Despite their commonality, these writers differ widely, Paquet argues, in their explorations of their Caribbean context, expressing sentiments ranging from nostalgia to ambivalence to antipathy. Challenging the notion of home as a celebrated sanctuary, Mary Seacole's *The Wonderful Adventures of Mrs. Seacole in Many Lands* "disengages the autobiographical subject from the Jamaican community and repositions her in the metropolitan heart of the empire" (62). As a result, Mrs. Seacole adopts a colonial perspective that precludes any sympathy for Jamaica. Claude McKay's two autobiographies divide his consciousness into African American and Jamaican portions. *A Long Way from Home* fashions McKay's persona as a citizen of anywhere except Jamaica, while *My Green Hills of Jamaica* celebrates him as a native son. Rather than a stable site, the Caribbean figures as an ever changing factor as individuals shape their life stories to achieve particular goals.

In *Scarring the Black Body*, Carol Henderson explores self-representation in the context of African American fiction. The body becomes the literal and figurative text employed by black writers to articulate a public self. While the larger society, Henderson writes, reinforces the notion of African Americans' inferiority by inflicting wounds and scars upon the black body, black writers use those body markings as "metaphor[s] for the reinvention of African American subjectivity" (7); they represent both the trauma of wounding and the process of healing. Henderson's critical paradigm combines "body woundedness," which centralizes the physical body as a text, with DuBois's concept of double consciousness and with methods used in cultural studies to examine the psychological and literary ramifications of wounding.

Henderson finds continuity in African American literary experience by linking wounding in the antebellum and postbellum eras. Slavery's harshness clearly represents a site of wounding for African Americans, and Henderson identifies Reconstruction (with its violent acts, such as lynching) as a continuation of the scarring of the black body. Viewed in this light, Toni Morrison's *Beloved* is about reconciling "the freed body and the enslaved soul/psyche" by acknowledging the physical and psychological wounds of slavery (88). Those psychological wounds are mirrored in fiction about the modern African American experience, where the trauma emanates from the urban experience. The characters in Ann Petry's *The Street*, Henderson writes, are "bruised by the many systems of oppression that regulate them to poverty, obscurity, and even death" (113).

Sterling Bland's exploration of slave narratives represents a middle ground between Paquet's study of autobiography and Henderson's examination of fiction. Bland distinguishes the fugitive slave narrative, which seeks to find meaning in an individual life and uses rhetorical strategies to that end, from the slave narrative in general, which uses an individual life to critique slavery. Using a DuBoisean double consciousness, writers of fugitive slave narratives create a public self that engages societal expectations of propriety and behavior, confronts distortions of the narrative produced by prefatory material and editing by abolitionists, and honors obligations to the masses of enslaved African Americans who need a spokesperson to articulate their experience.

Techniques of masking become key as the authors of fugitive slave narratives attempt to relate their experiences in their own voices while meeting the expectations of readers. The use of such techniques belies DuBois's assumption that the "warring ideals" can be resolved through a variety of rhetorical strategies to engage the conflict, for authors of fugitive slave narratives often fail to reconcile their obligations to their constituencies and themselves. In his *Narrative*, Frederick Douglass creates a voice that is simultaneously individual and dependent on the cultural moment. But in *My Bondage and My Freedom*, where Douglass articulates his identity as a public figure, Bland argues, "his ability to extend himself beyond the constraints of the rubric in which he was forced to write and the ways in which he was able to construct himself ultimately fell short of [his] vision of himself" (117).

All three authors view self-representation as more than an exercise in personal expression, identifying in the writings they examine an agenda that engages specific historical and cultural contexts. Paquet's examination necessarily takes into consideration the impact of colonialization on the way these writers view their homeland and their relationship to it. Similarly, Bland and Henderson ground their discussion of the articulation of a public self in the African American experience of slavery, and both cite the accumulation of assumptions about African Americans in the larger U.S. culture as a factor with which writers of fiction and fugitive slave narratives must contend.

Paquet's focus on the multiplicity found in Caribbean autobiography highlights the impact of a diasporic perspective on self-representation, while both Bland and Henderson focus on the individual within a U.S. society that consistently relegated African Americans to second-class status. Paquet's consideration of colonialization points to complex modes of self-representation, not just in relation to a homeland, real or imagined, but to a global context that features an ever changing relationship to colonial powers as well as other noncolonial states. Her interrogation of McKay's shift from downplaying to celebrating his Jamaican childhood reveals how changing international affinities affect the public self. Nevertheless, these studies provide a comprehensive examination of the personal narratives of a variety of people of African descent.

Crystal S. Anderson, Ohio University

Reconstituting the American Renaissance: Emerson, Whitman, and the Politics of Representation. **By Jay Grossman. Durham, N.C.: Duke Univ. Press. 2003. xii, 273 pp. Cloth, $59.95; paper, $19.95.**

Whitman Possessed: Poetry, Sexuality, and Popular Authority. **By Mark Maslan. Baltimore: Johns Hopkins Univ. Press. 2001. xii, 221 pp. $41.95.**

Calling Emerson and Whitman a crucial nineteenth-century (non)pair, Jay Grossman begins *Reconstituting the American Renaissance* by examining the constitutional debates to which both were, in some measure, responding. Grossman argues that "the distinction between the political and the literary is itself profoundly complicated in an American context in which language-making and nation-making are so profoundly inter-implicated" (4). The constituting to which his title refers is thus a witty evocation of the Constitution itself, the founding document from which Grossman's argument takes its origin, and another word for any kind of writing that depends on "an original foundational fluidity" (7). Describing "the nation's persistent conversation on the nature of political representation"—a "conversation," Grossman adds, that has not always been carried out verbally—*Reconstituting* finds in the Founders' "theme (and scheme) of representation" a structuring "rhetoric" for subsequent generations (2). Although Grossman's opening example is a narrow one, drawn from a 1999 Supreme Court decision involving the Census Bureau and its project of statistical sampling for purposes of congressional apportionment, this is not a book that assumes a reader with an extensive background in legal and political theory. Rather, its contribution lies in its understanding of the ambiguity of constitutional rhetoric and its compelling reading of nontotalizing, yet pivotal, episodes in the careers of Emerson and Whitman.

As it turns out, it is not necessary to share Grossman's passionate interest in the Constitution and the debates over its ratification to appreciate his reexamination of Whitman's indebtedness, or lack thereof, to Emerson. Following the intricate opening moves, *Reconstituting* reads Emerson and Whitman within larger discursive and material contexts, "structured by the concept of 'representation' in its multiple senses, only partially stabilized in the complex disagreements of the Founders" (6). For example, Emerson's use of his father's notebooks anchors a chapter on "Class Actions," and the discussion does indeed demonstrate that "[t]o examine the class-inflected dynamics present in the writings of these two men makes visible features of their relationship previously obscured" (121). The chapter concludes with a brilliant reading of Christopher Pearse Cranch's illustration of the "transparent eye-ball" passage in *Nature*, which furthers Grossman's argument that even as a visionary, Emerson sought to dominate his social inferiors. Throughout, Emerson is faulted for his class-based elitism and for standing above and apart, even from his own audiences. Whitman, on the other hand, is described as having inherited the socioeconomic position of a free white laborer, an inheritance that determines important features of his more democratic poetic, for example, its lack of irony. (Irony is conceived as a trope that depends on hierarchy.) Despite Grossman's initial overinsistence on the homogeneity of Whitman's class affiliation, a flesh-and-blood literary worker soon emerges, in no small measure because he is granted his "autocratic tendencies" (147). Grossman's concluding chapter offers a reading of the journalist–poet-to-be in New Orleans that is a classic of its kind, emphasizing "Emerson's and Whitman's shared reliance in their depictions of the human body on rhetorics associated with the practices of American slavery" (163).

Whitman Possessed also links the emergence of *Leaves of Grass* to a crisis of political representation in the antebellum period, but the book's focus, at least initially, is narrower; and rather than unsettling the disciple model, Mark Maslan invokes Emerson's understanding of poetic inspiration to argue that Whitman understood his creativity as emanating from forces beyond his control. Although this idea may seem overintellectualized and counterintuitive, it provides a useful purchase on Whitman's construction of sexuality and his seemingly grandiose aspirations for his poetry. Thus chapter 1 examines Whitman's indebtedness to the sexual-hygiene literature of his day, chapter 2 delves further into the model of Whitman and sexual agency developed therein, while the book's accumulating power emerges in chapter 3, in which a vampiric poet experiments with the language of blood. Here, in discussing "Masses and Muses," Maslan opens up a potential debate about the schism between Whitman's intentions and his effects, explaining that Whitman's insistence on his "representative function," and on the representative function of his language, can have the effect of "distancing us from the objects of representation" (137). A theoretical concluding chapter, "Lines of Penetration," addresses sexual and authorial agency in the writings of Derrida, Foucault, Judith Butler, and Leo Bersani. Though of interest in its own right, this chapter does not advance Maslan's historicized, Whitman-specific conversation. Moreover, this chapter leads to the conclusion that "literary critics in general need to understand sex and politics more contextually than poststructuralist theory permits" (170). Why invoke poststructuralist theory at such length, if only to dismiss it?

Maslan's combination of theoretical sophistication and contextual breadth produces consistently stimulating readings of familiar and unfamiliar texts. Yet because of his determination to present Whitman's career as itself a work of art, predicated on the partial disappearance of the desiring author, *Whitman Possessed* omits poems and passages from poems that might subvert the unity, and the severity, of the argument. This tendency to ignore contrary evidence leads to a statement such as the following, about Whitman's Civil War: "In fact, the sexual dimension of Whitman's relationship with the soldiers is, in his [Whitman's] view, integral to his ability to stand for them, and by standing for them he represents the nation" (136). This is a tantalizing statement, but Whitman's view needs to be challenged and tested by a fuller picture not only of his aspirations but also of his effects on the young men he desired. Notwithstanding its comparative insensitivity to this kind of interpersonal erotic issue, *Whitman Possessed* adds an important dimension to our collective understanding of why so many different readers have responded positively, as Maslan puts it, to "Whitman's genius for making everything hang upon what he doesn't tell us" (125).

Vivian R. Pollak, Washington University, St. Louis

Civil Wars: American Novelists and Manners, 1880–1940. By Susan Goodman. Baltimore: Johns Hopkins Univ. Press. 2003. xvii, 198 pp. $40.00.

Social Reform, Taste, and the Construction of Virtue in American Literature, 1870–1910. By Janice H. Koistinen-Harris. Lewiston, N.Y.: Edwin Mellen. 2002. iii, 190 pp. $109.95.

These two books take on the pedigreed quip that American society, apparently lacking manners, must also lack novels about them. Received from and reiterated by quotable America watchers from Alexis de Tocqueville to Henry

James to Lionel Trilling, this observation has it that the social thinness and professed egalitarianism of U.S. society offer insufficient behavioral grist for a form generated by the relatively stratified social relations of European society.

Susan Goodman's *Civil Wars: American Novelists and Manners* denies this outright. Arguing that manners are in fact "a defining quality in our literature," she assembles texts from a range of canonical figures (William Dean Howells, Henry James, Edith Wharton, Willa Cather, Ellen Glasgow, and Jessie Fauset) who "embraced the protean nature of manners and of novel writing" (xi, xii). Unlike much recent scholarship on taste and manners, Goodman's project leaves open the broader cultural construction of subjectivity, focusing instead on the literary elements of the novel of manners as "an evolving form, responsive to the persistent recomposition of American classes and culture and crucial to an understanding of American history" (xiii). In practice, this means that Goodman's archive briefly considers supplemental and comparative material but engages mostly with questions of theme and style, authors' lives, letters, and career-long preoccupations revolving around the "the twin questions of civilization and manners" (150). In the context of this world of letters, Goodman shows each of the writers in question to have participated in a project of enlarging the range of novelistic engagement with social conventions. Her foci include Howells and "middle-class family life"; James and the "encroachment of modernity"; Wharton and "the commodification of an increasingly international culture"; Cather and "the lives of indigenous peoples"; and Glasgow and "the rural poor" (11).

Foregrounding questions of taste and manners leads Goodman to a number of new perspectives on the literary production of her subjects. Wharton, for example, becomes an author whose career significantly began with the publication of a domestic manual, *The Decoration of Houses*. Wharton's fiction then seems to hover around this particular aesthetic aperture, at the intersection of material culture and social behavior, from which Goodman examines Wharton's existence between France and America as one that lent "a spatial dimension to manners as well as history" (63). Howells, whose prudery in print was a cherished topic even among his supporters, becomes a figure finely registering the social idiosyncrasies of nascent managerial capitalism by laying bare "the political and commercial significance of manners," in which "the tipping of a hat brim might betray an entire system of power" (17). Following the trail of represented manners to the pages of the *Crisis* and the work of its then literary editor Jessie Fauset, Goodman elaborates on their varied functions, which advocated, on one hand, a discourse of demure social endogamy—polite separatism for safety's sake—and, on the other, racial uplift as a project of self-mastery in which justice would be achieved through the acquisition of polished social carriage.

Working along different textual lines, Janice Koistinen-Harris traces a trajectory with analogous endpoints. In *Social Reform, Taste, and the Construction of Virtue in American Literature*, Koistinen-Harris complicates the socioaesthetic discourse of taste, pursuing it from late-nineteenth-century journalism aimed at the white upper and middle classes to organs of African American uplift in the first decades of the twentieth century. Bringing together the historical study of late-nineteenth-century texts with a Bourdieu-inflected inquiry into the social field constellated by taste, Koistinen-Harris reads the aesthetic prescriptions of the rhetoric of uplift as central in determining social status. Her main concern is a version of class identity that is both economically and discursively constructed at the intersection of "economic resources and identity—between money and virtue" (5). While Goodman's readings show manners to be a wrongfully neglected subject, Koistinen-Harris's analysis foregrounds the abundance of pedagogical discourse attesting to anxiety over their putative absence. Koistinen-Harris's readings of uplift tracts and progressive journalism suggest that the reformist gaze, contrary to theories that focus on its interpolating tendencies and surveilling imperatives aimed at the masses, just as frequently "addressed middle- and upper-class standards and behavior—and often in critical terms" (7). This reverse angle makes her account one in which the classes view the masses in order to keep tabs on their precarious selves. Koistinen-Harris's account presents a reflexive ethics of reform writing that can't help but also turn its didactic faculties on the reader, complicating accounts of uplift discourse as a disciplinary apparatus that regimented the marginalized while stabilizing the mainstream. "Instead of only legitimating readers, and underscoring their distinction from and superiority to less worthy others," Koistinen-Harris insists, reformist texts "clearly emphasize readers' own need to act responsibly" (29). This line of inquiry leads her through the pages of monthly magazines such as *Harper's*, *Atlantic*, and *Scribner's* and novels including James's *The Bostonians* and Howells's *Annie Kilburn* and *A Hazard of New Fortunes*. Her reconsideration of Charles Sheldon's wildly popular (at the time) novel *In His Steps* does the particular service of offering a nuanced discussion of a rarely mentioned text. Koistinen-Harris's account of publishing practices, like Goodman's, arrives at the pages of the NAACP's monthly *Crisis*, where the discourse of manners, previously a mechanism of disenfranchisement, was transformed into "a tool for undermining white prejudice" that functioned to "endorse the attainment of African-American civil rights" and "contest racist stereotypes of black inferiority" (128). Overall, Koistinen-Harris offers a multiperspective account of what is made distinct—and to whom—in the public pursuit of distinction, pointing finally to the subsequent imbrication in American journalism of aesthetic pedagogy with progressive ideology.

Both of these contributions demonstrate the importance of socioaesthetic considerations in studies of literary and journalistic production in the late-nineteenth and early-twentieth centuries. Through the respective literary and cultural focuses of their analyses, Goodman and Koistinen-Harris offer compelling accounts of the historical forces at work in the subtle technologies of form and formality.

Alex Feerst, Duke University

War Games: Richard Harding Davis and the New Imperialism. By John Seelye. Amherst: Univ. of Massachusetts Press. 2003. xv, 341 pp. Cloth, $80.00; paper, $24.95.

The Anarchy of Empire in the Making of U.S. Culture. By Amy Kaplan. Cambridge: Harvard Univ. Press. 2003. 260 pp. $35.00.

These two critical studies cry out for comparison and contrast, reflecting two similar periods of American history, two different approaches to American literary scholarship, and two double visions. In *War Games*, John Seelye writes a traditional literary biography, yoking the visions of a reporter-novelist's life to the changing sociopolitical environment of U.S. overseas adventures in the 1890s. Amy Kaplan's *The Anarchy of Empire* is an eclectic theoretical study with fascinating linkages between art and culture. Seelye uses history to explore the individual writer's life and values; Kaplan ranges broadly across a number of genres and authors to examine a politically controlling concept that defines thematics of narratives. But both ponder the same historical question: Why were we in Cuba, Puerto Rico, the Philippines, Africa? "Only connect," both studies insist, domestic American needs and imperialist drives.

Veteran scholars will recognize—perhaps with nostalgia—Seelye's critical stance. He writes a literary biography of an activist reporter-novelist, positioning the romantic, dashing persona of Richard Harding Davis (Rebecca's son) within the historical moments of expansionist overseas military adventures and as a continuation of the western frontier movement. For Davis, as for Kaplan, the climactic moment is Cuba, the charge up San Juan Hill. Seelye also fixes on much of Davis's journalism as well as some stories and two novels, *Captain Macklin* and *Soldiers of Fortune* (both 1916). Thus, *War Games* accomplishes a familiar task: reclaiming the reputation of a once famous writing life—think Fitzgerald or Hemingway—by discovering the "objective correlative" (209) and presenting literary anecdotes, close readings, influences (especially Conrad and Kipling), and potted historical summaries. The volume is beautifully illustrated with photographs and prints, especially Remington's, and draws on many forgotten critics of Seelye's (and this reviewer's, as well as *American Literature*'s) youth. Their names are no longer authoritative for present-day theorists, but there is a subtextual effort to reclaim, as with Davis, an honor roll: Thomas Beer, Van Wyck Brooks, Roger Burlingame, Henry Seidel Canby, Alfred Kazin, Grant Knight, Margaret Leech. Seelye's book is thoughtful, wide-ranging, and authoritative. He follows Davis's own map of his actual and his writerly lives, from Henry Stanley's Africa to Owen Wister's West to Theodore Roosevelt's Caribbean. Not without repetitious comments on sport, clubland, dinner parties, and military maneuvers, *War Games* enriches as an appreciative essay.

Amy Kaplan's *The Anarchy of Empire*, while similar to Seelye's book, asks how "dominant representations of national identity at home are informed and deformed by the anarchic encounters of empire, even as these same representations displace and disavow imperialism as something remote and foreign to U.S. nationhood" (16). Kaplan's critical foregrounding involves a dissimilar set of referents, employing names and theories of the present moment: Edward Said (obviously), Michael Harot, Antonio Negri, Ann Stoler, Laura Romero, Jackson Lears, Renato Rosaldo, Eric Sundquist (also, touchingly, Henry Canby).

Kaplan's project is deeply political, wide ranging, and tautly complex. Her book is part of a series of works under the general rubric Convergences, and parts of five of the six chapters have appeared in scholarly journals during the past decade. Kaplan ranges over a hundred years of literary and film productions, "[f]rom Catherine Beecher's *Treatise on Domestic Economy* to Orson Welles's *Citizen Kane* . . . [from] the crisis of masculinity in the 1890's to the rise of Jim Crow segregation. . . ."

This cultural history commences with a yoking of the separate domestic spheres of women's fiction to imperial ventures into foreign lands like Mexico and Asia. Then comes a brilliant chapter on the young Mark Twain's "imperial routes," leading to American exploits in Hawaii. The third section of this chapter, "The Double Discourse of American Imperialism," exemplifies Kaplan's deepest theory: "[T]he tension between the disembodied empire and the embodied American man is reproduced within the figure of masculinity itself, between nostalgia for the body and the spectacle of its display" (99). Frederick Jackson Turner gives way to Owen Wister, to Theodore Roosevelt, to Richard Harding Davis. The hero of Davis's *Soldiers of Fortune* is divided, as Seelye indicates, for such romantic warriors secure colonialist holds overseas simultaneously with homeland corporate power structures. The new woman partakes in both imperial structures, the horrors of the late-nineteenth-century hearts of darkness.

At the halfway point of these studies looms San Juan Hill, the still point of American imperialist narrative and iconography, also encompassing race. Chapter 4, "Black and Blue on San Juan Hill," reinforces and extends Seelye's climax. Kaplan interestingly conflates the military-economic incursion of Cuba with the Reconstruction era, employing the concept of wars reinterpreting previous wars. Thus, the charge up San Juan Hill produced a mythic, heroic president as soldier and connected race, manhood, nation, and empire. In a chapter packed with iconic and unnoticed figures alike, Kaplan quotes Davis's famous description of Theodore Roosevelt leading his rough riders, then analyzes the nearly obscured presence of African American soldiers in the combat picture. The discussion extends to U.S. interventions in Puerto Rico and the Philippines; then, having established the "Paradigm of Doubleness" (51), Kaplan moves on to her penultimate section, "Birth of an Empire," focusing on film's reordering of the imperial twists and themes. Griffith's *The Birth of a Nation* (1915); Oscar Micheaux's response, *Within Our Gates* (1920); and, surprisingly, Orson Welles's *Citizen Kane* (1941); as well as an early film set in the Philippines, *The American Soldier in Love and War* (1903), receive rich and provocative readings.

Kaplan's final chapter, as coda, is an appreciation of the life, work, theory, and influence of W. E. B. DuBois and his "imperial cartography," setting "an aesthetic analogue" of the anarchy of empire that maps Africa and America within a double vision, culminating in his novel *Darkwater*.

These books examine and reclaim writers on the margins of American culture, perhaps not sufficiently attending to the realistic thrusts. Seelye solidly locates one author within an imperialist network, while Kaplan questions ("I have been arguing" is a recurrent phrase) the anxiety-ridden doubling of this cultural history—both informing and menacing. Seelye seeks clearly to explain Davis's constructed adventure romances, while Kaplan deconstructs varieties of American imperialist double narratives that in 2004 remain murky, dark waters, as DuBois terms his novel.

Eric Solomon, San Francisco State University

West of Emerson: The Design of Manifest Destiny. By Kris Fresonke. Berkeley and Los Angeles: Univ. of California Press. 2003. xii, 201 pp. Cloth, $49.95; paper, $19.95.

Marriage, Violence, and the Nation in the American Literary West. By William R. Handley. New York: Cambridge Univ. Press. 2002. xi, 261 pp. $60.00.

"Familiarity is a part of looking at the new," remarks Kris Fresonke in *West of Emerson*, "and it is the ability to have seen it already" (2). In *Marriage, Violence, and the Nation in the American Literary West*, William Handley approaches the same idea from a different direction: "The challenge . . . is the willingness to incorporate what one was not looking for," the willingness to see a familiar subject with "estranged eyes" (230–31). These fine books both find new routes to conceptions of nationhood through old and new western maps of wonderous explorations, picturesque landscapes, Turnerian pioneers, violent conflicts, individual freedom, romantic history, manifest destiny, legacies of conquest, and imperialist agendas. Because national self-conceptions and values are revealed in representations of the West, Americans saw the West, in Fresonke's words, as "a national-theological proof, a region that proves we exist" (5). Fresonke explores how representations of the West by mid-nineteenth-century travel writers and key figures from the so-called

American renaissance depend upon the metaphoric "design argument [that] transformed mere scenery into national landscapes" (15). In his introductory chapter, "Western Unions," Handley claims that representations of western marriages in twentieth-century novels offer "competing allegories of national identity" (14).

Fresonke locates the underpinnings of the rhetorical "logic" of the Age of Jackson in arguments from "design" about westward expansion. Such arguments, writes Fresonke, "[read] aesthetic qualities and divine volition in the orderly appearance of the world" and are popularized by politicians as the "cheerful and providential" (15) notion that "there [is] order in American nature, and God put it there for Americans to profit by" (10). Fresonke demonstrates that Western explorers such as Lewis and Clark, Zebulon Pike, Stephen Long, and William Emory carried west with them "a particular theological argument" that provided them with a narrative for expansion (8). Seeking to describe unfamiliar landscapes, explorers turned to genres, tropes, and metaphors from design that assumed the "United States' imperial fate" (10). "How else to narrate a landscape that welcomed its absorption into an empire," asks Fresonke, "than to describe in picturesque aesthetics its immemorial longing to do so?" (10).

Fresonke moves from travel writers to those scions of nature writing, Emerson and Thoreau. Though they "could easily recognize political opportunism in Jacksonian rhetoric," Emerson and Thoreau nevertheless turned to the design argument to celebrate the national landscape and westward expansion, reflecting "the dilemma . . . in exposing the expansionist politics in manifest destiny while remaining committed to the nation" (15). Bringing Emerson and Thoreau into conversation with popular writers, Fresonke believes, allows her to decenter the American renaissance. "Westerns . . . helped create some of our 'Easterns,'" she suggests (2); "one of the correctives of this book is to point out that our regions are promiscuous, cross-breeding, interdependent, and obsessed with one another" (12).

Like Fresonke, Handley examines apparently strange bedfellows, demonstrating the "cross-breeding" between best-selling authors Zane Grey and Owen Wister, "literary" writers Willa Cather and Wallace Stegner, and authors who inhabit a space in between, such as F. Scott Fitzgerald and Joan Didion. Nina Baym demonstrated over twenty years ago that the national obsession with individualism and the lone male in the wilderness has led critics to overlook recurrent and equally significant literary patterns. Handley builds on Baym's insight, declaring that "[a]gainst expectation, the popularly embraced fiction examined in this study is filled not with examples of free individualism but with forced choices and constraints, tragic marriages, environmental hardships, group conflict and identity confusion, murder, failure, and accidents" (24). Because the West has "function[ed] as national allegory and because marriage has served culturally and historically as an analogue to national union," the portrayal of marriage is center stage in the literary West and, according to Handley, "only betokens trouble" (18). Handley reads "the troubled particulars of romance and marriage in relation to American nationalism" (24), concluding that the conflicted marriages "in the literary West so often separate, even as they participate in, the double helix between love and nation, becoming allegories of a failed national metaphor of unity in a region, where many Americans hoped to locate common identity" (34).

In *Marriage, Violence, and the Nation*, Handley challenges the myth of the "cowboy" West, but rather than offering an alternative paradigm, he explicitly and implicitly explores the complex act of creating literary meaning and its relationship to historical reality. In Handley's view, and I agree, popular westerns, even formula westerns, are "ideologically complicated" and richly reward imaginative analysis rather than reductive dismissals (225). "What literature has to offer anyone who reads it closely," Handley asserts, "is the demanding, unavoidable ambiguity and estranging effect of literary expression itself" (230), and he demonstrates this point in detailed and inventive readings of important and still widely read texts. Most valuable is the way he brings these readings to bear on a larger question of the relationship between literature and history, "this dilemma between the claims of representation and the claims of 'reality'" (230). In a polemical afterword exploring "the impasses between [western] historians and literary critics," (227), Handley advocates a "return to literary complexity" (233). These two fine books convincingly prove Handley's point that "reality is narratively malleable" and support his argument "for understanding how and why narrative continues to matter" (232).

Melody Graulich, Editor, *Western American Literature*

Cold War Orientalism: Asia in the Middlebrow Imagination, 1945–1961. By Christina Klein. Berkeley and Los Angeles: Univ. of California Press. 2003. xiv, 316 pp. Cloth, $55.00; paper, $21.95.

Embracing the East: White Women and American Orientalism. By Mari Yoshihara. New York: Oxford Univ. Press. 2003. x, 242 pp. Cloth, $55.00; paper, $19.95.

Christina Klein's *Cold War Orientalism* investigates the global imaginary of integration: the hierarchical cultural order linking countries under U.S. influence. Analyzing the other side of the culture of containment, Klein describes ways in which "middlebrow" intellectuals and artists translated U.S. foreign policy objectives into affective ties, aesthetics, and ideological values for American audiences during the Cold War.

Breathtakingly well documented, convincingly argued, and a pleasure to read, this book strikes a refreshingly just note in its sounding of the relationship between what is on- and off-screen, claiming neither too much nor too little for the significance of cultural texts in the workings of the political economy. In one chapter, Klein examines how the editors of *Reader's Digest* and *Saturday Review* nurtured in Americans feelings of personal commitment to international affairs and promoted the profile U.S. policymakers wished to project, celebrating individuals they saw as representing the best of America in Asia. In another chapter, she links James Michener's *Voice of Asia* to the development of international tourism, in turn situating tourism within Washington's efforts to make friends abroad. A chapter links *South Pacific* with international adoption, both of which projected a family structure onto U.S.-Asia relations, one in which the nationality of those arrogating parental authority was not a matter of indifference. Another studies the narrative of modernization in *The King and I*, dimming the charitable light in which the film implicitly casts U.S. foreign aid. In her sixth chapter, Klein turns to *Flower Drum Song* and *Hawaii*, analyzing both as mediating the representations of Asians in the United States and promoting a new tolerance for Asian immigrants within the existing framework of American society: global integration turned within.

Cold War Orientalism is excellent and indispensable for anyone interested in Cold War culture. This said, it does not fully live up to its title. Klein suggests that containment dominates our understanding of U.S. Cold War culture, framing her project as a revisionist response. We thus get only the "integration" narratives. A consideration of both sides of this discourse, one including works that served to morally and ethically contain, and exclude, the humanity of those in the socialist or communist world—placing *these* in *their* context— would have been welcome. A thoroughgoing analysis of how the one is writ through the other at the level of U.S. mass culture is a burning avenue for study. I should note also that Klein's investigation devotes less energy to inspired readings of the cultural works themselves. Where she does turn to close readings, whether of films or texts, the observations are insightful, but they do not go as deeply into the works as they might. Klein ultimately seems less interested in this sort of investigation than in the exposition of linkages between texts and the rest of the world. That this one book does not do it all, though, is no derogation of its value as it stands.

Mari Yoshihara's *Embracing the East* brings a comparably rich and careful analysis to an examination of white women's role in constructing U.S. orientalism from the 1870s through the 1940s. Highly original in its approach and extremely suggestive for work in a range of related topics, this book crafts a nuanced analysis of white women's influence in generating and mediating U.S. gendered discourse on Asia, investigating in turn how this engagement enabled white women to empower themselves both within U.S. society and in relation to Asians.

Yoshihara's project bears the fruit of careful archival research and an analysis both flexible and powerfully wrought. An insightful study on its own terms, *Embracing the East* employs a meticulous and evenhanded methodology that can serve as a model for analyses of material culture and interdisciplinary work in general. The first chapter traces the feminization of orientalist consumption, highlighting the pivotal role of middle-class women in popularizing orientalism in U.S. culture through the consumption and domestication of cultural artifacts. Another chapter studies a group of women artists' "Asian" prints, while the next looks at the New Woman's propensity for performing as Asian women heroines on stage and screen. The following four chapters are structured around particular individuals and texts: Amy Lowell and her "Asian" poetry; Agnes Smedley's life and her account of her experiences in China; Pearl S. Buck's immensely influential *The Good Earth*; and anthropologist Ruth Benedict's study of Japanese national character, *The Chrysanthemum and the Sword*.

The diversity of objects in Yoshihara's study—novels and figurines, patterns of middle-class consumption, marketing practices and scholarly discourse, fashion trends and modernist poetry, to name only a few—echoes the range of orientalist culture itself. Especially given the wide net Yoshihara casts for her analysis, her readings are arrestingly precise. The book draws connections between sites as dissimilar as displays of "Oriental" merchandise in department stores in the 1890s and Smedley's radical political and personal engagement with the Chinese Revolution, in a manner that manages to do justice to the specific contexts without ever losing the thread of the larger investigation.

These two projects share a number of characteristics and virtues: they explore Asia's importance to U.S. culture and are welcome additions to American studies scholarship, they adjoin global analyses generated in Asian American studies, and they eloquently demonstrate the value of studying multiple forms with the resources of multiple disciplines. Written for scholars, the language of each is also suitable for students, and both texts include wonderful visuals.

Early on, both Klein and Yoshihara cite Edward Said's *Orientalism* as a point of departure for their own work. Said presents his aims in that study as exposing the sources of orientalism's views, reflecting on its worldly, historical importance, and proposing "intellectual ways for handling the methodological problems that history has brought forward." These books also achieve those objectives within distinct discursive sites. Framing their analyses within national and historical boundaries, they reveal important shifts in orientalist discourse as well as the relevance of the overarching framework. Among their other achievements, they are valuable contributions to the ongoing collective critique of orientalism.

Seung Hye Suh, Scripps College

A Sense of Things: The Object Matter of American Literature. By Bill Brown. Chicago: Univ. of Chicago Press. 2003. xii, 245 pp. $32.00.

Surface and Depth: The Quest for Legibility in American Culture. By Michael T. Gilmore. New York: Oxford Univ. Press. 2003. xiv, 217 pp. $35.00.

A Sense of Things is a story of America's passion for material objects at that climactic moment in the 1880s and 1890s when it threatened to engulf us. While Bill Brown's book is deeply informed by recent efforts in cultural studies, it is ultimately about "something stranger than a history of a culture of consumption." By granting things a kind of "interiority" or "subjectivity," Brown proposes a poetics of the thing wherein objects' relations to each other are linked to the prosaic yet powerful fetishism proposed by literature, in which objects fascinate, enthrall, and oblige us to have a relation to them. The ways in which we use objects "to make meaning, to remake ourselves, to organize our anxieties and affections, and to sublimate our fears and shape our fantasies" are not reducible to the commodity relations that dominate everyday life but are, Brown contends, "overwhelmingly aesthetic, deeply affective," entailing "desire, pleasure, frustration, a kind of pain."

Two fires frame the literary analyses that make up the heart of Brown's book. Between these defining blazes, Brown meditates, with both originality and lucidity, on the encounters with things staged in Norris's *McTeague*, Jewett's *The Country of the Pointed Firs*, and James's *The Spoils of Poynton*. Brown's "tale of possession" clarifies the role of objects in the American literary registers of naturalism, regionalism, and realism, tracing the fate of the object as it passes into American modernism. Thus, Brown reads Norris's compulsion to attain a sense of "material thingness," via iterative narration and descriptive repetition, as foreshadowing the more radical narrative techniques of Stein and Faulkner; similarly, he sees Jewett's "poetics of attachment" and revelation of the "logic whereby an everyday object becomes a cultural thing" as anticipating William Carlos Williams's, Marcel Duchamp's, or Georgia O'Keeffe's capacity to render objects luminous through a process of dislocation. Finally, while Brown's readings emphasize the ways in which objects and subjects quicken each other at the turn of the nineteenth century, these readings occasionally, and hauntingly, mark the estrangement of objects and subjects. Brown's "Coda" brings the book full circle in a reading of James's final novel, *The American Scene*, where modernity figures as a "disaster site" and objects unable to escape their status as commodities speak directly to James, voicing their longing for "the aura of history," and for "the peace to become historical."

Brown describes *A Sense of Things* as a "disciplined, self-disciplinary experiment" in which he returns to some fundamental questions about literature and literary form. It should meet the most exacting scholar's requirements for a clearly written, well-argued book. Yet Brown is as much a poet as a critic, and this richly speculative work demonstrates that the poet's unpredictable and at times elusive path to knowledge is revealing, astonishing, and absolutely necessary.

While Brown's claims about American literature as such remain provisional, or at least understated, Gilmore's engaging work offers a comprehensive reinterpretation of the United States' literary and cultural inheritance. In *Surface and Depth*, Gilmore traces the history of the American fervor for legibility—from the Puritan's fanatical desire to inscribe order on the apparently blank continent to our own imperialist objectives—in order to "demonstrate the existence of a thematic tradition and to enrich understanding of that tradition by connecting it to a larger imperative." Gilmore's attempt to reclaim a central literary and cultural tradition seems to situate *Surface and Depth* in a line stretching back to such studies as F. O. Matthiessen's *The American Renaissance*, yet Gilmore's work offers a searching critique of such master narratives by acknowledging just how much they have blocked from sight. "American visibility," he remarks in his introduction, "has necessitated and produced American *in*visibility." American receptivity to cinema, "a technology of visible surfaces," and psychoanalysis, "a technique for sounding the human depths," encourage Gilmore, in thinking about our relationship to legibility, to pursue uncanny connections between apparently unconnected materials. Cooper's frontier narratives predict the sensory hyperreality and scopic powers of the cinema, for example, and Hawthorne's plumbings of the psyche in *The Scarlet Letter* anticipate the work of psychotherapy.

Gilmore's diachronic reading of the American obsession with legibility reveals two related but not identical lines of descent. The uncritical faith in linguistic transparency that characterizes the writing of the Declaration of Independence is reinscribed in popular literary genres such as the western, the detective tale, and celebrity fiction, while elite, or "high," works of art highlight the ambiguity and linguistic skepticism of the Constitution. Thus while nineteenth-century canonical works such as Hawthorne's *The Scarlet Letter* or Melville's *Moby-Dick* "engage the knowledge drive as a highly compelling social edict," they ultimately reject the "grammar of legibility" that provokes the figurative striptease performed by Fanny Fern's *Ruth Hall* in favor of "more distanced, guarded forms of disclosure." In the postcinema twentieth century, Gilmore argues, writers grapple with the will to legibility expressed in the "imperialism of images." The relationship between text and image as a way of knowing is most notable at the heart of Hemingway's *The Sun Also Rises*, where "language itself evolves into the medium of motion pictures." The image, however, turns out to be as unreliable a means as language for illuminating the truth: "night follows day with the same regularity that 'the sun also rises.'" Gilmore's analyses of those texts that illuminate even as they qualify the prevailing structures and values that have fashioned American experience are, however, less compelling than his brief but powerful readings of texts that more radically challenge or subvert these structures and values. Most important, Gilmore's readings of African American texts offer important counterexamples of the drive toward legibility while foregrounding race as the "limit of American knowing." In his final chapter on Douglass and Ellison, Gilmore argues that "illegibility" is the "originary impulse of this countertradition," meditating on the irony that the "most disadvantaged" artworks of a culture share with the most rarefied "a refusal of accessibility."

Sharing as their point of departure the American 1890s, Gilmore's and Brown's projects have little else in common. Both books, however, challenge many assumptions about premodernist and modernist thought and change the way we think about our culture, our literature, and our selves.

Marta L. Werner, D'Youville College

Sexual Violence and American Manhood. By T. Walter Herbert. Cambridge: Harvard Univ. Press. 2002. 256 pp. $27.95.

Male Sexuality under Surveillance: The Office in American Literature. By Graham Thompson. Iowa City: Univ. of Iowa Press. 2003. xxi, 248 pp. $39.95.

These two studies offer poignant and often fascinating analyses of heterosexual American manhood's debilitations and potential reformation. Each author takes a relatively long view on the literary and historical construction of American straight male sexuality. Herbert's *Sexual Violence and American Manhood* reaches as far back as the Revolutionary War and Thompson opens *Male Sexuality under Surveillance* with a deft reading of Melville's "Bartleby, the Scrivener." Both authors see sexuality and manhood as dynamic and constantly in process, although both also have firm explanations for the historical processes that have resulted in contemporary notions of masculinity. Herbert and Thompson each underscore the fact that straight masculinity is based on a rather devastating insecurity. For Herbert, men's anxiety produced by fears of their vulnerability and the relative disempowerment that follows from desiring another person conspire to instill a redemptive violence—which may take a literal form but, at the least, always organizes men's thinking about sexuality—at the core of straight manhood. For Thompson, the dominant, binary hetero-homo logic of sexuality results in an anxious straight masculinity "that displaces its own insecurity into the paranoia and fear that have, historically, marked the relationship between heterosexuality and homosexuality" (129).

The first noteworthy element of *Sexual Violence and American Manhood* is Herbert's willingness to turn his analytical gaze upon himself in the prologue and epilogue. He opens by examining his memories of an early childhood encounter with sexually violent literature, and he ends the book with a meditation on the ways in which "despotic," or "code," manhood has inevitably shaped, and deformed, his own sense of gender relations. These moments are significant because they exemplify one of Herbert's most trenchant and perhaps most disconcerting points: that men who commit sexually violent acts are not, as most of us would like to think, "wholly alien." "Far from standing at the margins of conventional manhood," Herbert writes, "these men are working at its troubled center" (166–67). Herbert's argument that violence is deeply ingrained in the cultural construction of manhood is integral because his intentions reach far beyond literary criticism and its core audience of scholars. *Sexual Violence* is a polemic whose ultimate goal is cultivating "democratic masculinities" that "surmount the paradoxes of misogynist braggadocio" by working toward a world in which "women and men engage each other on grounds of equality and mutual respect" (156).

To support his analysis of manhood's violent past and present, as well as his hoped-for democratic future, Herbert largely relies on rapidly sketched analyses and wide-angle historical contexts. He finds that the main culprits behind masculinity's troubled state are the unfortunately dominant "notion of warrior manhood" (70), the violent ways in which boys are socialized (106), and the ideologically powerful but false images of self-made men and economic independence. Although Herbert offers illuminating readings of canonical and popular texts, some readers may find themselves wanting a more fine-grained history or more detailed analysis of individual texts. Herbert, however, is not out simply to dazzle us with inventive interpretations (although there certainly are some, such as his takes on *Uncle Tom's Cabin*, *Native Son*, and Michael Powell's film, *Peeping Tom*, vis-à-vis Hitchcock's *Psycho*). Instead, Herbert's task is more passionate and more urgent: "Literary criticism is devoted here to an ethical project, that of . . . permitting us to see through and correct the injustices of a prevalent way of being masculine" (25–26).

Graham Thompson's *Male Sexuality under Surveillance* also has a polemical edge, but his book is a much more traditional scholarly study. Thompson offers lengthy and detailed readings of a range of well-known American male writers from the last 150 years and provides the carefully constructed footnote apparatus that typifies scholarly works (Herbert's book, by contrast, has scant footnoting). Thompson divides his study into three distinct periods, including the early "all male" business concerns of late-nineteenth-century incorporation; the post–World War II era of the gray-suited "organization-man" in which women become visible in "pink collar" jobs; and the 1990s high-tech industry, in which women work side-by-side with men in positions of equal responsibility. Operating from a Foucauldian paradigm, Thompson identifies the office as a visually determined space of surveillance. He couples this idea with a theoretical paradigm emerging from queer studies. As the American office space has developed, Thompson argues, "non-straight sexuality . . . [has been] made to bear the burden of its own visibility through inscription and exposure" (99) and, crucially, straight male sexuality is therefore always striving to position itself in hierarchical opposition to the cultural markers that supposedly signify homosexuality.

Many of Thompson's interpretations are both important and eye-opening. For instance, his readings of the homosocial male friendships that are eventually disavowed in literature written during the early period of incorporation are highly revealing (his texts are "Bartleby," *Silas Lapham*, and *Babbitt*). The analysis of Sloan Wilson's *The Man in the Gray Flannel Suit* as a book that traffics in interlinked 1950s paranoia of latent homosexuality and communist sympathies is also particularly enlightening. In addition to these impressive readings, Thompson (and this is true for Herbert as well) sees literature, both popular and canonical, as an important site where social identities are constructed, tried on, and even reimagined.

Recognizing literature's social utility is ultimately crucial because each author ends on a note of hope. Thompson finds reason for optimism in recent novels by Nicholson Baker and Douglas Coupland, which, he argues, disrupt the paradigm that he persuasively interrogates throughout his study. And for Herbert, "undo[ing] the sexual pathologies" that he shrewdly diagnoses "promises a world in which we can meet one another, and touch one another, and look at the truth together" (202).

Jeffory A. Clymer, University of Kentucky

Rewriting: Postmodern Narrative and Cultural Critique in the Age of Cloning. By Christian Moraru. Albany: State Univ. of New York Press. 2001. xviii, 230 pp. Cloth, $59.50; paper, $19.95.

Radiant Textuality: Literature after the World Wide Web. By Jerome McGann. New York: Palgrave. 2001. xv, 272 pp. $35.00.

Bakhtin's theories of textual heteroglossia are familiar to scholars in language-based fields. Imaginative writing's polyvalency is the focus of Christian Moraru's *Rewriting* and Jerome McGann's *Radiant Textuality*, which treat revision of model texts as a potentially productive strategy for writers and an inevitable activity for readers. Explicitly rejecting Terry Eagleton's claim that all writing is a reworking of other writing, Moraru focuses on postmodern novels that patently revise nineteenth-century texts in order to serve as "self-acknowledged vehicle[s] for ideological criticism." While this strategy is not unique in modern and postmodern criticism, Moraru's decision to treat novels that "intensively" rework an urtext *is*. In studying postmodern rewrites, Moraru's goal is to answer those critics on the Left and Right who see postmodern fiction as mere recycling in our age of cloning.

McGann covers similar ground in his exploration of textual "radiance," the proliferation of meaning that readers discover in poetic texts. McGann reveals his understanding of textual instability in an indirect yet fascinating manner. As editor of the electronic *Rossetti Archive*, he became incrementally aware of the nature of "paperspace," or textual layout, as a result of translating poetic texts and graphic images into digital form. The computer's singular ability to provide scholars a tool to play with—or "deform"—text and image makes visible aspects of traditional texts heretofore unnoticed. The operation of textual "deformation" can result, McGann claims, in a "dramatic exposure of subjectivity" on the part of scholars, critics, and editors.

Rewriting and *Radiant Textuality* are structured similarly: both consist of earlier published articles and writings grouped into multiple parts. Moraru's two initial chapters explore his notion of contemporary "counterwriting," making clear that while some narrative retelling is mere recycling, authors such as E. L. Doctorow, Ishmael Reed, and Kathy Acker do not borrow out of what Stephen Greenblatt calls "imaginative parsimony." Dismissing those, like John Barth, who merely stress the aesthetic aspect of postmodern retelling, Moraru aligns himself with Gilles Deleuze's notion that "re-petition opposes re-presentation."

Subsequent chapters disclose how a variety of contemporary authors use "intentional echoing" of earlier texts to produce sociocultural critique. Moraru explores traces of Poe in novels by Paul Auster and Ishmael Reed, and retellings of Hawthorne in Auster and Acker. Other authors who rewrite earlier stories include Charles Johnson, Trey Ellis, Mark Leyner, and Bharati Mukherjee. An epilogue revisits the book's overarching theme: that far from being "blank parody," the version of postmodernism in *Rewriting* is progressive art capable of "asserting, changing, and reasserting—renarrating—identity." As such, it counters Eagleton's, Fredric Jameson's, and Jean Baudrillard's "Xerox degree" image of writing as cloned, "self-same" pastiche.

McGann's record of constructing the electronic *Rossetti Archive* takes the reader on a journey through a series of epiphanies he experienced translating traditional texts to digital format. One intriguing revelation is that the alleged linearity of imaginative print texts is actually mirrored in the hypertextuality of digital equivalents. Taking us chronologically through the archive's planning and construction, McGann recreates his growing sense that traditional ways of treating imaginative texts such as poems (but all literary genres are implicated) are inadequate. This aspect of *Radiant Textuality* challenges its readers to rethink the relation between paper and digital writing, forcing us to face, as McGann has, the authentic yet hidden "theoretical structure of paper-based textual forms."

While McCann's early chapters, "The Alice Fallacy" and "The Rationale of Hypertext," illustrate the centrality of a reader's "dialogue" with the text, later chapters stress how textual "deformation" dramatizes the "idiosyncratic" nature of the reader's relationship with a text. Embracing "the objective instability of the subjects of our study," McGann calls for a criticism capable of framing the "n-dimensional space" of creative texts, the "multivariate" nature of art works. Because "[a]esthetic space is organized like quantum space," McGann calls for the adoption of a quantum poetics able to reflect, and reflect upon, textual phenomena that shift and change.

While Moraru and McGann adhere to the notion that repetition and difference in imaginative writing lead to what McGann calls a "dynamics of ambiguity," textual "rewriting" is not precisely the same as textual "radiance." McGann's experience with digitized texts reveals the inherent instability of textual codes and meaning, which can lead scholars and critics away from traditional notions of textual authority to a profound awareness of the role of subjectivity not only in criticism but also in such "informational" endeavors as editing. McGann does not consider the implications of poetry's ability to "radiate" meaning beyond its metacognitive potential for scholars, while Moraru's work explicitly focuses on prose narratives whose "radiant" retelling creates a surplus of meaning that is intentionally political.

Rewriting is a pleasure to read, as Moraru's writing is accessible and nimble. Although focusing on American texts, Moraru invokes familiar and less well-known theorists—often continental—to support his claims. While *Rewriting* contains a number of typographical and other textual errors, it is professionally written and researched. *Radiant Textuality* is also a valuable text, and readers should not be put off by the dense and, at times, overly technical language in the introduction, parts of which might have been better placed in an appendix for readers familiar with digital programming. Overall, however, McGann's writing is nuanced and provocative, bound to challenge many readers' ideas about the role of computer technology in humanities scholarship, the nature of traditional texts, and the power of "deformation" to reveal unseen aspects of imaginative writing.

Victoria Ramirez, Weber State University

Brief Mention

Editions

To Find My Own Peace: Grace King in Her Journals, 1886–1910. Ed. Melissa Walker Heidari. Athens: Univ. of Georgia Press. 2004. xxxvii. 247 pp. $39.95.

A versatile nineteenth-century New Orleans writer, King produced several histories, novels, short stories, biographies, and articles. She was lauded for transcending the local-color genre and for her depictions of both white and black women in a variety of locations. These journal entries record her travels across the United States and Europe, reveal her thoughts on political issues as well as her personal trials, and provide a more informal, candid portrait of King than her published autobiography. Heidari's introduction provides historical context for the letters, showing how they convey the complex position of Southern women writers after the Civil War.

The Correspondence of William Carlos Williams and Louis Zukofsky. Ed. Barry Ahearn. Middletown, Conn.: Wesleyan Univ. Press. 2003. xxiii, 574 pp. $65.00.

The letters in this collection, exchanged during the thirty-year friendship between two influential figures in American modernist poetry, discuss the personal lives of each man and reveal their thoughts on the state of publishing and poetry in America, shedding new light on their own work and the work of contemporaries like Cummings, Aiken, Eliot, and Pound.

The Letters of Robert Duncan and Denise Levertov. Ed. Robert J. Bertholf and Albert Gelpi. Stanford, Calif.: Stanford Univ. Press. 2004. xxxv, 857 pp. Cloth, $99.00; paper, $39.95.

The intimacy, loyalty, and lively intellectual exchange captured in this correspondence reveal the intense bond between Duncan and Levertov and depict the state of American poetry and cultural history in the mid-twentieth century. In nearly five hundred letters, Duncan and Levertov address spirituality, the importance of poetry, and their political and ethical differences. The editors provide a comprehensive introduction, notes, chronology, and glossary of names.

General

The Threads of "The Scarlet Letter": A Study of Hawthorne's Transformative Art. By Richard Kopley. Cranbury, N.J.: Univ. of Delaware Press; Associated Univ. Presses. 2003. 201 pp. $39.50.

In this study of intertextual influences on *The Scarlet Letter*, Kopley finds echoes of authors such as Edgar Allan Poe, James Russell Lowell, and Ebenezer Wheelwright in Hawthorne's literary imagination. The final chapter suggests that Hawthorne's borrowing of formal conventions, plot, and thematic structure from works like *Robinson Crusoe*, *The Salem Belle*, and *Arthur Gordon Pym* helped him define his own novel's investment in "providential" themes.

Rhetoric and Resistance in Black Women's Autobiography. By Johnnie M. Stover. Gainesville: Univ. Press of Florida. 2003. vii, 244 pp. $55.00.

Stover draws on literary texts by four nineteenth-century African American women (Harriet Wilson, Harriet Jacobs, Elizabeth Keckley, and Susie King Taylor) to demonstrate how words, rhythms, sounds, silences, looks, and posture convey veiled meanings. Stover argues that black women's language is a "mother tongue," incorporating elements of the oral traditions of West African Yoruba culture, which serves as both a mode of expression and a linguistic and physical stance of subversive resistance to the oppression these women faced as slaves and servants.

Nightmares of Anarchy: Language and Cultural Change, 1870–1914. By Wm. M. Phillips. Lewisburg, Penn.: Bucknell Univ. Press. 2003. 233 pp. $47.50.

Nineteenth-century anarchism is often understood in relation to debates and concerns of the period, including fears of degeneracy and revolution, loss of autonomy in the modern era, and social and economic changes. Phillips contextualizes anarchist rhetoric in the cultural discourse of late-nineteenth- and early-twentieth-century Britain and the United States. His analysis of fictional and nonfictional works by Henry James, Ford Madox Ford, Frank Norris, Charlotte Teller, and Joseph Conrad provides a comprehensive discussion of how anarchism functioned as a scapegoat for social problems, the effects of its reliance on violence, and how its logic and ideals of individual liberty shaped modernist understandings of the twentieth century.

Collaborators in Literary America, 1870–1920. By Susanna Ashton. New York: Palgrave Macmillan. 2003. ix, 223 pp. $65.00.

Ashton traces collaborative authorship in America in the late nineteenth and early twentieth centuries, analyzing it in relation to book history, labor practices, and rapid changes in the literary marketplace. Examining works by Henry James, William Dean Howells, and Mark Twain, among others, Ashton attributes the production of collaborative works during this period to authors' anxieties about increasing competition in the publishing world.

Eudora Welty and Walker Percy: The Concept of Home in Their Lives and Literature. By Marion Montgomery. Jefferson, N.C.: McFarland. 2004. 214 pp. Paper, $38.50.

While both Welty and Percy called the Deep South their home, their conceptions of and relationships with it were quite different. Welty was firmly rooted to her community in Jackson, Mississippi, but Percy lived a more nomadic existence before settling in what he called the "noplace" of Covington, Louisiana. Montgomery explores the friendship between these authors, the different ways they represented home in their fiction, and how they understood the *homo viator*, or "man on his way."

Wakeful Anguish: A Literary Biography of William Humphrey. By Ashby Bland Crowder. Baton Rouge: Louisiana State Univ. Press. 2004. xvi, 403 pp. $44.95.

Interweaving literary analysis and biographical detail with collections of unpublished letters, interviews, photographs, and journal entries, Crowder chronicles the life of this melancholic and prolific Southern writer. Crowder traverses the narrative worlds of Humphrey's short fiction, from the northeastern settings of his early and late works to the fictional landscape of Red River County in East Texas (an imaginary space modeled on his own native Texas community). Crowder also analyzes Humphrey's novels and his memoir, *Farther Off from Heaven*, which deals with the death of his father, a loss that haunted his life and work.

On a Silver Desert: The Life of Ernest Haycox. By Ernest Haycox Jr. Norman: Univ. of Oklahoma Press. 2003. xx, 307 pp. $39.95.

This candid biography of the accomplished writer of literary westerns is a tribute from son to father. Haycox Jr. writes about his father's difficult childhood, his passion for writing, and his success in both the literary and business worlds of Portland, Oregon. Haycox Sr., who wrote over two hundred short stories and twenty-four novels, was a regular contributor to *Collier's* and the *Saturday Evening Post*. He is noted for incorporating historical events into his fictional westerns and helping to bridge the gap between literary and film genres. John Ford and Cecil B. DeMille adapted his work in classic film westerns such as *Stagecoach* and *Union Pacific*.

Uncommon Readers: Denis Donoghue, Frank Kermode, George Steiner, and the Tradition of the Common Reader. **By Christopher J. Knight. Toronto: Univ. of Toronto Press. 2003. xiii, 506 pp. $50.00.**

Knight presents the unique critical independence of these three intellectuals by tracing their careers and backgrounds. He highlights the interests of each critic—from the imagination, canonicity, cultural politics, and theology to their debates with poststructuralism. In bringing together their politics and interests, Knight also traces broader genealogies: of the review essay as a genre, the role of the public critic, and the importance of the common reader.

Patterns of Power in American Political Fiction. **By Thomas J. Kemme. Lanham, Md.: Univ. Press of America. 2003. viii, 261 pp. Paper, $41.00.**

Through close readings of such classics of political fiction as Edwin O'Connor's *The Last Hurrah*, Gore Vidal's *Lincoln, A Novel*, Allen Drury's *Advise and Consent*, and Robert Penn Warren's *All the King's Men*, Kemme shows how politics combine with literary art to create fiction that is both serious and popular. Although Kemme's style and approach to politics are rooted in the perspectives of political science, he offers both political and literary frameworks through which to read, analyze, and teach political fiction.

Existential America. **By George Cotkin. Baltimore: Johns Hopkins Univ. Press. 2003. x, 359 pp. $39.95.**

This sweeping survey traces the genealogy of existential philosophy in the United States from its literary antecedents in the works of eighteenth- and nineteenth-century figures such as Edwards, Melville, Dickinson, and William James to its transatlantic migration in the works of Kierkegaard, Sartre, de Beauvoir, and Camus (who were embraced by New York intellectuals) to its evolution in the works of Wright, Ellison, Mailer, and photographer Robert Frank and, finally, to its presence in the feminist and political protest movements in the 1960s and in contemporary popular culture, particularly in such films as *Fight Club* and *American Beauty*.

Gravity Fails: The Comic Jewish Shaping of Modern America. **By James D. Bloom. Westport, Conn.: Praeger. 2003. xvi, 192 pp. $62.95.**

This study delves into the transformative role of pioneering Jewish comedians and artists in shaping Americans' self-representations in the twentieth century. Examining the work of artists like Woody Allen, Mel Brooks, Lenny

Bruce, Gilda Radner, Philip Roth, Jerry Seinfeld, and Stephen Sondheim, Bloom describes how Jewish comedy affected entertainment, commerce, politics, art, science, and the discourses of race, sex, and history in America.

Christianity and the Mass Media in America: Toward a Democratic Accommodation. By Quentin J. Schultze. East Lansing: Michigan State Univ. Press. 2003. viii, 440 pp. $84.95.

Schultze outlines five concepts (conversion, discernment, communion, exile, and praise) that serve as rhetorical guides to this study of the complicated relationship between Christianity and the mass media in U.S. political and cultural life. Addressing the debates between Christianity and the mass media over issues such as depictions of sex and violence on television, biased journalism, censorship, and government regulation, Schultze considers how Christianity and the mass media have borrowed from each other to shape American sentiments and to foster a sense of national unity and community.

Literature after Feminism. By Rita Felski. Chicago: Univ. of Chicago Press. 2003. ix, 195 pp. Paper, $18.00.

Do women and men read differently? What is the relationship between literary and political value? These are some of the questions that frame Felski's analysis of how feminism has transformed the way people read in the twenty-first century. Using popular literary examples, Felski addresses a wide audience who may be unfamiliar with feminist literary criticism.

Collections

George Washington's South. Ed. Tamara Harvey and Greg O'Brien. Gainesville: Univ. Press of Florida. 2004. x, 345 pp. $59.95.

Historians, anthropologists, and literary critics consider the emergence of regional identity in the American South through the figure of George Washington. As a Virginia planter, general, and president, his experiences reflect the diversity of the South in the eighteenth century.

Booker T. Washington and Black Progress: "Up from Slavery" 100 Years Later. Ed. W. Fitzhugh Brundage. Gainesville: Univ. Press of Florida. 2003. viii. 227 pp. $55.00.

Marking the centenary of the publication of Washington's autobiography, this collection illuminates aspects of Washington's life and work that have not received adequate critical attention. Topics include his strategies of self-presentation, masculinity, relationship to secular notions of racial uplift, and thoughts on economic development.

Mencken's America. Ed. S. T. Joshi. Athens: Ohio Univ. Press. 2004. xx, 244 pp. Cloth, $49.95; paper, $22.95.

Joshi has brought together articles by one of the most renowned and controversial journalists and cultural critics of the twentieth century. These essays
from *Smart Set, American Mercury*, and the *Baltimore Evening Sun* are characteristic of Mencken's caustic style. Included, for example, are six articles
on "the American" in which Mencken reflects on the flaws of his fellow citizens, as well as articles on cities in the American landscape and on morality,
religion, politics, art, literature, and culture. The collection concludes with
explanatory endnotes and a glossary of names mentioned in the articles.

*Imaginary (Re-)Locations: Tradition, Modernity, and the Market in Contemporary Native
American Literature and Culture*. Ed. Helmbrecht Breinig. Tübingen: Stauffenburg Ver-
lag. 2003. 297 pp. Paper, EUR 39.00.

German and American scholars and writers of Native American literature
reconsider here what it means to be an indigenous writer in North America
after the "Native American Renaissance" of the 1960s. These essays on cultural and political identity formation in the United States, Canada, and Mexico
examine issues of nationalism, mixed-blood identity, border zones, the use
of Native images in film and fiction, and "post-Indian" tricksterism. Among
the writers discussed are Louise Erdrich, N. Scott Momaday, Leslie Mar-
mon Silko, and Gerald Vizenor (who also wrote a scholarly piece for this
collection).

Resources for American Literary Study, Volume 28. Ed. Jackson R. Bryer and Richard
Kopley. Brooklyn, N.Y.: AMS Press. 2003. vii, 317 pp. $89.50.

Founded in 1971, *Resources for American Literary Study*, now a cloth-bound
annual, remains a key resource for archival scholarship in American literature. This volume's range of articles spans fugitive-slave running in *Moby-
Dick* to an analysis of "transatlantic mentoring" through correspondence exchanged between Israel Zangwill and Emma Wolf. Previously unpublished
correspondence between various authors from the nineteenth and twentieth
centuries are also included, along with a comprehensive book review section
and an index to the previous volumes.

Reprints

North Carolina Slave Narratives: The Lives of Moses Roper, Lunsford Lane, Moses Grandy, and Thomas H. Jones. Ed. William L. Andrews. Chapel Hill: Univ. of North Carolina Press. 2003. 279 pp. $27.95.

Each of the four pre-1865 slave narratives in this collection was widely read in the antebellum era and influenced the abolitionist movement at home and abroad. In bringing these four narratives together, Andrews demonstrates how contemporary readers might see in them the roots of an African American literary tradition, as well as the prototype for an emerging black middle class. These stories detail the social, economic, and racial dynamics of antebellum North Carolina and how these four men were able to attain freedom.

"The Dead Letter" and "The Figure Eight." By Metta Fuller Victor. Durham, N.C.: Duke Univ. Press. 2003. 388 pp. Cloth, $74.95; paper, $21.95.

Written in the 1860s under the pseudonym Seeley Regester, these two classic stories by the first American author of detective novels combine elements of Poe's gothic mystery with the genre of domestic fiction. Victor's pioneering style has influenced many generations of detective writers, male and female. An introduction by Catherine Ross Nickerson offers insight into the tales as well as commentary on the mystery's popularity among middle-class readers in the nineteenth century.

"That Affair Next Door" and "Lost Man's Lane." By Anna Katharine Green. Durham, N.C.: Duke Univ. Press. 2003. 445 pp. Cloth, $74.95; paper, $21.95.

In these two late-nineteenth-century mystery tales, Green's amateur detective-narrator, Amelia Butterworth, is the first female sleuth in American fiction—unmarried, opinionated, and in constant rivalry with police detective Ebenezer Gryce. These narratives show how Green's inventive narrative and stylistic devices, like matching the wits of a professional detective with those of a keenly perceptive lay person, paved the way for future writers of the genre.

Anthologies

Reading the Roots: American Nature Writing before "Walden." Ed. Michael P. Branch. Athens: Univ. of Georgia Press. 2004. xxxi, 408 pp. Cloth, $54.95; paper, $24.95.

This anthology of early ecocritical literature begins with Renaissance explorers and concludes with the New England transcendentalists. By shifting the focus from Thoreau, most commonly identified as the father of American nature writing, to the period that anticipates and influences his work,

Branch has created a new space for critical and pedagogical intervention in ecocriticism. The anthology includes a range of genres and authors, a variety of landscapes, different nations and cultures, and diverse ideological views. Detailed headnotes and a comprehensive bibliography of primary and secondary sources are provided.

Bibliographies and Guides

A Bio-Bibliography of Clarence S. Day Jr., American Writer, 1874–1935. By Patrick Coyne and Edward Moran. Lewiston, N.Y.: Edwin Mellen. 2003. viii, 208 pp. $109.95.

Edith Wharton's "The House of Mirth": A Casebook. Ed. Carol J. Singley. New York: Oxford Univ. Press. 2003. viii, 337 pp. Paper, $22.00.

Louis L'Amour: An Annotated Bibliography and Guide. By Halbert W. Hall. Jefferson, N.C.: McFarland. 2002. vii, 302 pp. $55.00.

Toni Morrison's "Song of Solomon": A Casebook. Ed. Jan Furman. New York: Oxford Univ. Press. 2003. ix, 276 pp. Cloth, $39.95; paper, $15.95.

The Cambridge Companion to Crime Fiction. Ed. Martin Priestman. New York: Cambridge Univ. Press. 2003. xvii, 287 pp. Cloth, $65.00; paper, $23.00.

Reference and Research Guide to Mystery and Detective Fiction, Second Edition. By Richard J. Bleiler. Westport, Conn.: Libraries Unlimited. 2004. xi, 828 pp. $78.00.

The Cambridge Companion to Science Fiction. Ed. Edward James and Farah Mendlesohn. New York: Cambridge Univ. Press. 2003. xxvii, 295 pp. Cloth, $60.00; paper, $24.00.

Index of American Periodical Verse, 2001. Ed. Rafael Català and James D. Anderson. Lanham, Md.: Scarecrow Press. 2003. xiv, 682 pp. $95.00.

Hispanic Literature of the United States: A Comprehensive Reference. By Nicolás Kanellos. Westport, Conn.: Greenwood. 2003. x, 314 pp. $75.00.

The Cambridge History of American Literature, Vol. 5: Poetry and Criticism, 1900–1950. Ed. Sacvan Bercovitch. New York: Cambridge Univ. Press. 2003. xi, 624 pp. $95.00.

The Cambridge History of American Literature, Vol. 6: Prose Writing, 1910–1950. Ed. Sacvan Bercovitch. New York. Cambridge Univ. Press. 2003. xx, 620 pp. $95.00.

Announcements

Nineteenth Century Studies Association Article Prize

The Nineteenth Century Studies Association (NCSA) is accepting applications for the annual NCSA Article Prize, awarded in recognition of excellence in scholarly studies on subjects from any discipline focusing on any aspect of the long nineteenth century (the French Revolution to World War I). The winner will receive a cash award of $500 to be presented at the annual meeting of the NCSA in March 2005. Articles published between 1 September 2003 and 31 August 2004 are eligible for the 2005 Prize and may be submitted by authors or by a publisher of a journal, anthology, or volume containing independent essays. Multidisciplinary essays are especially encouraged. Essays written partly or entirely in a language other than English must be accompanied by translations in English. Submissions should be mailed by 15 October 2004 to Professor Kevin Lewis, Department of Religious Studies, University of South Carolina, Columbia, South Carolina 29208. Inquiries for further information may be directed to Professor Lewis at kevin@sc.edu, but electronic submissions will not be accepted. Applicants should provide an e-mail address for acknowledging receipt of their submissions.

John Carter Brown Library Research Fellowships

The John Carter Brown Library will award approximately twenty-five short- and long-term Research Fellowships for the year 1 June 2005–31 July 2006. Short-term fellowships (some of which have thematic restrictions) are available for periods of two to four months and carry a stipend of $1,600 per month. These fellowships are open to foreign nationals as well as to U.S. citizens engaged in pre- and postdoctoral, or independent, research. Graduate students must have passed their preliminary or general examinations at the time of application and be at the dissertation-writing stage. Long-term fellowships, primarily funded by the National Endowment for the Humanities (NEH) and the Andrew W. Mellon Foundation, are typically for five to nine months and carry a stipend of $4,000 per month. Recipients of long-term fellowships may not be engaged in graduate work and ordinarily must be U.S. citizens or have resided in the United States for the three years immediately preceding the application deadline. All fellows are expected to relocate to Providence and be in continuous residence at the Library for the entire term of the fellowship.

The John Carter Brown Library is an independently administered and funded center for advanced research in history and the humanities located at Brown University. The library's holdings are concentrated on the history of the Western Hemisphere during the colonial period (c. 1492 to c. 1825). Research proposed by fellowship applicants must be suited to the holdings of the Library.

The application deadline for fellowships for 2005–2006 is 10 January 2005. For application forms or additional information, write to Director, John Carter Brown Library, Box 1894, Providence, Rhode Island 02912; telephone: 401-863-2725; fax: 401-863-3477; e-mail: JCBL_Fellowships@brown.edu. The Web site is www.JCBL.org.

Join the MLA
and Join us *in*
P★H★I★L★A★D★E★L★P★H★I★A

One of the largest humanities organizations in the world, the Modern Language Association represents members in more than a hundred countries, publishes an internationally acclaimed bibliography, and hosts an annual convention on professional and scholarly issues.

After a forty-year absence, the MLA convention will return to Philadelphia this December. The convention will feature more than 750 sessions over a three-day period from 27 to 30 December. In addition to forums and special events, the convention will host more than 150 book and educational exhibits and a job information center for applicants and interviewers. Become a member now and get access to early online registration at reduced members' rates and special discounts on hotel prices and airfares.

Philadelphia offers an array of cultural activities. Visit the Franklin Institute Science Museum or the Philadelphia Museum of Art; take a walk through Independence National Park or around Rittenhouse Square; and reserve early for a trip to the Barnes Foundation.

Every MLA Member Receives

- Six issues of *PMLA*

- Four issues of the *MLA Newsletter*

- A complimentary copy of the sixth edition of the *MLA Handbook for Writers of Research Papers*

- Web access to a regularly updated list of members

- Web access to a searchable list of convention sessions

- A copy of *Profession*, an annual collection of articles on the field

- Reduced registration fees at the annual convention

- Membership in divisions and discussion groups concerned with scholarly and teaching interests

- Significant discounts on the *MLA International Bibliography* and on more than 200 books and pamphlets published by the MLA

- Participation in MLA-sponsored group insurance plans

- Eligibility to vote for officers, members of the Executive Council, members of the Delegate Assembly, and members of division and discussion group executive committees

Join the

MLA at

www.mla.org

MLA 2004
PHIL★DELPHIA

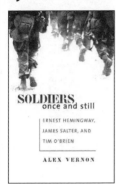

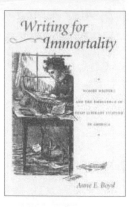

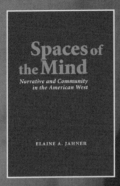

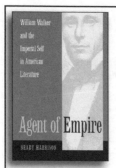